THE CLANS
and their connected family names

BUCHANAN
Bouchannane
Colman
Donleavy
Donlevy
Dove
Dow
Dowe
Gibb
Gibson
Gilbert
Gilbertson
Harper
Harperson
Lennie
Lenny
Macaldonach
Macandeoir
Macaslan
Macauslan
Macausland
Macauslane
MacCalman
MacCalmont
MacCamon
MacCamond
MacChruiter
MacColman
MacCormack
MacNuyer
MacWattie
MacWhirter
Masterson
Murchie
Murchison
Rish
Risk
Ruskin
Spittal
Spittel
Walters
Watson
Watt
Weir
Ynill
Yuille
Yule

CAMERON
Chalmers
Clark
Clarke
Clerk
Clarkson
MacClerich
MacGillonie
MacIldowie
MacKail
MacIerie
MacMartin
MacOnie
MacPhail
MacSorley
MacVail
Martin
Paul
Sorley
Taylor

CAMPBELL of ARGYLE
Bannatyne
Burns
Denoon
Denune
MacDermaid
MacDermid
MacDairmid
MacGibbon
MacIver
MacIvor
MacKellar
MacNichol
MacOran
Maclause
Mactavish
MacUre
Tawesson
Thomas
Thomason
Thompson
Ure

CHISHOLM
Chesholme
Chisholme

COLQUHON
Cowan
Culchone
Kilpatrick
Kirkpatrick
Macachounich
MacOwan

CUMIN
Buchan
Comyn
Cummin
Cumming
Cumyn
Niven

DAVIDSON
Davie
Davis
Davison
Dawson
Dow
Kay
Macdaid
Macdade
MacDavid

DRUMMOND
Begg
Brewer
MacRobie

FARQUHARSON
Brebner
Bremner
Coutts
Farquhar
Findlay
Finlay
Findlayson
Grassich
Hardie
Hardy
Leys
Lyon
MacCaig
MacCardney
Maclaw
MacCuaig
MacEarachar
Mac Farquhar
MacGuaig
MacHardie
MacHardy
MacKerchar
MacKerracher
Macindlay
Mackindlay
Reoch
Riach
Tawse

FERGUSON
Fergus
Fegusson
MacAdie
MacFergus
Mackerras
Mackersey

FORBES
Bannerman
Fordyce
Lumsden
Walters

FRASER
Frazer
Frescell
Friseal
Frizell
Frew
Macgruer
Macimmey
MacKennie
MacKin
Mackimmie
MacShimes
MacShimmie
MacSimon
MacSymon
Sim
Sime
Simon
Simpson
Sume
Symon
Tweedie

GORDON
Adam
Adie
Edie
Geddes
Grassich
Huntly
Mill
Milne
Moir

GRAHAM/GRAEME
Allardice
Bontein
Bontine
Buntain
Bunten
Buntine
Doig
Graham of Menteith
Graham of Montrose
MacGibbon
Menteith

GRANT
Gilroy
MacGilroy
MacIlroy

GUNN
Gallie
Gaunson
Georgeson
George
Henderson
Jameson
Jamieson
Johnson
Kean
Keane
Maclomas
MacCorkill
MacCorkle
MacIan
Mackarres
Macteamish
MacKean
MacOmish
MacRob
MacRobb
MacWilliam
Mann
Manson
Nelson
Robinson
Robson
Sandison
Swanson
Will
Williamson
Wilson
Wylie

KENNEDY (ULRIC)
MacOurlic
MacUlric
MacWalrick

LAMOND
Black
Brown
Burdon
Lamb
Lambie
Lammie
Lament
Lamondson
Landers
Lemond
Limond
Limont
Lucas
Luke
Lyon
Macalduie
MacClymont
Macgilledow
MacGillegowie
Macilwham
Macilwhom
Macilzegowie
MacLamond
MacLucas
MacLymont
MacPatrick
MacPhorich
MacSorely
Meikleham

MAC ALLASTER
Alexander
MacAlaster
MacAlester
MacAllister
MacAllaster

MAC ARTHUR
Arthur
Campbell of Strachur
MacArtair
MacCarter

MAC AULAY
MacAulay
MacCall
MacPhedran
MacPhedron
MacPheidiran

MAC BEAN
Bayne
Bean
Binnie
MacBain
MacBean
MacBeth
MacBheath
Macilvain
MacVean

MAC COLL
Colson
Coulson
MacKail

MAC DONALD of CLAN RANALD
Allan
Allanson
Currie
MacAllen
Mackechnie
MacKeochan
MacKissock
MacKissock
MacMurrich
MacVarish
MacVurie
MacVurich

KENNEDY (ULRIC) — listed above

MAC DONALD of GARAGACH and KEPPACH
MacGillivantic
MacKillip
MacKilip
MacKillop
MacRanald

MAC DONALD of GLENCOE
Johnson
Kean
Keane

MAC DONALD of THE ISLES
Houston
Howison
Hughson
Hutcheson
Hutchison
Hutchinson
Isles
Mac Donald of Sleat
MacHugh
MacHutchen

MAC DONELL of GLENGARRY
Alexander
Sanderson

MAC INTIRE
Mactear
Tyre
Wright

MAC DUFF
Duff
Fife
Fyfe
Spence
Spens
Wemyss

MAC INTOSH
Adamson
Ayson
Clark
Clarke
Clarkson
Clerk
Crerar
Dallas
Doles
Elder
Esson
Easson
Glen
Glennie
Hardie
Hardy
MacAy
MacCardney
MacClench
MacConchy
MacFall
Macglashan
MacHardie
MacHardy
Mackay
Mackeggie
Mackillican
Macintosh
MacLerie
MacNiven
Macniven
MacNamell
Macoul
Macowl

MAC DUGAL
Carmichael
Conacher
Cowan
Dougall
Dowall
Dowell
MacConacher
MacCoull
MacCowan
MacCulloch
MacDougal
MacDulothe
MacGugan
MacGugan
Machowell
MacKichan
Maclintock
MacLucas
MacLugash
Macnewan

MAC GILLIVRAY
MacGillivoor
MacGilivra
MacGilvray
Macilvrae

MAC IVOR
Macglasrich
MacIver
MacUre
Ure

MAC GREGOR
Black
Brewer
Caird
Comrie
Dochart
Fletcher
Gregor
Gregorson
Gregory

MACKAY
Bain
Bayne
MacCay
MacCrie
Macghee
Macghie

MAC MILLAN
Baxter
Bell
Brown
MacBaxter

MAC DONALD of GLENGARRY / MAC LENNAN
Logan

MACLEOD
Beaton
Beton
Bethune
Malcolmson
Norman
Tolmie

MACKENZIE
Kenneth
Kennethson
MacBeolain
MacConnach
MacIver
MacIvor
MacKerlich
Mackinney
MacMurchie
MacMurchy
MacVanish
MacVinish
Murchie
Murchison

MACKINNON
Love
Mackinning
Mackinven
MacMorran

MAC INNES
Angus
Innes
MacAngus
MacCansh
MacCaush
MacMaster

MAC LACHLAN
Gilchrist
Lachlan
MacGilchrist
MacLaghlan
MacLauchlan
MacLaughlan

MAC LAURIN
Laurence
Law
Low
Maclaren

MAC LEAN
Beaton
Beton
Bethune
Black
Lean
MacBeath
MacBeth
MacBheath
MacRankin
MacVeagh
MacVey
McVey
Rankin

MAC LEAN (continued)
(Greig)
Grier
Grewar
Grierson
Grigor
King
Leckie
Lecky
MacAdam
Macara
Macaree
MacChoiter
MacCrowther
MacGregor
MacGrory
Magrowther
Magrudger
Maegruther
Macildny
MacLiver
MacNee
MacVie
MacNish

MAC INTOSH — (second col)
Mackie
MacPhail
Macquey
Macquoid
Macvail
Neilson
Paul
Polson
Scobie
Williamson

MAC NAB
Abbot
Abboton
Bayne
Dewar
Gilfillan
Macandeoir
Macindeor

MAC PHEE
Duffie
Duffy
MacDuffie
Macfee
Mache
MacGulfie
Machaffie

MUNRO
Dingwall
Foulis
MacCulloch
Machulich
Munro
Munroe
Vass
Wass

SKENE
Carston
Carnie
Dis
Dise
Dyse
Dives
Hallyard
Skene

MAC NACHTAN
Hendrie
Hendry
Kendrik
MacBrayne
MacHendry
Maceol
MacHendrie
MacHendry
MacHenry
MacHenrick
MacKnight
MacNachden
MacNachten
MacNaghten
MacNair
Mac Naver
MacNauchton
MacNaughten
MacNaughtan
MacNaughton
Niven
Weir

MAC PHERSON
Carson
Cattanach
Clark
Clarke
Clarkson
Currie
Gillespie
Gillies
Gondie
Gow
Lees
MacChlery
MacCurroch
MacGilchrist
MacGoun
MacGown
MacKeith
MacLeish
Maclene
Maclise
MacMurdo
MacMurdoch
MacMurrich

MURRAY
Fleming
Murray
Small
Spalding

OGILVIE
Christie
Findlater
Gilchrist
MacGilchrist
Mill
Milne
Ogilvie
Ogilvy
Sturrock

ROBERTSON
Collier
Colyear
Donachie
Dunnachie
Inches
Maclagan
Maclagan
MacConnechie
MacConichie
MacDonachie
Macinroy
Maclagan
MacRob
MacRobbie
MacRobert
MacRobie
Reid
Robertson
Roy
Stark
Tonnochy

STEWART
Bannalyne
Boyd
France
Garrow
Jameson
Jamieson
Lennox
MacLamie
MacIoy
Macglashan
Mackinlay
Mackirdy
MacLewis
MacMichael
MacMunn
Monteith
Monteith
Stewart
Stuart

SUTHERLAND
Broom
Cheyne
MacConnechy
MacConichie
MacDonachie
Macinroy
Maclagan
Mackay
Mackeygie
Mackillican
Macintosh
Maclerie

MAC NICOL
Nicol
Nicoll
Nicholl

MAC QUARIE
MacCorrie
MacCorry
MacGorrie
MacGorry
MacGuaran
MacGuire
Macquaire
Macquire
MacWhirr
MacWhirr
Murdoch
Murdoson
Wharrie

MAC RAE
MacCrea
MacCraw
MacCreath
MacCrie
MacGrath
Macra
Macrach
MacRaith
MacRath
Rae

ROSE
Geddes
Rose

ROSS
Anderson
Andrew
Dingwall
Fair
Gillanders
MacCulloch
Machulich
Mac Taggart
MacTear
MacTier
MacTire
Ross
Tagart
Vass
Wass

MAC NIEL
MacGugan
Macguigan
MacNeilage
MacNeiledge
MacNeil
MacNelly
MacNair
MacNaver
MacNeur
MacNider
MacNiter
MacNeil of Barra
MacNeill of Gigha
Neal
Neil
Neill
Neilson

MAC PHARLAN
Allan
Allanson
Bartholomew
Caw
Fereen
Galbraith
Griesck
Gruamach
Kinnieson
Lennox
Mac Aindra
Mac Allan
Maclae
MacCause
MacCondy
MacEoin
MacErracher
MacFarlan
MacFarlane
MacGaw
MacGeoch
Macgreusich
Macinstalker
Mac Jock
Mac James
Mackinlay

MATHESON
MacMath
MacPhun
Matheson
Mathie

MENZIES
Dewar
Macandeoir
Macindeor
MacMenzies
MacMunn
MacMonies
Means
Mein
Meine
Mengues
Mennie
Meyners
Minn
Minnus
Monzie

SHAW
Ayson
Esson
Easson
MacAy
MacHay
Shaw

SINCLAIR
Caird
Clyne
Linklater
Lyall
Sinclair

URQUHART
Mavor
Urquhart

THE CLANS

OF THE

SCOTTISH HIGHLANDS

THE CLANS

OF THE

SCOTTISH HIGHLANDS

THE COSTUMES OF THE CLANS

R.R.McIAN

Text by James Logan

Foreword by Antonia Fraser

CHANCELLOR
PRESS

First published in Great Britain by Webb & Bower (Publishers) Ltd
and distributed by WHS Distributors

Designed by Malcolm Couch

This edition published in 1983 by Chancellor Press
59 Grosvenor Street
London W1

Clans of the Scottish Highlands first published 1845 and 1847

This redesigned one-volume edition with additional material
© 1980 Webb & Bower (Publications) Ltd
Foreword © 1980 Antonia Fraser

ISBN 0 907486 38 X

Printed in Hong Kong

Foreword

It might be said of *McIan's Costumes of the Clans* as Walter Bagehot said of a royal marriage: that it provides a brilliant edition of a general fact. In 1845 the passion for tartan, the clans and things Highland altogether was certainly a general fact. The young Queen Victoria had paid her first visit to Scotland in 1842 and no holiday taken by a distinguished person has had more tumultuous consequences. By 1848 the building of Balmoral itself was under way. On the subject of the life led there by the Queen and Prince Albert we may best quote James Logan, who wrote the text for the *Costumes of the Clans*: in Scotland "Her Gracious Majesty and Illustrious Consort unbend the bow of Royal Etiquette amid the quietness of a mountain retreat, breaking the monotony of seclusion by healthful pursuits peculiar to a Highland life; deriving entertainment from the athletic and convivial performances of their Gaelic subjects."

Nor was the passion for the costumes of the clans – whatever their form – confined to the British Isles. By 1820 it was rampant in the United States. A Glasgow firm wrote to W. Wilson junior, who amassed one of the earliest sample books of tartan fabrics: "Tartans are much worn in America and seen at all seasons, tho' best in the Fall; the patterns best adapted are large clan patterns for gentleman's wear." Most in demand was Colquhoun, with MacDuff, Bruce, Mackenzie and Glenorchy following. However, even if the material was not exactly any known tartan, there would be no particular problem: "that is not cared for here" added the writer cheerfully.

McIan's *Costumes of the Clans* is in fact dedicated, with her own permission, to Queen Victoria. The names of the Queen and Prince Albert, together with the Royal Dukes of Sussex and Cambridge, head the list of the original subscribers. How strange such a conjunction of Hanoverian princes and homage to the Highlands would have seemed a hundred years earlier! The wretched hunted remnants of the Forty-Five would have been amazed to find such a volume dedicated to the great-niece of Butcher Cumberland, their persecutor.

Queen Victoria herself, however, found nothing incongruous in the situation, despite the fact that the *Costumes of the Clans* was specially issued to commemorate the centenary of the tragic rising. Brought up in an age of security, she calmly ignored the fact that the Forty-Five had been aimed at substituting the Stuart dynasty of Bonnie Prince Charlie for that of the Hanoverians. Instead she was innocently proud of her own Stuart descent (from James I), reserving her frowns for the Tudor Queen Elizabeth I ("she cut off the head of our ancestress Mary Queen of Scots"). By 1845 the rehabilitation of the Stuart name was complete.

In the eighteenth century, in contrast, the ferocious government legislation which followed the defeat of Bonnie Prince Charlie at Culloden brought about the nadir of Highland society. The vanquished Highlanders were not only forbidden to bear arms – a cruel stipulation to a tribal people – but also the wearing of their clan dress. These prohibitions represented an attack on the whole Highland way of life, a systematic form of repression following military conquest. As a result, for a generation the Highlands resembled that Abyssinia described by Gibbon: "the world forgetting by the world forgot." It was, from the Scottish point of view, an unhappy state of oblivion.

It was noticeable that when Dr. Johnson made his fascinated and fascinating tour of the Highlands in 1773, he was able to refer to the state of the local inhabitants, together with their mountains and islands, as being equally unknown with "that of Borneo and Sumatra". Yet already a few years earlier the successful publication of the *Works of Ossian*, purporting to be founded on original Highland documents, had demonstrated a new romantic English taste for such things. In 1782 the Act of Disarming was repealed. Of equal significance was the death in 1788 of he who had once been termed Bonnie Prince Charlie. He died abroad, bankrupt, dissipated and without legitimate heirs except a brother, who as a celibate Catholic Cardinal clearly intended to give his Hanoverian cousins no trouble; in fact he accepted a pension from them. The way was clear for the family of King George III to start draping itself in tartan, much as the Americans were described as doing in the nineteenth century. By 1789 three of the King's sons were painted in Scottish dress.

The formation of a Highland Society in London in 1778 was another indication of a new and gentler mood. Most momentous of all, however, in the rediscovery of romantic Scotland was the influence of Sir Walter Scott. From the publication of his poem *The Lady of the Lake* in 1810 onwards, Scott's works turned the public imagination northwards in a way for which it is difficult to find a parallel, except perhaps in the rise of Chinoiserie when European travellers rediscovered the Far East.

The theatre was a particularly striking example of Scott's artistic dominance, although, ironically enough, it was one which did not benefit the author himself. In the absence of any form of protective copyright where drama was concerned, the Waverley novels were pillaged remorselessly by other writers to provide successful plays. *Rob Roy* in particular proved such a popular quarry, that by the month of June in its year of publication there existed no fewer than five versions of it on the stage – none of them paying a penny to Sir Walter.

This piratical Scottification of the stage was, as we shall see, to have a strong influence on McIan.

To Sir Walter, also, was owed that visit of King George IV to Edinburgh in 1822 which inaugurated a new era. George IV was the first reigning monarch to visit Scotland since the seventeenth century when Charles II had, regrettably if understandably, taken a dislike to a country ruled by critical Presbyterian preachers. George IV, cheerfully adipose in yards of tartan, found a very different kind of society – and a very different welcome. Only Byron wrote sarcastically of the general acclaim, alluding to "tours, huzzas and Highland dresses" and pointing out that "hired huzzas redeem no land's distresses".

But Byron was wrong: for the Scottish tourist industry – and the term is hardly anachronistic for that was exactly what Scott, single-handedly, had created – did at the time and has continued ever since to do a great deal to redeem the land's distresses. Highland holidays rapidly became extremely fashionable. Sir Robert Peel was a typical convert. He rented a lodge in Inverness-shire from Lord Lovat, to recuperate from political strains. Eilean Aigas was a particularly exotic retreat, sat on a rocky island in the middle of the river Beauly; Sir Robert was quickly so enamoured both of the place and the surrounding terrain, that he succumbed to the feelings of many other lovers of the Highlands, in hoping that the area would remain unvisited by all except him. He reported with approval that a neighbour lived "in Terror of the magnificent scenery being discovered and explored by Tourists and adopts the only precaution against their intrusion – that of denying himself the comfort of a Road". The date is August 1849, but the sentiments (and the remedy) are common to our own day.

Eilean Aigas' Highland Gothic charms had been further enhanced by the tenancy of two brothers who called themselves John Sobieski and Charles Edward Stuart and claimed to represent the legitimate royal line of Bonnie Prince Charlie. Their pretensions were however received with nothing but grace in a society already so intoxicated by Highland myths. And the brothers themselves added to these myths in 1829 by the publication of *Vestiarum Scoticorum*. Like the Works of Ossian, this account of fifty-five different setts of tartan had no real historical validity, but it had a great deal of charm and fantasy, and was illustrated with all the enthusiasm of the best kind of Victorian amateur.

The first work of James Logan, *The Scottish Gael*, published in 1831 was of more scholarly interest; although the Sobieski Stuarts, for the sheer energy and delight of their imagination, should not be denied their place in the history of the Highlands. Logan was born in Aberdeen about 1794, the son of a merchant, and began to study law like many another ambitious young Scot. When his skull was fractured, probably by the accidental blow of a hammer while he was watching Highland games, Logan turned to drawing. Then, still repeating the pattern of eager Scots, he made for London. There he enjoyed the patronage of Lord Aberdeen, and was able to study drawing in connection with the Royal Academy. After working in an architect's office he began to earn his living as a free-lance journalist.

Although Logan's pen was at the service of the English capital, his first love was for the North. He was briefly secretary of the Highland Society in London and then in 1826 he set off on a prodigious tour of the Highlands themselves, armed only with a knapsack and a notebook. The result was *Scottish Gael*, of which the subtitle was *Celtic Manners*, and which constitutes an interesting record of the Highland way of life so long hidden from the English view. *Scottish Gael* sold well at thirty shillings a copy (Logan, according to the practice of the time, sold the copyright for a hundred guineas). What was more, Logan was allowed to dedicate the work to William IV, taking the opportunity to present a volume to the monarch in full Highland dress.

Logan's next venture introduced him to the artist Robert Ronald McIan (the christian names are given variously in reference books as Ronald Robert, with other deviations of Ranald and Roland, but this version, used in the obituary of McIan written by a close friend for the Art Journal, is to be preferred). McIan too was a Scot who had found his original livelihood in the south; but unlike Logan, McIan had begun life as a professional actor, working in companies at Bristol and Bath. He was born in 1803 and was therefore some ten years younger than Logan, but he played the role of the Dugald Cratur in one of the many versions of *Rob Roy* before he was eighteen. McIan was a colleague and friend of the actor William Macready; but so bouyant, even manic, was McIan's nature that Macready made it a condition of their acting together that McIan should not have a lethal weapon available on the stage. Coming to London, McIan formed part of Macready's troupe at the Covent Garden Theatre.

It was, indeed, from this address that in 1835 he submitted his first picture to the Royal Academy and had it accepted. Like McIan's own nature, the themes of his pictures were dramatic, or, as a friend wrote after his death, he was at his best when depicting scenes of violence and human conflict. He was therefore, from his own point of view, born into exactly the right age for acceptance in established artistic circles, particularly when this talent for depicting conflict was joined with a profound love of his native Scotland, its history and its traditions. For the pervasive influence of Sir Walter Scott had been felt as much in painting as in drama.

William Allen, a class-mate of the great Wilkie, led the way. Disappointed by his lack of success with the oriental scenes he loved to paint, Allen was inspired by his friendship with Scott to turn his hand to incidents in the lives of Robert the Bruce, Mary Queen of Scots and John Knox. The success of this rich new seam in Scottish painting was crowned when Allen was elected President of the Scottish Royal Academy in 1838. McIan's work fitted easily into a world eager to receive works with such titles as *The Battle of Culloden*, *A Highland Feud*, *The Covenanter's Wedding*, *The Jacobite Hiding Place*, not forgetting such more mundane aspects of Scottish life as *The Highland Whisky Still* (exhibited in the Scottish Royal Academy in 1843).

Encouraged by his success, McIan proceeded to give up the stage for painting, although he retained all his old friendships with his fellow-actors; being ever ready to lend money to "a brother of the buskin". A man of highly attractive if frequently wild (not to say drunken) temperament, McIan stood in contrast to the far more peppery and difficult Logan. Logan never failed to quarrel with his benefactors, or indeed his immediate neighbours: even the efforts of the Prince Consort could not ensure Logan keeping his place in the Charterhouse, a charitable foundation which gave him accommodation. Logan was finally expelled, not only for his "free and unrestrained life" but for criticising the bench of governors, who happened to be a body of bishops.

Like McIan, Logan drank, but in his case his head was so excessively weak (possibly the effect of that early blow of the hammer) and his nature so quarrelsome that the results were sometimes disastrous. Nor did Logan suffer fools gladly. In fact, he did not suffer fools at all. One of his advertised habits was to quit the company of anyone the instant they bored him – without giving any explanation, he would simply turn on his heel and leave. The convivial love of oysters for which he was also famous scarcely made up for these rebuffs, particularly as the oysters often had to be paid for by others.

McIan, already luckier than Logan in his temperament, enjoyed the further advantage of a very happy marriage. Fanny McIan, for many years a teacher in the Female School of Design at Somerset House, was also an artist in her own right (some of her early pictures were, in modest Victorian fashion, submitted under her husband's name). One of her pictures, *The Empty Cradle*, went straight to the heart of her own age, as we know from Macready. Calling on Fanny in April 1843, he found her at work on a picture of a cradle, which was lying in her studio. Like so many Victorians, Macready had lost a baby. "I looked for the child," he wrote in his *Journal*, "and not thinking of what I said, uttered: 'The Cradle is empty.' 'Yes.' I could not speak and the tears welled to my eyes, and I thought of that blessed one with whom I have so often wished to be companioned . . ." But Fanny McIan's *Highlander defending his Family at the Massacre of Glencoe* was generally felt to be her masterpiece, and was the subject of engravings.

From the base of this happy marriage, McIan himself was able to venture forth and enjoy considerable success in London society. His role there is probably well expressed by the fact that he attended the famous Eglington Tournament dressed as a jester. McIan also had a special passion for singing and recitation, due no doubt to a wish not to let his dramatic talents rust. On at least one occasion, McIan was so carried away by his own performance ("We are no fou'/We're not that fou'/But just a drapie in our ee") that a servant hastily asked his hostess if he should fetch the gentleman a cab and get him home . . . . Another vivid vignette of McIan's social progress has him attending the opening day of the Royal Academy's Annual Exhibition. Dissatisfied with the poor hanging of his own pictures, McIan overcame his chagrin by dragging along critics to admire his friends' work. Should any terrified critic try to escape, the artist's eyes "flashed lightning".

McIan did have in common with Logan the need and enjoyment of Highland tours to amass the materials of his art. But in McIan's case, such a tour was an occasion for yet more conviviality, and yet more recitation. He would pass the days visiting, sketching – and holding forth about – such sites as the island burying-ground of the Macnabs, Blair Atholl, the pass at Killiecrankie, and Glenfinnan where the march of the clans took place. Later, as one companion put it, "there was singing in the taverns at night". Furthermore, McIan loved the Scottish present as much as the Scottish past, enjoyed shooting and fishing, and couldn't pass a river "without peering for a salmon".

When the time came for Logan to join with McIan in *The Costumes of the Clans of Scotland*, something of the dramatic and excitable nature of both men went into the production of this remarkable and colourful work. McIan has certainly used his experience of the stage to depict no mere lay figures draped in tartan, but highly lively, even leaping, characters. It is always said that his own actor and actress friends sat for these portraits: certainly there is a life and variety here which alone sets *The Costumes of the Clans* apart from most other books on the subject.

All Logan's knowledge and love of the Highlands has also gone into the production of a text which, even if it is not always accurate according to later researches on the subject of tartan (ever a controversial topic) it remains agreeably readable. The book certainly deserved the success it enjoyed at the time and it is pleasant to record that Logan and McIan went on to produce another work together, their extravagant temperaments apparently not precluding them from a satisfactory artistic partnership. *The Highlanders at Home*, sub-titled *Gaelic Gatherings*, followed in 1848.

Alas, neither Logan nor McIan were destined to enjoy that kind of respected old age which crowned the existence of so many successful Victorians. Logan died in 1872 at the age of nearly eighty, but he existed after his expulsion from the Charterhouse as a result of the intermittent patronage of Highland Societies, a hand to mouth life brought about by his own difficult nature. James Cruickshank, who edited his Collections for the Spalding Club, summed him up after his death as follows: "something of a genius, partially a failure, but notably a pioneer. . . ."

McIan, who might have hoped for a better fate, died in 1856. He was only fifty-three, but he had fought with a wasting disease for two years. There was however general agreement that for a man of McIan's highly strung disposition, the death of so many of his friends in the Crimean War was another severe blow which contributed to his final collapse. Fortunately McIan's pictures of the Cameron Highlanders still constitute one permanent memorial to his art.

The Costumes of the Clans of Scotland constitute another. "The heather grew in his heart" wrote a contemporary of McIan. "And there was no music he loved so well as the bag-pipe on the wild hill-side." It is to be hoped that this reissue of McIan's finest composite work will recapture something of this spirit of high Victorian romance. It will also demonstrate that ardent and loving approach to Scottish history which animated both Logan and McIan. Both men have been in their graves for over a hundred years: yet through their eyes, we can still admire a Highland way of life and what Logan optimistically described as "the graceful flow of Oriental drapery with more than the advantages of European attire": that is to say, the costumes of the clans of Scotland.

Antonia Fraser
October 1979

Contents

Plates

THE CLANS

THE CLANS

OF THE

SCOTTISH HIGHLANDS,

ILLUSTRATED BY APPROPRIATE FIGURES, DISPLAYING THEIR

DRESS, TARTANS, ARMS, ARMORIAL INSIGNIA, AND SOCIAL OCCUPATIONS.

FROM ORIGINAL SKETCHES,

BY R. R. McIAN, ESQ.

With Accompanying Description and Historical Memoranda of Character, Mode of Life, &c. &c.

BY JAMES LOGAN, ESQ.

F. S. A. SC. COR. MEM. SOC. ANT. NORMANDY, ETC.

AUTHOR OF " THE SCOTTISH GÄEL," INTRODUCTION TO THE " SAR OBAIR NAM BARD GÄELACH," ETC.

LONDON:

ACKERMANN AND CO., STRAND.

The

HIGHLAND SOCIETY OF LONDON is incorporated "for the preservation of the Martial Spirit, Language, Dress, Music, and Antiquities of the Caledonians, and rescuing from oblivion the valuable remains of Celtic Literature."

In accordance with these desirable objects, the Society has afforded to this work, the peculiar advantage of its patronage, and as a mark of the great respect which the proprietors entertain for so patriotic a body, and as an indication of their high sense of the honour done them, This acknowledgement is offered to the Comunn-Ghaelach

By the Society's most obedient

and obliged Servants,

ACKERMANN AND CO.

To

Her Most excellent Majesty,

THE QUEEN,

Who has graciously deigned to visit the

Country of

THE CLANS,

And patronised their Manufactures & Costume

This work is with permission dedicated by

Her Majesty's

Most dutiful Subjects and Servants,

ACKERMANN AND CO.

LIST OF SUBSCRIBERS.

HER MAJESTY THE QUEEN.
HIS ROYAL HIGHNESS PRINCE ALBERT.
HIS ROYAL HIGHNESS THE DUKE OF CAMBRIDGE, K.G.

HIS ROYAL HIGHNESS THE LATE DUKE OF SUSSEX, EARL OF INVERNESS.

His Majesty the King of the French.

THE ROYAL LIBRARY, MUNICH, BAVARIA.
THE ROYAL ACADEMY IN LONDON.
THE HIGHLAND SOCIETY OF LONDON.

HIS GRACE THE DUKE OF SUTHERLAND, K.G., &c.

HIS GRACE THE DUKE OF MONTROSE, K.T.

THE MOST HON. THE MARQUIS OF BREADAL-BANE, K.T.

THE RIGHT HON. THE EARL OF DERBY.

THE RIGHT HON. THE EARL OF ABOYNE.

THE RIGHT HON. LORD WARD.

THE RIGHT HON. LADY DUFF.

BARONESS DE ROTHSCHILD.

BARON J. DE ROTHSCHILD, PARIS.

SIR JOHN CATHCART, BART.

SIR CHARLES FORBES, BART., OF NEWE AND EDINGLASSIE.

THE LATE SIR FRANCIS MAC KENZIE, BART., OF GAIRLOCH.

GEN. SIR HECTOR MAC LEAN, K.C.B., OF COLL.

THE LATE SIR NEIL MENZIES, BART., CHIEF OF CLAN MEINNICH.

HUGO, PRINCE OF SALM-REIFFERSCHEIDT, PRAGUE.

COUNT FRANZ XAVIER AUERSPERG, PRAGUE.

LE COMTE NÁKÓ DE NAGY SZENT MIKLOS, HUNGARY.

Artice, Robert, Esq., Jamaica.

Babcock, W. R., Charleston, South Carolina.

Berroll, R., Esq., Hague.

Beasley, W., Esq., Dublin.

Cabbell, Benjamin Bond, Esq., M.P., F.R.S., S.A., &c.

Cabbell, Thomas, Esq., Temple.

Campbell, Alexander, Esq., of Monzie, M.P.

Campbell, A. F., Esq.

Campbell, Dr. Charles, Jamaica.

The Chisholm, Chief of Clan Siosal, &c.

Clendinning, Miss, Westport.

Cobbett, Pitt, Esq., Walburton.

Colquhoun, W. H., Esq.

Coulthard,——Esq., Wells.

Daniel, Henry, Esq.

Davidson, Duncan, Esq., Chief of Clan Dhai', &c.

Davies, H. D., Esq.

Dickens, Charles, Esq.

Dickenson, L., Esq.

Dower, William, Esq., Stronduff.

Downie, Robert, Esq., of Appin.

Doyle, W., Esq., Dublin.

Drew, Mrs., Promenade, Cheltenham.

Drummond, Mrs. Henry Dundas.

Dunbar, John, Esq., Forres.

Elliott, S. M. Dr., New York.

Ellis, John, Esq.

Eyton, J. Walter King, Esq., F.S.A.L., & Sc. Leamington.

[Subscribers continued

Fairfull, Alexander, Esq., Jamaica.

Farquharson, James, Esq., of Invercauld, &c.

Fingzies, J. K., Esq., Jamaica.

Forbes, Alexander, Esq.

Forbes, Arthur, Esq., of Culloden.

Gildowie, James, Esq.

Gooden, James, Esq., Tavistock Square.

Gordon, John, Esq., Jamaica.

Gordon, Robert, Esq.

Graeme, A. Sutherland, Esq.

Grant, Charles, Esq., Clyde Bank, Rutherglen.

Gray, W., Esq., Wheatfield, Bolton.

Guthrie, David Charles, Esq.

Hart, Samuel, Sen., Esq., Charleston, South Carolina.

Hamilton, Miss.

Hammill, Miss, Everton Crescent, Liverpool.

Huth, C. F., Esq.

Hutton, Captain Thomas, F.G.S., Bengal Army.

Jenkins, Thomas, Esq., Jamaica.

Johnstone, Lockhart, Esq., Worcester.

Ladbrooke, Mrs.

Lang, David, Esq., A.M., &c.

Littledale, Miss, Daventry.

Logan, John, Esq., Jamaica.

Lomax, John, Esq., Accrington.

Longlands, Henry, Esq., Charlton, Kent.

Mac Alpin, Colonel.

Mac Arthur, Major.

Mac Bain, Alexander, Esq.

Mac Bean, Donald, Esq., Jamaica.

Mac Connell, John, Esq., Hobart Town, Van Dieman's Land.

Mac Donald, Angus Bain, Esq.

Mac Donald, James, Esq., Kinstair.

Mac Gregor, John, Esq., Jamaica.

Mac Gregor, of Glengyle.

Mac Kenzie, John, Esq.

Mac Kinnon, Captain Duncan, 68th Regiment.

Mac Kinnon, William Alexander, Esq., M.P., F.R.S, Chief of Clan Fhi'nnon, &c.

Mac Kintosh, Mrs., 125, Stephen's Green, Dublin.

Mac Laren, John, Esq., Bloomsbury Street.

Mac Laurin, Daniel, Esq., Lombard Street.

Mac Lean, Lachlan, Esq.

Mac Leod, General Charles, C B.

Mac Neil, Major, W. Gibbs, New York.

Mac Nab, Dr. G., Jamaica.

Mac Neil, Sir John, Dublin.

Mac Niell, William W., Esq., Larne, Co. Antrim.

Mac Phee, J. Cameron, Esq.

Mac Pherson, Clunie, Chief of Clan Chattan, &c.

Mac Quarrie, Captain Lachlan.

Macready, W. C., Esq.

Matheson, James, Esq., of Achany, M.P., &c.

Maule, Colonel, 79th Regiment Cameron Highlanders.

Meikleham, William, Esq., LL.B., &c., Glasgow.

Menzies, Duncan, Esq., London.

Menzies, Sutherland M., Esq.

Michell, Henry, Esq., Jamaica.

Monypenny, Thomas Gybbon, Esq., Rolvenden, Kent.

Moore, John W., Esq., Philadelphia.

Murray, John, Esq., Dundalk.

Napier, R., Esq., Glasgow.

Nash, Dr. F., Worcester.

Nicholls, C., Esq., Petersburg.

Nicholson, Samuel, Esq., 43, Dame Street, Dublin.

Peel, Rev. J.

Riggs, George W., Esq., D.C., Washington, United States.

Robertson, Divie, Esq., Bedford Square.

Robertson, E. W., Esq., Chester Square.

Robertson, Gen., of Struan, Chief of Clan Donchadh.

Rogers, Arnold, Esq.

Rolland, Stuart Erskine, Esq., 69th Regiment.

Rose, Hector, Esq.

Ross, Alastair, A.M., &c.

Rushout, Miss H., Burford House, Tenbury, Worcester.

Shubrick, General, Leatherhead.

Sinclair, Robert, Esq.

Skene, William F., Esq., F.S.A., &c., Edinburgh.

Stewart, Duncan, Esq.

Strachan, J., Esq., M.D.

Stuart, Charles, Esq., of Balachulish.

Templeman, John, Esq.

Towerzey, Alfred, Esq.

Tulloch, James, Esq., F.R.S., S.A.

Urquhart, Beauchamp C., Esq., Chief of Clan Urquhart.

Veith, Anton, Esq., Prague.

White, J. C., Esq., New York.

Wiley, J., Esq., New York.

Wiley, George P., Esq., New York.

Wilson, John, Esq.

Wilson, William, Esq., Pyon House, Herefordshire.

Introduction

THERE is no more extraordinary spectacle in Europe than that of the Gaël of Scotland, who retain a language the most ancient, and once the most widely diffused, and preserve the manners and customs which distinguished their ancestors in ages the most remote. Among all the habitudes which characterize this "peculiar people," none is more remarkable than their fond adherence to a garb the most primitive.

This we feel worthy of ample illustration, and a subject the interest of which is not confined to Great Britain. It has repeatedly employed the pens and pencils of authors and artists, but it has never been treated as in the present work, and, from the want of correct data, the most glaring improprieties have been committed.

Long has it been known as the striking attire of a warlike Scot, and the well-adapted dress of a pastoral people; both hemispheres have witnessed, with admiration, the exploits of the Highlanders, while their social and domestic manners have commanded respect wherever they have been located.

During the late Peninsular war, and at Waterloo, where the British troops displayed their wonted prowess, the Highland regiments attracted the particular notice of even the great Napoleon : other Scottish corps behaved with equal bravery, but it was the peculiar dress which so distinctly marked the battalions of Caledonia.

The natives of several countries have retained the antiquated form of their garments, and appear in the now unsuitable and grotesque habiliments of their ancestors : the Gaël adhere to the costume of their fathers, not merely as a venerated badge of national distinction, but as being best fitted for their circumstances : and it is a flattering compliment that those who are not natives take pride in assuming the garb of a North Briton.

In the various modes of its arrangement this is undeniably the most picturesque and original costume in Europe, partaking of the graceful flow of Oriental drapery, with more than the advantages of European attire, and which can be worn in great plainness, but is susceptible of being carried to the highest enrichment. It is, indeed, more usually considered as a military uniform than a civil costume, and its admirable adaptation for the fatigues and hardships of war is incontrovertibly admitted ; while it is certainly the best adapted for the country and the laborious avocations of its inhabitants. This was so evident to President Forbes, of Culloden, that he memorialized the government in strong terms against passing the act which made it felony to wear this much loved dress; one of his reasons why it should not be proscribed was, that it enabled them to bear the inclemency of the weather ! The statistics of our armies afford abundant proof of the truth of this assertion ; they show that, in the intense cold, during campaigns in Holland, the Highlanders suffered incomparably less than others; and the kilt being bound tightly round the loins, its advantages in a rapid and protracted march have been witnessed in the retreat of Corunna, and elsewhere.*

Societies which have for their object the encouragement, by premium to those who wear this costume habitually, and with most propriety, and those noblemen and others who individually exert themselves in the promotion of its

* On this subject may be consulted Dalrymple's Memoirs, Stewart's Sketches of the Highlanders, the Scottish Gaël, Collect, rebus Albanicis, Skene's History of the Highlanders, Naval and Military Gazette, 1834, &c.

use, are benefactors to the country, holding forth substantial inducement to prosecute the national manufacture, and continue a dress the most convenient and economical, and greatly conducive to the preservation of health; while the sociality of the meetings connected with the object, where all classes mix in cordial animation, has a most beneficial effect.

In the army this national uniform keeps alive, in a surprising degree, the *esprit du corps;* and the tartan being, as it were, a Highlander's coat armour, he is especially careful that it shall in nowise be dishonoured.

A great advantage of this dress is its lightness, the limbs being left at perfect freedom, thus enabling the inhabitant of the mountaneous region to pursue with facility his laborious occupation, ascend the mountains, traverse the glens, and bound over the bogs with agility ; indeed, in the address which the Hon. Archibald Fraser, of Lovat, delivered, when seconding the motion of the late Duke of Montrose for the repeal of the act prohibiting this dress, he drew particular attention to its suitability in this respect. In 1782 this obnoxious and absurd law was repealed, and the Celts expressed their unbounded joy in vocal gratitude and congratulation. Donchadh bàn nan orain (fair Duncan of the songs) lamented, in touching strains, the infliction of so galling a reproach on a loyal people, and we give an abstract from a translation by Mr. D. Mac Pherson, a poet of no mean talents.

"Though compelled," says the bard, " to assume the breeches as our dress, hateful to us in the fashion by which our legs are now constrained : heretofore we moved boldly and erect with our belted plaids ; alas ! we are now disgraced. Since we have appeared in this detested garb, we can scarcely recognise each other at feast or fair. I have seen the day I would answer the man with contempt who should tell me that I ever should wear so unmanly a costume—so foreign to my kindred. Now our heads are thatched with dingy hats, and our backs with clumsy cassocks. Our smartness and picturesque appearance are gone. Alas ! how unfit is the dress for ascending our mountains, and coming down from the heights. We blush in it, when in presence of the fair. We are like slaves disarmed and humbled, without dirks, guns, swords, cross-belts, or pistols, and are scorned by the Saxons. Our indignation is great," &c. His ode on the restoration of the dress gave another opportunity for displaying the deep attachment of the people to their " native weeds." " The hated costume made our youths appear without sprightliness or graceful carriage ; they were utterly spiritless. Now all our hills re-echo to sounds of joy, and our men appear in their beloved tartans—the clothes that display the strife of colour, in which the carmine prevails : the banner again waves o'er the heads of the valiant. The Gaël now proudly looks up and appears as becomes him. The debt of gratitude to the noble Graham shall not be forgotten. Many a noble current flows in his veins, the heir of the great Montrose."

The rigid and long continued proscription of the Breacan, or Highland dress, during which numbers were banished for wearing it, produced an ignorance of its component parts and arrangement which has never been wholly removed. The present work is intended to accomplish this object, so highly desirable to artists and the general inquirer.

No branch of home manufacture has so long received the public patronage as this : it has, indeed, from its intrinsic beauty and qualities, combined with the attractive character of the costume, progressed very much in general favour, to the discomfiture of the prophets who pronounced " its tasteless regularity and vulgar glare" as sufficient to prevent for ever its adoption anywhere save in the Highlands.* Accurate data will be furnished on the clan tartans. We are aware that on this subject some differences of opinion exist, and the recent splendid work of John Sobieski Stewart exhibits great variations from the received patterns. Those will be given which are acknowledged by the present chiefs and clans, and which tradition and long prescriptive use have invested with a legitimate claim.

Mr. Mac Ian does not intend to restrict himself in these sketches to modern costume, but will introduce a useful variety by those of different dates. Some figures will appear in the Breacan an fheile, or belted plaid, and in the half belted, or imitation of this more ancient form, the shoulder plaid and others. There will also be illustrations of the Black Watch, or old 42nd, and other Highland troops, and the very ancient garment called the Leinn-croich, or saffron coloured shirt, the robe which distinguished a gentleman.

Some of the sketches will represent individuals who have in any way distinguished themselves, when authentic portraits can be procured. The figures will be variously armed, and the weapons will be drawn from the best specimens preserved in the armories of chiefs, or in other public and private collections. Amongst them will be seen the two-handed, or great sword, the true Claidheamhmor (claymore), as well as the common broadsword and accompanying target. The bow and arrow will also be given, a favourite weapon of the Cateran, or light-armed band, and the cautious deer-stalker, which, although in partial use to a much later period, was, it appears, last employed in Highland warfare at the great clan battle of Maolrua', fought 1688, between the Mac Intosh and Mac Donald of Keppach.

The female costume will afford subjects of great interest. That singular but long disused garment, called the Arasaid, will be represented in this work, it is believed, for the first time; and this portion will be varied by the other peculiarities of old and modern dress.

* Pinkerton, &c.

THE CLANS

THE CLANS.

SIOL AUSLANICH—CLAN BUCHANAN.

THE seanachies, or genealogists of this clan, derive it from Auslan bui', son of O'Kyan, an Irish prince, who came to Scotland in the time of Malcolm II. anno 1016, and obtained the lands of Buchanan, in the county of Stirling. It was the usage of the Celts to give distinctive appellations to individuals and tribes from the localities where they might reside, and the district occupied by this clan bears a Gaëlic name. Mac Auslan is, however, an original patronymic, which a branch of the clan yet retains, Gillebrid, seneschal to the Earl of Lennox, who flourished 1240, being the first who was styled "de Buchanan." His father, Mac Beth, obtained a grant of Clâr innis in 1225; but it must be borne in mind that lands were held in undisturbed possession long before the feudal tenure by charter was introduced. Various other grants were, from time to time, made to the lairds of Buchanan, who, up to 1682, when the last chief died without male issue, numbered twenty-two. One of these charters, dated 1564, confirmed possession of both Clareinch and Kepinch, with the bell and alms of St. Kessog! A branch of this clan who possessed the lands of Lennie, held them by the preservation of a large sword, with which their ancestor had first acquired them. Whoever had the custody of this weapon, and a tooth of St Fillan, were presumed to have a good right to that estate.

The family of Arnprior, an old cadet of the Buchanans, obtained that property in this manner. The Menzies' had been, for many generations, proprietors of part of the parishes of Kippen and Killearn, in which the above estate is situated, and in the reign of James IV. he who was then laird became aged and was without children, circumstances which induced Forrester of Cardin, a neighbouring gentleman, to give the old man great annoyance, and at last to threaten, on an alleged debt, that, if he did not assign to him the house and lands, he would possess himself of them by force of arms. In this extremity Menzies offered, for protection during his life, to leave Arnprior to one of the Chief of Buchanan's sons, an offer which was cheerfully accepted, and the terms very satisfactorily performed.

The Highlanders have been accused of indifference to everything but the acquirement of martial renown; but we find Sir John Buchanan, in 1618, "mortifying" £6,000 Scots, for the mainte-nance of three students of theology in the university of Edinburgh, and an equal sum to that of St. Andrew's for maintaining three students of philosophy there.

Among those of the name who have been distinguished in literature, the great George Buchanan stands pre-eminent. He was a son of Buchanan of Moss, a cadet of the family of Druimikill, and was born in 1506. In his "History of Scotland" we find evidence that Gaëlic was his mother tongue, and if he spoke it with as much elegance as he did the Latin, it is much to be regretted that he did not condescend to leave posterity some specimen of the vernacular. He particularly notices the Highlanders' partiality to the Tartan.

The military history of this clan is very honourable. Sir Maurice, the Chief, would not sign the bond of fealty to King Edward I. of England, 1296, to which so few had courage to withhold their names, and he stood firmly in the Bruce's favour throughout his wars, at first so disheartening.*

After the battle of Agincourt, France applied, in virtue of the ancient league between the two countries, for reinforcement, and, in 1420, 7,000 men were sent over, among whom were a number of this clan. In the heat of the battle which ensued at Beauge, Sir Alexander Buchanan, meeting the Duke of Clarence, pushed towards him, and, escaping his thrust, pierced him through the left eye, on which he immediately fell, when the fortunate knight, seizing the Duke's cap, or coronet, bore it off on his spear's point ? This is contrary to other accounts, which represent the great constable, the Earl of Buchan, as having killed the Duke of Clarence, but Buchanan of Auchmar, the historian of the clan, gives the authority of the Book of Pluscardine Abbey, and the tradition has always been that, for this signal service, the French king granted the victor a double tressure flory as an augmentation of his coat-armour, and for crest a hand holding a cap of honour.

Buchanan and Lennie both fell at Flodden, in 1513, and the clan fought bravely for Queen Mary at Pinky, 1547, as well as at Langside. Sir George Buchanan had command of a regiment during King Charles's wars, and the clan acquitted themselves with their usual valour at Dunbar and Inverkeithing, but the chiefship becoming extinct in

*Auchmar's History, but a Malcolm de Buchanan attached his name.

24

BUCHANAN

the direct line, and the affairs of the clan getting into some confusion, they do not appear in their former prominent position during the troubles of the "'15 and 45."

The Mac Mhaolanich, or Mac Millans, a branch of this clan. settled at Cnap, in Argyle, but in consequence of the slaughter of a person of some note, called Marallach mòr, they were obliged to seek refuge in Lochaber, where they were named Mac Gille Veol. Locheil found them useful auxiliaries, as they could take 100 good men into the field, who were ready to engage in the most desperate enterprizes.

The country possessed by this clan stretches on the north side of Loch Lomond, about eighteen miles, and the house of Buchanan on its bank, is now the mansion of His Grace the Duke of Montrose.

The CATH-GHAIRM, or war-shout, used for the purpose of mustering the clan, or rousing its courage, is "Clàr innis," a small island in the lake. On raising this cry, fifty Buchanan heritors, with their followers, could be assembled in a few hours.

The ARMORIAL BEARINGS are, on a field, or, a lion rampant, sable, armed and langue'd, gules, within a double tressure, flory counterflory fleur-de-lis, of the second. Crest, a hand couped, holding a ducal cap, within two laurel branches, disposed orlewise, proper. Supporters, two falcons proper, belled or. Motto above, "Audaces juvo," and beneath, "Clarior hinc honos."

The SUAICHEANTAS, or Badge, is Dearcag monaidh, Bilberry plant, *vaccinium uliginosum.*.

Buchanan of Lennie is representative of the old Chiefs.

"The tartan of the Buchanans, as here shewn, contains that peculiarity of colour which has, about the Pass of Balmaha and Loch Lomond side, generally procured it the name of the breacan bhui. The figure is arrayed in a large loose plaid and philibeg; being two separate articles. The jacket, or doublet, is of the same fashion as that in the figure of Mackinnon, only buttoned and belted. The buttons on the jacket are peculiar to the Highlands. The sporan bears the Cath-ghairm of the clan—Clàr innis. The hose, being cath-dath, are gartered high, and were sketched from a pair worn by Paul Mc Coll, a shepherd in the employment of Monzie; the brogues have been described before. The bonnet is a small, flat one. The badge in the bonnet denotes the wearer's clan; the two feathers, his near affinity to the Chief. The beard, to which the Celtic race was so attached (witness the act of parliament to compel the Irish Gaël to cut it off), is from an authentic portrait of Rob Roy, in the possession of Herbert Buchanan, Esq., of Arden. It may surprise our southern readers to tell them that a Highlander thus habited has in his dress eighteen yards of cloth!"—*Mr. Mc. Ian.*

NA CAMSHROINAICH—THE CAMERONS.

WERE it consistent with the plan of this work to enter more particularly into the history of a clan, there is here a seductive opportunity for ample detail and expatiation. The Camerons are an aboriginal clan, and the patronymic is derived from an ancestor whose visage must have been remarkable; cam-shron signifying crooked nose, the *s* being quiescent. From Donald Du', who flourished in the end of the fifteenth century, the clan has been since distinguished as the race of Mac'onuill Du', or the son of Donald the black; but it seems the Locheil branch is not the eldest, the tradition being that it was by intermarriage with the Mac Martins, of Letterfiunlay, that the property in Lochaber was first acquired. The Camerons proper were anciently called Clan mhic Ghili'n Obhi, the children of the son of the follower of Ovi, an heroic band whom we find mentioned in some fragments ascribed to Ossian, the unrivalled bard of Cona.

Aonghas, who married a sister of Bancho, slain by Macbeth in 1020, is held to have been the undoubted ancestor of the line of Lochiel, and the family genealogies present a long series of succeeding chiefs who distinguished themselves highly in the wars and other transactions of their country. John fought in the army of Donald, Lord of the Isles, at the battle of Harlaw, in 1411; but the Camerons subsequently abandoned the cause of those powerful chiefs, who, therefore, visited them with direful vengeance: Donald Du' and his renowned son, Allan, extricated the clan from the state of depression into which it had fallen, the latter acquiring the lands of Locharcaig and Lochiel, which he retained possession of, notwithstanding that Clan Ranald laid claim to them as ancient property vesting in his person, but by accepting feudal charters of the lands forfeited by the Mac Donalds, they were the means of sapping the power of that branch of the clan. Various other possessions were obtained, and under the prudent management of Allan, the clan rose very rapidly in importance, although he was engaged in several feuds, one of the most determined being with the Mac Intoshes. He supported Ian Mudartach when that enterprising leader assumed the chiefship of Clan Ranald, and having been with the Mac Donalds when they gave so signal a defeat to Lord Lovat in Glenlochie, 1544, whom they killed with almost every one of his followers, Huntly marched to Lochaber with a force which could not be withstood, and seizing Locheil and Keppach, he caused them both to be beheaded at Elgin.

CAMERON

The Camerons were afterwards engaged in various feuds with neighbouring clans which were conducted with different success. They joined the Earls of Huntly and Errol, who took arms for their own protection against the king's troops, and were of great service in obtaining the victory over Argyle at Glenlivat, but for his share in this rising Locheil was outlawed, and lost part of his estate, which was never afterwards recovered.

Sir Ewen Cameron, born in 1629, was one of the most renowned chiefs of this or any other clan, many of his adventures appearing more like romance than matters of reality. From his youth he showed the strongest attachment to the Stewart family, and obtained repeated thanks for his loyal services. He was the only chief who never submitted to the authority of Cromwell, and it is remarkable that when he had suppressed the Scottish insurrection in favour of the royal family, by disarming, imprisoning, and fining the leading men, the Camerons were allowed to retain their arms on the simple promise of peaceable conduct, and "no oath was required of Lochiel but his word of honour to live in peace." Reparation was even ordered to be made to him for the wood destroyed by the garrison of Inverlochie; the losses which his tenants had sustained were to be made good, and an indemnity was to be given for all crimes and depredations which had been committed by his clan! His character must, indeed, have made a strong impression on the stern Protector! So continually did he harass the garrison at Inverlochie that the troops remained in a state of siege, and they could only obtain peace by these concessions. The agreement was entered into between Locheil and the governor, the soldiers being drawn up to receive the Camerons, with all the formality of a treaty between two independent states. Locheil joined Dundee at Killicrankie, 1689, although then far advanced in life, and died in 1719, at the patriarchal age of ninety, never having lost a drop of blood in any battle or personal encounter.

His grandson, the celebrated Lochiel of 1745, was a counterpart to Sir Ewen. His father had joined the Earl of Mar in 1715, for which he was forfeited, but young Locheil was the first to muster his clan for prince Charles, and during his brief campagne this heroic and amiable chief acquired the respect of both parties. His humane and conciliatory disposition was displayed in exertions to alleviate the evils of the war, and he most determinedly punished all acts of insubordination and plunder; on one occasion, it is said, going so far as to shoot one of his own men caught in the act of theft. After the battle of Culloden, in which he was severely wounded, he escaped to France, where King James gave him the command of a regiment formed of his expatriated countrymen.

He died in 1748, and his son, John, returned to Scotland in 1759, where he lived respected on his paternal property, which had been restored. His son, Charles, succeeded to the family estates, and the present chief is Donald Cameron, Esq., late captain in the guards, who married the Lady Vere.

The military force of the Camerons was estimated at 800, both in 1715 and 1745, men whom Drummond of Hawthornden describes as "fiercer than fierceness itself!"

The ARMORIAL BEARINGS are or, three, bars, gules.

The SUAICHEANTAS is the Dearcag fithich, Crowberry, *Empitium nigrum*, but there is a prevalent belief that a slip of oak is the proper badge. The former is seen in the gronnd near the figure.

PIOBAIREACHDAN. Spaidsearachd, *i. e.*, the march of Lochiel, is the favourite salute to the chief. Ceann na drochait mhòr, or the end of the great bridge, is another piece which is said to be a Cameron composition, and they claim that piob'rachd which, in a former number, we have given to Black Donald Ballach of the Isles.

The suppression of the Colleges for pipers, of which the Mac Cruimins, Mac Artairs, and others, were hereditary masters, has tended much to the misappropriation of Clan music, but we believe the above is correctly awarded to the Mac Donalds.

The figure represents a young man dressed in the style prevalent in the middle of the last century, when wigs were in use. The chief garment is Breacon, which is worn in the mode usually termed the belted plaid. It is of the pattern claimed as the appropriate *sett*. The hose are ca' da', or formed of cloth of the tartan worn by the 79th, or Cameron Highlanders, which is a design furnished by Sir Allan Cameron of Errachd, who raised this distinguished corps in 1794. The gun is painted from one of those taken from the Highlanders in the two last rebellions, many of which were preserved in the small armory in the Tower, now destroyed. It is of Spanish manufacture, as most of the Highlanders' muskets formerly were. The sword is from a fine "Andrea Ferrara" the property of Henry Longlands, Esq., Charlton, Kent.

NA CAMBEULICH—THE CAMPBELLS OF ARGYLE.

It has long been the practice of Scottish genealogists to deduce families from Norman or Saxon ancestors, and the latinising of proper Gaëlic names by the early chroniclers has led to a very general belief that their conjectures were correct. The founder of

CAMPBELL of ARGYLE

this clan is represented to have been a certain person styled De Campo Bello, who came to England with William the Conqueror, but in the Roll of Battle Abbey, which was a list of all the knights who composed that prince's retinue, this name is not to be found, and its appearance in Scottish record is always in the form which it still retains. Gilliespuig Cambel is witness in a charter granted to the town of Newburgh, in 1266, and the appellation Kambel is found among the signatures to the Ragman Roll in 1296.

The appellation is personal, and is composed of the words cam, bent, or arched and beul mouth, and the individual so distinguished, was of the race of Dairmid o Duibhne, who is much celebrated in traditional story, and was contemporary with the heros of Ossian, an antiquity which few clans can claim with equal confidence, but the Campbells do not come forward very prominently in national history until the time of Robert the Bruce. Their chief possession was Lochau, but Sir Nial Cambeul, Mac Chaillain môr, having fought strenuously for that monarch, was rewarded by many grants of forfeited lands, while by marrying the king's sister he acquired a superiority in the Highlands which his descendants not only maintained, but extended over almost all the surrounding clans. They had a long and severe contention with the Mac Dugals of Lorn, whose power they materially abridged, and they were long rent by a feud respecting the chiefship, which was keenly disputed by the Mac Arthur branch of the clan; but it was finally established in the barons of Lochau, anno 1427.

Many families of note sprung from the great clan of Argyle, the most distinguished of whom is that of Glenurchai', subsequently Earls, and now Marquis of Breadalbane, in Perthshire, whose ancestor was a son of Duncan, first Lord Campbell of Lochau, who was created 1445. The Earldom of Argyle was conferred on Caillain or Colin, in 1457. Gilli'-Espuig, or Archibald, his son, was Lord High Chancellor, Lord Chamberlain, and Master of the Household to James IV., whom he followed to Flodden, where he fell with that chivalrous monarch, leading the van of the army, anno 1513 Archibald fifth Earl was zealous for the reformation, and with the Prior of St. Andrews, afterwards the Regent Moray, he concluded a negociation with the Lords of the congregation, which the queen mother violated, when they joined the reformers, took possession of Edinburgh, and were mainly instrumental in settling the Protestant religion by Act of Parliament, 1560. Argyle notwithstanding espoused the cause of Queen Mary, and commanded her army at Langside, but his brother, Sir Colin, took the side of the young king and the barons who opposed his mother.

In the commencement of the 17th century Archibald seventh Earl, was at the age of eighteen, sent in command of an army against the Popish Earls of Errol and Huntly, by whom he was completely defeated, 1594. He engaged in the suppression of an insurrection of the Mac Donalds, and he was also commissioned to act against the Mac Gregors' with fire and sword. His son Archibald was the chief leader of the Covenanters; he had placed the crown on the head of Charles II., but notwithstanding his evident loyalty he was on the restoration charged with treason in having given his countenance to Cromwell's assumption of the Protectorate, condemned and beheaded.

The Marquis of Montrose having ravaged Kintire, Argyle went in pursuit of him with the largest army he could muster, when he was attacked at Inverlochie and defeated with great slaughter, no fewer than 1500 of his family and name having fallen. Archibald, his successor, was steady in his adherence to King Charles, for whom he acted so vigorously, that Cromwell forbade him the privilege of his act of grace and pardon. Having refused to take the oath prescribed by the Test Act, 1681, otherwise than according to his own view of its intent, he was condemned to death, but made his escape from Edinburgh Castle in the disguise of a page, holding the train of his step-daughter, Lady Sophia Lindsay, and retired to Holland. When the Duke of Monmouth attempted to excite an insurrection in England 1685, Argyle was induced to land in the west of Scotland with some forces to act in co-operation. At Cambelton he issued a proclamation, in which he averred that they were constrained for the common safety to take up arms in the name and fear of the great God, for their own and country's relief—for intolerable grievances and oppressions, and for the defence and re-establishment of the Protestant religion. His forces were, however speedily dispersed, himself taken prisoner, and beheaded like his father, 30th of June, 1685, with circumstances of particular harshness and indignity.

It has been observed that this nobleman perished on the scaffold, for the very same line of conduct that was a few years afterwards pursued by the men, who are yet distinguished by the appellation of the glorious patriots who seated King William on the throne!

Argyle's eldest son Archibald returned with William of Orange, and by that monarch was elevated to the rank of Duke. His son and successor, John was celebrated for his military abilities, and gave proofs of his valour, when Colonel of a regiment of foot at the early age of seventeen, and he commanded the army which checked the rebellion under the Earl of Mar, at Dunblain, in 1715. John, the fifth duke, was created an English peer, by the title of Baron Sundridge, of Coomb Bank. The present Duke, John, Douglas, Edward, Henry, succeeded on the death of his brother in 1836, of whom a circumstance is deserving of record in this place, redounding as it does so creditably to him, and offering so striking a contrast to the feelings and proceedings of other highland proprietors. When the rage for ejecting the highland tenantry, and turning vast tracts of land into sheep farms was so much the rage, it was strongly urged on his Grace to expel the inhabitants of the isle of Rum, and let it to a south country farmer for the pasturage of sheep, as a much more lucrative stock than the old inhabitants. "No," said his grace, "if they are desirous to leave I shall not object to their doing so, but I will not attempt to displace them, for I cannot forget that it was to these people, who furnished me a company, that I was indebted for my captaincy when a young man."

Scott's beautiful poem of Glenera must be familiar to our readers. It commemorates a shocking occurrence, but as the detail is not consistent with the fact, it may be well to relate the circumstance as it happened. Gilliespuig-ruà, the first Earl of Argyle, had a daughter Elizabeth married to Lachlan Cattanach of Duart, chief of the Mac Leans, with whom she lived very unhappily, and their discord became so great that Lachlan, in his barbarous wish to rid himself of the unfortunate lady, left her one evening on a rock which the sea covered at high tide, in order that she might be swept away during the night. Providentially her shrieks were heard by the crew of a passing boat, who rescued her, on which a divorce took place, and she married Campbell of Achnambrea. This happened in 1490, and the place in the Sound of Mull which was to be the scene of her death, is since pointed out as the Lady's Rock. The friendship of the Campbells and Mac Leans does not seem to have been destroyed through this atrocious deed, for the families soon after intermarried; Lachlan, however, who lived to a very old age, was killed in his bed when in Edinburgh, by a stab from the hand of Campbell of Calder, in revenge for his usage of the unhappy lady, and for an attempt he had made on the life of his brother, Ian-garbh, first laird of Lochnell.

The Campbells are a very numerous clan in the West Highlands, most part of Argyleshire being their property. In 1715, Marshal Wade reported their military strength as 4000; in 1745 it was estimated at 5000, and the Argyle militia embodied to act against Prince Charles Edward, materially contributed to the discomfiture of his army at Culloden. The 91st is the Argyle regiment, but they do not wear the highland dress.

The chief seat of the Dukes of Argyle is at Inverary, a splendid mansion in one of the most delightful situations.

The ARMORIAL BEARINGS are quarterly first and fourth, gyrony of eight, or and sable, for the name of Campbell; the second and third are for the lordship of Lorn, viz. arg, a galley, sails furled, sable, flag and pennons, gules. Behind the shield are placed in bend dexter, a baton gules, semee of thistles or, ensigned with an imperial crown proper, and thereon the crest of Scotland, borne as hereditary master of the royal household. In bend sinister, a sword proper, hilt and pomel, or, indicative of the office of Lord Justice General. Crest, a boar's head, fesswise, couped, or. Supporters, two lions guardant, gules. Mottoes, above the shield, *in more Scottorum*, "Ne obliviscaris," and on a compartment beneath, "Vix ea nostra voco."

The SUAICHEANTAS, or Badge, is the Alpine plant, Garbhag an t-sleibh, Fir club moss, *Lycopodium selago*. Many assert that the Roid, or sweet gale is the proper plant, but as it is not an evergreen it could not serve the purpose of a badge in all seasons unless, indeed, it were used when prepared as if for a hortus siccus.

The artist, in accordance with the character of the family of Argyle, who were distinguished as staunch adherents of the "solemn league," has exhibited the figure in the character of one of those doughty opponents of prelacy, poreing over the sacred volume to strengthen his resolution to stand for the covenanted work of Scotland's reformation.

He is also, as was the practice with those worthies, provided with his trusty broadsword, as if prepared for an attack by Clavers and his formidable dragoons.

James Campbell, a private in the highland regiment, has been celebrated for his heroism at Fontenoy, having with his broadsword killed no fewer than nine men—making a stroke at the tenth, his left arm was carried off by a cannon ball! To the honour of the Duke of Cumberland he rewarded this brave man although a Celt, with a lieutenant's commission.

CAMPBELLS OF BREADALBANE.

THE CAMPBELLS trace their descent to an antiquity equal to that of any of the clans. Diarmid, a warrior celebrated in Ossianic poetry, is the progenitor of this surname, and tradition represents the Campbells as Barons of Lochow since the fifth century.

The immediate ancestor of the Breadalbane family was dark Sir Colin (Cailain dubh), third son of Duncan, first Lord Campbell of Lochow, ancestor of the ducal house of Argyle, his mother being a daughter of Robert, Duke of Albany, Regent of Scotland. He was born about 1400, and his father settled on him the lands of Gleannurchaidh (Glenurchy). He married one of the three daughters of the Lord Lorn, by whom he got the third part of that extensive property; and from that acquisition the Long-fada, Lymphad, or Galley, was quartered in the armorial shield. He visited many foreign countries, distinguishing himself by his valour, and when in Palestine he was made one of the Knights of Rhodes.

His son, Sir Duncan, obtained crown charters of the lands

of Glenlyon, Finlarig, Port of Loch Tay, &c., and married Margaret, daughter of the Earl of Angus, with whom he received, as dowry, 600 marks, two gentlemen of rank becoming sureties for its payment. Gilleaspuig, or Archibald, his second son, was ancestor of the Campbells of Glenlyon. Charters of several other lands were granted to Sir Colin, third of the name, 1551 to 1564. This chief was one of the first noblemen who took an active part in the Reformation: he sat in the Parliament of 1560, which established the Protestant doctrines, and was subsequently appointed a commissioner for finally settling the system of church government. His son, Sir Duncan, continued to increase the family possessions, and obtained from King Charles I., the office of heritable keeper of Mamlorn Forest, and the Sheriffship of Perthshire for life; he was also created a Baronet of Nova Scotia, 1625. His fifth son, Gilleaspuig. or Archibald, was ancestor of the Campbells of Monzie, pronounced Monee.

Sir Robert, who flourished 1640, had several sons besides his successor, who were the respective founders of the branches of Mochaster, who succeeded to the chiefship, Auchlyne, Glenfallach, and Glendochart. From daughters of his successor, Sir John, are descended the Campbells of Airds, Ardchattan, &c.

Sir John Campbell, of Glenurchy, Ian Glass, so named from his swarthy complexion, obtained, in 1681, a patent creating him Earl of Breadalbane and Holland, Viscount Taymouth and Pentland, Lord Glenurchy, Ormelie, Benederaloch and Weik. Sir John was of the greatest service in the operations carried on in favor of Charles II.; and at the Revolution his great influence with the clans enabled him to prevent a rising in the Highlands in favour of the exiled family. He was an admirable politician; and it was said of him that he was cunning as a fox, wise as a serpent, but slippery as an eel.[*1] In 1657, he married Lady Mary Rich, daughter of the Earl of Holland, with whom he received £10,000.—a considerable sum in those days. It is said that the long journey from London to Breadalbane was performed in the plain old way, her ladyship riding on a pillion behind her lord, while on the back of a strong gelding was placed the marriage portion, which was paid in coin; a sturdy Highlander, well armed, at each side being appointed as a guard.[*2]

In 1806, the British title "Baron Breadalbane, of Taymouth," was conferred, aud, in 1831, the dignity of Marquis. The present munificent and highly respected chief of the Breadalbane Campbells takes an active interest in all objects of public utility, and warmly patronises the national observances, for which the Gaël have so unchangeable a predilection. Justly proud of an imposing retinue of devoted clansmen, a body of them has been always mustered to grace the Royal cavalcades. When Prince Leopold visited Taymouth, 1238 picked men, under arms, and in the national costume, welcomed him in front of the castle– a number which might easily have been doubled: and a considerable body was marched for duty when King George IV. honoured Dunedin (Edinburgh) with his presence, in 1822. It is unnecessary to attempt any description of the late scenes at the Ballach of Loch Tay, where there was such a numerous assemblage, and scenes of Highland parade and festivity—more like the dreams of romance than reality.

Breadalbane sent 500 men to Mar's army in 1715; they were 1000 strong in 1745; and in the late war three fencible battalions were quickly enrolled, amounting to 2300 men.[†]

The ARMORIAL BEARINGS are quarterly, 1st and 4th gyrony of 8, or, and sable, for Campbell; 2nd, or, a fesse checky azure and argent, for Stewart; 3rd or, a lymphad, sails furled, sable, for the Lordship of Lorn. Crest, a boar's head erased proper. Supporters, two stags proper, attired and unguled, or. Motto, "Follow me"—a call to which several of the cadets have responded in the characteristic spirit of clanship. Auchlyne says, "with heart and hand;" Achalader, "with courage;" Glenfallach, "thus far," in allusion to his crest—a dagger piercing a heart; Barcaldine, "paratus sum," &c.

The SUAICHEANTAS, or Badge, as now worn, is the Roid, or Sweet gale; many, however, maintain that it should be the Garbhag an t-sleibh, *lycopodium selago*, Fir club moss.

The BREACAN, or Tartan, is of the classs denominated uaine, green, but it is enriched by a double stripe of yellow, differing, as will be shown in a following number, from the Argyle pattern.

The CATH-GHAIRM, or Battle-shout, used in former times, is not precisely known; Siol Diarmid an tuirc!—the race of Diarmid of the boar—was a rallying cry for all Campbells; but the bearer of the Crois-taradh, or warning cross—at which signal a clan flew to arms— always named the place of rendezvous.

The PIOBAIREACHD—a species of music peculiar to the Highlanders and the bagpipes—is called Bodach na Briogais, and originated in a very singular circumstance. The Earl of Caithness was deeply in debt, and in 1672, finding Sir John Campbell, of Glenurchy, a creditor to a large amount, which he had no hopes of ever being able to pay, he renounced his own property and titles in favour of Sir John, in liquidation of the debt, on condition that he should assume the name and arms of Sinclair. He was accordingly created a peer by that title, and proceeded to take possession of his newly–acquired estates; Sinclair of Geis, heir male of the family, opposed him with an armed force, but was defeated, with great slaughter, in a pitched battle, on which occasion, the piper composed the above fine spaidsearachd, or march, in ridicule of the Sinclairs, which, from the exclamation that "Bodach na briogais," the fellow with the breeches was running, shows that Sinclair wore that garment so disliked by the Highlanders. The Campbells were ultimately driven out of the country by the Sinclairs, and the Earldom was restored as a dignity which could not be disponed to another. Glenurchy, however, for some time retained the lands, and was solaced for his disappointment by the titles which he acquired as before related.

The ancient seat was the Castle of Coalchuirn (Kilchurn), on the side of Lochow, originally the residence of the chiefs of Clan Gregor, but rebuilt in 1440, by the Lady of Black Colin, during his absence in the Holy Land. It was subsequently much enlarged, and the ruins still attest its former splendour; but since it was occupied by a garrison, placed there to overawe the disaffected after 1746, it has been untenanted. His successor, Sir Colin, of the sixteenth century, built

CAMPBELL of BREADALBANE

Edinample, and founded, in 1580, the splendid castle where the present Marquis resides. Its proper appellation is Ballach, which signifies a pass, or opening, but Taymouth is descriptive of its locality. It is situated near the boundary of the estate, and its site was determined in this manner. Sir Colin was desirous of erecting it in a more centrical position, but the seanachaidh, elders, or councillors, represented that, when placed on the frontiers of the property, if molested by their neighbours, they could more easily retaliate, and could, with more facility, extend their territories in that direction, and the result proved the justice of their policy. So little did a chief—notwithstanding his patriarchal power—feel justified in opposing the wishes of his clansmen, that the point was yielded without opposition. A family history, in M.S., written 1598, tells us that, besides these works, he also built "the haill ludging of Perth within the close, the four kernellis of the castell of Ilan Keilquhirne, and the north chalmeirs thairoff;" and adds, that "he was ane greate Justiciar all his tyme, throch the quhilk he sustenit that deidly feid of the Clan Gregor ane lang space. And besydis that, he causit execute to the death mony notable lymmars, and beheided the Laird of Mac Gregor himself at Keanmoir, in presence of the Erle of Atholl, the Justice Clerk, and sundrie uther nobillmen." The latter observation is meant to show his sovereign

rule in his own barony, where he had "power of pit and gallows"; i. e, heritable privilege to imprison and execute.

Sir Duncan, his successor, was fond of building and embellishing his mansions, having, besides the above, Finlarig, Loch-dochart, Achalader, and Barcaldine; from this partiality he obtained the *sobriquet* of Donchadh nan Caisteal, Duncan of the Castles. It was the maxim of the Highlanders, that it was always better to trust to "a bulwark of bones, than a castle of stones."

The Burial-place of the Breadalbane family was originally the ancient kirk of Dalmally, which they built in 1440, placing over the door the coat of arms; since 1508, it has been the ancient chapel of Finlarig.*

The figure appears in the costume nearly as now worn; but the sword belt is appropriately under the plaid. He carries dirk and pistols, and wears the buckles which distinguished the gentleman and courtier of the last century, and is retained in the Highland regiments. The Glengarry bonnet is, however, a late introduction, but the taste of many leads them to prefer it to the more legitimate form. The whole figure, with these exceptions, reminds us of the chiefs who so chivalrously embarked in the cause of the unfortunate Prince Charles Stewart.

*Archæologia Scotia.

CLANN SIOSAL, OR THE CHISHOLMS.

THE claim of this clan to a Celtic origin has been very confidently opposed by some writers; but their opinions, formed on different grounds, arise in consequence of a confusion of names, an insufficient knowledge of the Gaëlic language, and a want of due consideration of Highland and Lowland usages. Chisholm is the Saxon name of a property on the border of Scotland, and the proprietor is designated from his estate, but no such name exists in the Highlands. The vernacular appellation is Siosal, and the translation of that word is one of the numerous similar corruptions introduced by the capricious ignorance of chroniclers and fanciful heralds. Chisholm of Chisholm is very improperly substituted for An t-Siosal, The Chisholm.

Again—those who came to understand the original appellation found, by a fertility of imagination, that the race of Siosal descended from the English Cecils; but the ancestors of that family were Cambrian knights, who bore the appropriate name of Sytsylt and Seisylt, long after the Chisholms appear in the pages of national history; and the coat armour, on which so many fortify their belief of family connexion, is entirely dissimilar.

Harald, or Guthred, Thane of Caithness, flourished in the latter part of the twelfth century. Sir Robert Gordon gives him the

surname of Chisholm; and the probability is, that it was the general name of his followers. He married the daughter of Madach, Earl of Athol, and became one of the most powerful chiefs in the north, where he created continued disturbances during the reign of William the Lion, by whom he was at last defeated and put to death, his lands being divided between Freskin, ancestor of the Earls of Sutherland, and Ma'nus, or Magnus, son of Gillibreid, Earl of Angus.* It seems that, from the rigourous prosecution to which the followers of Harald were subjected, they were compelled, as was the case with several other clans in troublous times, to seek for new possessions; and Strathglas offered an eligible position for a high-spirited clan maintaining their independence.

These proceedings occurred about 1220; but we do not find other notice of the Chisholms until 1334, when the clan was of such importance as to induce Sir Robert Lauder, of Quarrel Wood, who was Constable of Urquhart Castle, on the bank of Lochness, to seek its alliance by giving his daughter and heiress in marriage to the Chief. There are, indeed, the signatures of Richard *de* Chesehelm and John *de* Cheshome, in Roxburgh and Berwick shires, attached to the deed called Ragman's Roll, 1296; † but none of the Siosailich submitted to this degradation of betraying their country's independence.

* History of the Earls of Sutherland, fol.   Lord Hailes. Annals.   † Prynn.

CHISHOLM

Robert, the son of this marriage, acquired Quarrel Wood in right of his mother, and succeeded to the important trust of the keeping of Castle Urquhart. He obtained the honour of knighthood, and was taken prisoner, with King David II., at the unfortunate battle of Neville's Cross, 1346. He lived long after his release; and his piety is attested by a well-preserved deed, dated Inverness, the feast of the Epiphany of the Holy Cross, 1362, in which he grants, for the salvation of his own soul, and those of his ancestors and successors, six acres of arable land lying within the lands of the old castle of Inverness. The piece of ground thus bestowed is still, in part, the property of the Kirk Session; and its proceeds being devoted to relieve the poor, it was called Tir na bochd; now, corruptly, Diribught, "the poor's lands." Many charters and exchanges of property between the different chiefs, the Scottish kings, and nobility, took place, which shows that their possessions were very extensive.*

They occasionally got into misunderstandings with the bishops and chapter of Moray, respecting their lands in that county. In 1369 these clergy made complaint that Robert, Lord of Quarrel Wood, had "wrongously intromitted" with some of their property; and, in 1398, John de Chesehelm was charged to give up the lands of Kinmylies, which were the church's patrimony.

The form of an act of homage, 1368, for certain lands, is preserved, which is somewhat curious:—" In camera domini Alexandri Dei gratia Episcopi Moraviensis apud struy presente tota multitudine Canonicorum et Capellanorum et aliorum, ad prandium ibi invitatorum. Alexander de Chisholme fecit homagium junctis manibus et discooperta capite, pro eisdem terris," &c. About this time, Uilan, or Wyland, *hodie* William, " venerabilis vir et dominus," was treasurer of Moray, and appears to have been a very active official.†

John, who was chief at the end of the fourteenth century, had an only child, Morella, who married Alexander Sutherland, Baron of Duffus, and she carried away so much of the property, that the male heir was greatly reduced, having little more than the "country" of Strathglas. From this marriage the house of Duffus carry the addition of the boar's head in their armorial coat.

An indenture for the settlement of the respective lands was entered into, in 1403, between Margaret de la Aird, widow of Alexander, late chief, then designed from the place of his residence, " of Comar," his successor, Thomas, and William Lord Fentoun, heirs portioners, by which we find the property lay, not only in Inverness and Moray shires, but in the counties of Perth, Forfar, and Aberdeen.

In 1513, we find Uilan of Comar, assisted by Alastair Mac Ranald of Glengarry, storming the castle of Urquhart.

In 1587, the chiefs, on whose lands resided broken men, were called upon to give security for their peaceable behaviour, among whom appears "Cheisholme of Cummer."

After the battle of Killicrankie, 1689, Erchless Castle was garrisoned for King James, and it required considerable exertion, on the part of General Livingstone, to dislodge the Highlanders, and prevent them from regaining possession of it, having besieged it with a large force. Ruarai', or Roderic Mac Ian, had signed the address of 102 chiefs and heads of houses to George I., expressive of their loyalty, but no notice being taken of it, he engaged very actively in the

rising under the Earl of Mar, 1715, Chisholm of Cnocfin, an aged veteran, heading the clan at the field of Dunblane, in requital for which his estates were forfeited and sold. In 1727 he procured, with several other chiefs, a pardon under the privy seal; and Mac Kenzie of Allangrange, who then possessed the lands, "disponed" them the same year to Chisholm of Mucherach, who again conveyed them to Roderic's eldest son, and entailed them on his heirs male.

This chief, so devoted to the family of Stewart, joined his fortune with that of Prince Charles, 1745, and Colin, his youngest son, was appointed colonel of the Clan Battalion.

Alexander, who succeeded to the family honours and estates in 1785, left an only child, Mary, married, to James Gooden, Esq., London; and, dying in 1793, the chiefship and property, agreeably to clan law, and by the deed of entail, devolved on his youngest brother, William, who married Elizabeth, eldest daughter of Duncan Mac Donell, Esq., of Glengarry, and left two sons and a daughter. On his death, 1817, he was succeeded by the elder son, Alexander William, late member of parliament for Invernessshire, who was doomed to fill a premature grave, September, 1838, and of whose amiable life an interesting memoir has recently appeared.

The succession now rests on his brother, Duncan Mac Donnell (Gaëlice, Doncha' Mac Dhonuill), who inherits, in an eminent degree, the patriotic characteristics of a Highland chief; while he actively promotes all objects in which his countrymen are interested, he cordially supports those institutions beneficial to society in general.

The Chisholms of Cromlics, in Perthshire, were a distinguished branch of this clan, and were remarkable for giving three bishops of Dunblane in succession, who were most strenuous opposers of the Reformation, which involved them in continued trouble, and led to the loss of their patrimony, and the expatriation of William, who became Bishop of Vaison. By the marriage of Jane, only daughter of Sir James Chisholm of Cromlics, to James, second son of David Lord Drummond, the lands were carried to the family of Viscount Strathallan, and gave him the second title.

The Armorial Bearings of the Chisholm are on a shield gules, a boar's head couped, or. Crest, a dexter hand couped at the wrist, holding a dagger, proper, on which is transfixed a boar's head couped, of the second. Supporters, two savages wreathed about the head and loins, and bearing knotted clubs, proper. Mottoes: above the escutcheon, " Feros ferio:"—underneath, " Vi aut virtute."

The Suaicheantas, or Badge, is Rainneach, *Filix*, Fern.

The Piobaireachd, or Gathering, is Failte Siosalaich Sthrathglas, the Salute or Welcome to the chiefs, a fine piece of pipe-music, composed in praise of their noted hospitality.

Erchless Castle, the family seat, is an old baronial mansion, situated in a picturesque locality in Strath-glas, or the Grey-valley.

---

* Family History, 4to. MS.   † Registrum Moraviensis.

The burial-place was in the chancel of Beaulieu Priory, now in ruins; but there is no monument, except a mural slab erected in memory of Alexander, who died 1793, by his only daughter. The late chief was buried, by his own desire, on a verdant mount, surrounded by venerable trees, near the castle, where several of his remote ancestors likewise repose.

The military force of this clan, in 1745, amounted to 200 men, but their " following" must have been formerly much greater.

After the disastrous battle of Culloden, Prince Charles was obliged to trust his life to the honour of his devoted followers, and three poor individuals of this clan concealed and supported him in a cave, and safely conveyed him to the coast of Arisaig, resisting the temptation of £30,000 offered for his apprehension. Hugh Chisholm, otherwise Mac Lea, one of these faithful Highlanders, having shaken hands with the Prince when parting, made a vow, which he religiously observed, that his right hand should never be offered to another.

One of the chiefs having carried off a daughter of Lord Lovat, placed her for safety in an islet in Loch Bruiach, where she was soon discovered by the Frasers, who had speedily mustered for the rescue. A severe conflict ensued, during which the young lady was accidentally slain by her own brother! A plaintive Gaëlic song records the sad calamity, and numerous tumuli mark the graves of those who fell.

The figure is represented in the attire in which the chief usually appears when present at festivals and national meetings. This costume is the court-dress of a Highlander; and the Chisholms' plain tartan is as proud a passport to the presence of royalty as the splendid uniform of the British guards. The black velvet jacket contrasts well with the red-coloured kilt, and, by wearing the imitation of the old belted plaid, the breast is left free, and neither ornaments nor arms are hidden. The pistols are remarkable for size, but they are painted from a genuine old family pair. The brogs are of a pattern frequently worn by gentlemen.

THE COLQUHONS.

LIKE many other families, the Colquhons seek to derive themselves from an Irish progenitor. We are told, by their genealogists, that Conoch, one of the reguli of the sister isles, came to Scotland in the reign of Geirg'ear mòr, or Gregory the Great, 875—891, and obtaining certain lands from that monarch in the county of Dunbarton, he named them Conochon, which was subsequently corrupted to Colquhon.

It is, however, to be observed that to transfer personal appellations to locality was not a Celtic practice, but the contrary; and hence a more reasonable account of the settlement of this clan in the part of the country which they have so long possessed can be given. Umphred de Kilpatrick received a grant of the lands of Colquhon in the above county from Alexander II., when, according to custom, he was distinguished by the name of his property. Luss, situated on the side of Loc Lomond, was then in possession of the old Earls of Lennox, and it was not until the time of King David Bruce, 1329—1370, that these lands became the property of the Colquhons.

Sir Robert Kilpatric, of Colquhon, married the daughter and sole heiress of Umphred de Luss, whence he was described as Dominus de Colquhon et de Luss, and the family has since been styled by either title indifferently.

The sanguinary battle of Glenfruin has been referred to in the account of Clan Gregor. Sir Humphry was then chief of the Colquhons, and having been active in the measures adopted to coerce the Mac Gregors, those of Balquhidder, were not slow to make retaliation. Anxious to terminate the feud, Alastair of Glenstræ, their chief, went to Luss, in 1602, that he might negotiate with the laird on the part of his clansmen, who at the time were under the leading of his brother, and he was accompanied by 200 of his friends and clansmen. The interview was apparently amicable, for Glenstræ and his retinue took their leave, and marched homewards for Rannach. It seems, however, that Colquhon did not confide in their friendly disposition, for he speedily collected a body of his own followers, the Buchanans, Graemes, and others amounting, it is said, to 500 horsemen and 300 foot, and pursued the Mac Gregors, who had gone by the way of Glanfruin, where there was then no road, and coming up with them about the middle of the valley, he made an immediate attack. Alastair appears to have expected some molestation: his men were in two divisions, and while he maintained the combat with the one, his brother made the circuit of a hill with the other, and attacked the assailants in the rear.

The battle was maintained with desperate courage on both sides, but the Clan Gregor was at last successful, routing their enemies with great slaughter. It is said that in the battle and pursuit no fewer than 200 Colquhons were slain, but although many of the Mac Gregors were dangerously wounded, the only persons killed were Iain glas, brother of the chief, and another! Luss escaped from the field, but the castle in which he had taken refuge being stormed, he was there slain. He had been twice married, first to a daughter of the Earl of Glencairn, and secondly to a daughter of Lord Hamilton, but leaving only a daughter, the succession devolved on his brother Alexander.

Several burgesses of Dunbarton had been present at the conference, and some of them were engaged in the battle which ensued. A number of scholars also had gone out to witness this " Highland pageant" in the glen of Luss, and from curiosity they followed in the pursuit to Glenfruin, where they were unhappily slain, a circumstance which added greatly to the indignation which was excited against the Mac Gregors. The Colquhons made an extraordinary appeal to the sympathies of the king. Besides a formal petition, sixty widows, mounted on white ponies, and clad in " weeds of woe," proceeded to court, bearing on poles no fewer than 220 bloody shirts, which they presented, with expressions the most doleful, to his majesty, loudly crying for speedy vengeance on the murderers of their husbands and sons. King James whose natural horror of war and bloodshed was so remarkable, became roused to exasperation, and immediately proscribed the whole race of Mac Gregor, by an act which otherwise so crushed them that they were not able again to molest the Colquhons.

John, son of Alexander, was created a baronet of Nova Scotia by king Charles I. in 1625. Sir Humphry, eighteenth chief, sat in the parliament of 1707, and, jealous of the independence of Scotland, he voted against every clause in the Act of Union.

Having but one daughter, Anne, his sole heiress, who married James Grant of Pluscardine, second son of Ludowick, chief of that clan, he surrendered his baronetcy for a new patent, which in the event of a failure of heirs, male, of his own body, settled the reversion of his estate and honours on his son-in-law and his heirs, with this condition, that they should assume the name and armorial insignia of Colquhon. The baronetship was vested in the person, but whenever he or his heirs should succeed to the Grant estates, those of Colquhon were to be relinquished in favor of the younger brother. Sir Humphry died in 1718, and his son-in-law, in virtue of this settlement, became Sir James Colquhon, of Luss; but next year on the death of his brother, he succeeded to the paternal inheritance and resumed the name, when Luss went to his second son, Ludowick. On the death of Sir James Grant, Ludowick surrendered the lands and honour of Colquhon to his younger brother, James, and became Laird of Grant. Sir James Colquhon died in 1786, and was succeeded by his eldest son, James, who, to avoid the inconvenience attending so singular a disposition of title and property, resigned his patent for a British baronetcy.

He died in 1805, and Sir James, his successor, a spirited and indulgent landlord, married Janet, daughter of the late Right Hon. Sir John Sinclair, Bart., and died in 1836. The present Sir James Colquhon, Bart., twenty-second chief, is Lord Lieutenant of the county.

The Luss estates extend for several miles along the west side of Loch Lomond, and the family mansion, Ros-dù', is situated on a beautiful peninsula, as its name indicates.

The ARMORIAL BEARINGS, argent, a saltire ingrailed, sable. Crest, a hart's head couped, gules. Supporters, two greyhounds, argent collared sable. Motto, " Si je puis."

SUAICHEANTAS, or Badge, Braoileag, nan con, Bear berry, *Arbutus uva ursi.*

This " veritable effigy " of the Colquhons, appears with a common flat bonnet, in which is appropriately fixed the clan badge, and the figure has no neckcloth, a " band " being seldom worn but at court, and on high occasions. The doublet is taken from the portrait of Prince Charles Stewart, in possession of Henry Pratt, Esq., St. John's Wood. The plaid, fastened by a brooch, is of the full size and the trews are painted, according to the description minutely given in the " Scottish Gaël ;" they are fastened round the loins, and had a square piece which hung down in front.

Alexander, fifteenth chief's third son, is ancestor of the respectable family of Tillyquhon, in the same country, who assumed the degree of baronet, as representing the line of the chiefs, on the death of Sir Humphry, in 1718.

CLANN GHUIMEIN—THE CUMINS.

MANY Scottish Clans who do not follow the corrupted traditions of the mediæval bards, and claim an Irish origin, labour to prove a Norman descent. Both have been assigned to the Cumins by different writers, but the assertion may be made with equal confidence and more probability, that this clan is ab origine a Gaëlic race.

Among the earlier instances of the occurence of this name in the annals of Caledonia, are those of Cumin Abbat of the famed Icolumkil, or Iona, who flourished in the year 597; and of another, who filled the same distinguished office, in 657, and bore, from his complexion, the adjunct albus, in gaëlic, bàn, or fair; and it would seem that, to one or the other, the church was dedicated, from which Kil Chuimein, the original appellation of Fort Augustus, in Invernesshire, was derived. The traditionary account places them at a

COLQUHON

period before the reach of other record, in Badenach, of which they became the powerful lords, and from whence they were at last expelled, after severe contention, by the clan Vurich, or Macphersons, in the time of Robert the Bruce. Genealogists adhering to written documents, do not recognise these assertions, but inform us that the first possessions which they obtained in Scotland were in the County of Roxburgh, during the reign of David I.; and the orthography of Comyn, we are told, is most correct.

The tragical death of John the Red Cumin, who was killed by Robert the Bruce, before the high-altar of the minor friars' monastery at Dumfries, must be familiar to all readers of national history: in his son terminated the male line of the chief family; and, about the same time, the collateral branch, who held the Earldom of Buchan, also became extinct.

From Sir Robert Cumin, fourth son of John, Lord of Badenach, who died about 1275, are descended the Cumins of Altyr, Logie, Auchry, Relugas, &c., all families of great respectability in the north of Scotland.

The Cumins of Altyr, the chiefs of the ancient clan, have charters extending to the time of King David Bruce, who reigned from 1329 to 1369, by which many lands and various privileges were conferred upon them:—one of the latter is an exemption, granted by King James V, for the chief, his kin, clansmen, and friends from attending the Sheriff Court of Moray.

The power of the Cumins was effectually crushed by King Robert Bruce, but not without the most vigorous resistance. So formidable was the opposition which this clan offered to his authority, that, it was with great difficulty he could repress the aggressions of these intractable and powerful barons; but the sanguinary engagement at Inverury, in which the king, although very ill, took the field in person, obtained the victory, and ravaged the possessions of the Earl of Buchan and his numerous confederates, effectually checked their turbulent and ambitious career.

Barbour, Archdeacon of Aberdeen, in his valuable political life of "The Bruce," wherein he chronicles the checquered events of that monarch's life, gives a graphic detail of this engagement, and the consequent operations. This venerable historian, whose versification will bear comparison with that of Chaucer, whom he preceded somewhat in point of time, describes the battle with curious particularly, and tells us that, when the small folk, saw their lords retiring, they took to rapid flight, when the king

> " Chaisyt tham with all thair mayn ;
> And sum thai tuk and sum has slayn,
> The remanand war fleand ay ;
> Quha had gud hors gat best away."

Buchan fled to England, and the whole district was burnt.

> " And heryit was in sic manner,
> That efter that wele fifty yer,
> Men menyit " the herschip of Bouchane."

In the neighbouring churchyard of Bourtie, lies an effigy of a warrior, which is said to be a memorial of one of the Cumins, who was slain in this battle.

The Cumins are numerous in Aberdeen, Banff, and Morayshires; but a considerable number changed their name to Farquharson, as being descendants of Ferquhard, son of Alexander, the sixth of Altyr, who lived in the middle of the fifteenth century.

They were induced to do this, from a feeling very strong in those of Celtic race, in consequence of being prevented, for some reason, from burying their relatives in the family cemetery. It is from them that the Farquharsons of Balfluig, Haughton, and others in the County of Aberdeen are descended.

Mac Intosh, of Tirini, lived near the residence of Cumin, Lord of Badenach, and his lady having been presented by Mac Intosh with a bull and twelve cows, Cumin began to consider himself too near so powerful a chief. He, therefore, resolved to humble his neighbour, and, inviting him to his castle, he treacherously murdered Mac Intosh and his company. They seem to have been rather an offensive race; for Alexander Mac Pherson, called the revengeful, slew nine principal men of the Cumins, in a cave to which they had retired for shelter, in requital for their repeated depredations.

The ARMORIAL BEARINGS of the Cumins, or Cumings, as the name is now spelt, are azure, three garbs, or. Crest, a lion rampant, holding a dagger in his dexter paw, proper. Supporters, two wild horses, argent. Motto, " courage."

The SUAICHEANTAS, or Badge, is Lus mhic Chuimein Cumin plant, *Cuminum*.

Sir William Cumin Gordon, of Altyre and Gordonston, County of Elgin, Bart., is the representative of the ancient Lords of Badenach, and inherits the estates and honours of the extinct Baronetage of Gordonston.

The figure represents a shepherd, whose dress being modern and similar to some of the previous illustrations, requires no particular description. The utility of an ample plaid, as convenient shelter from the rough weather experienced in an alpine district, is evident. The broad bonnet also defended the face from sun and rain, whereas the " Glengarry " leaves it exposed to both, and seems contrived by some who wear it, in what is thought the smartest form, to carry the wet down the neck.

CUMIN

CLANN DHAIBHIDH—THE DAVIDSONS.

THERE seems to be no traditional knowledge of the individual from whom the patronymic of this clan is derived. He bore a scriptural name, and "the offspring of David" became numerous and powerful in Badenach, where their possessions lay. If little be known of their more remote history, they distinguished themselves throughout the fourteenth century by the protracted and sanguinary feuds which they maintained with such bravery and determination, that they were almost exterminated before they could be effectually suppressed.

The Clan-Chattan, which comprehends a number of subdivisions, was engaged in a war respecting the lands of Glenluie and Locharcaig with the Camerons, who at last came down to Badenach, about 1296, in hostile array, and great force. They were met, at Invernahavan, by the Mac Intoshes, Mac Phersons, and Mac Dhai's, who drew up in order of battle to oppose the farther progress of the enemy. This operation, in a Highland army, was to be performed with a very careful attention to the military privileges of the respective clans, many sad disasters having been the result of an oversight in such a matter. On this occasion an unfortunate dispute arose between the Mac Phersons and Davidsons as to the post of honour, each claiming the right to lead the van, and Mac Intosh, who had the chief command, the quarrel with the Camerons being his own, was appealed to, and gave his award to the latter. Cluny, the disappointed chief, immediately withdrew his men, and the Clan-Chattan thus weakened, met with defeat. The influence of the bards among the Gaël is well known—one of the profession, purposely sent, it is said, by Mac Intosh to the camp of the Mac Phersons, repeated a poem, or address, which sarcastically represented their conduct as the effect of cowardice, and not a sense of honour. This so incensed their feelings, that they immediately attacked the Camerons, who were defeated, and pursued with great slaughter to the verge of Lochaber.

The Camerons being thus reduced, the Mac Dhai's and Mac Phersons commenced hostilities on their own account. The former had lost their chief, Lachlan, and seven (or nine) sons at this battle of Invernahavan, and felt otherwise indignant that the award of precedency should be disregarded ; both parties were implacable, and the disorder occasioned by this feud must have been exceedingly great, for the Earls of Crauford and Dunbar were sent by a royal commission to quell it. Although provided with a military force, they found that to subdue these stubborn clans would be no easy task, and to reconcile them impossible ; but they at last got them to submit to a proposal which was agreeable to their chivalrous spirit. Thirty men on each side were to be selected, who, armed with swords only, should decide their claims by judicial combat, his majesty, Robert III., being umpire. This led to the battle of the North Inch of Perth, fought in 1396, with which extraordinary event Sir Walter Scott has made every one acquainted. From some cause one of the Mac Phersons was absent, but no one of the Mac Dhai's would

relinquish the honour of the impending conflict. Luckily for the ardent heroes, a volunteer, in the person of Henry the blacksmith of the wynd, or lane, known among the Highlanders as the Gobh-crom, enabled them to begin the work of death, which ended in the slaughter of twenty-nine Davidsons. The survivor preserved himself unhurt, but finding no companion left to battle by his side against the redoubted Harry with ten surviving, but desperately wounded, Mac Phersons, he threw himself into the Tay, swam across, and made his escape, unscathed and unpursued.

Since this unfortunate epoch in the history of the clan, it has almost been lost sight of. All who belonged to it seem to have felt, with indescribable mortification, that they who had ever distinguished themselves in warlike prowess, and had so vigorously maintained their position and asserted their rights, were now humbled in the presence of royalty, before the assembled chivalry and beauty of the land, and compelled to relinquish pretensions at a tribunal to which they had themselves agreed to submit. They may have given all the merit to the sturdy smith, who entered the lists and fought with a coolness which enabled him the better to cope with men infuriated by the spirit of revenge, and eager to achieve a triumph for which they had so long contended ; and doubtless they all repented the day when it was agreed that " St. John's town" should be the scene of the last act in the tragic feud ! They never resumed their wonted spirit, and the abeyance into which they fell must have led, in a great measure, with the similarity of name, to the supposition that it was the Mac Kays who were here engaged.

It is believed that the chief, with some part of his followers went northwards. and settled in the county of Cromarty, on the property called Davidston, but unfortunately about twenty years ago many documents were destroyed by fire which might have thrown light on the family history. Davidston was sold about 100 years ago, and the beautiful estate of Tulloch, in Ross-shire, was purchased from the Baynes in 1753, and at this place is the residence of the chief, who is hereditary keeper of the royal castle of Dingwall. The ancient abode was at Inver na h-avan, where the battle took place, on a fine plain at the confluence of the Truim with the Spey.

Davidsons of Cantra, in Nairnshire, is one of the most respectable and public-spirited cadets of this family.

The ARMORIAL BEARINGS are azure, on a fess between three pheons, arg. a stag couchant gules, attired with ten tynes, or. Crest,

DAVIDSON

a falcon's head, couped, proper. In addition, Tulloch carries the insignia of the Baynes, the Mac Donalds of the Isles, Andersons of Udale, Fergussons of Kilkerran, &c.

The SUAICHEANTAS, or Badge, is that common to the whole Clan-Chattan: Lus nam Braoileag, Red whortle berry, *Vaccinium vitis idea.*

The peculiarity in this sketch is the manner in which the plaid is put on. It is a mode of wearing it chiefly observable among the western Highlanders, and is particularly suitable for the stormy climate to which the figure is represented as being exposed. The two corresponding ends of the plaid are fastened together as it hangs over the shoulders: then passing the part so joined around the neck,

the back of the plaid being previously drawn over the head, it is retained in that position, forming a sort of cowl, or hood, and thus the whole body is enveloped so that the wearer has a comfortable protection from the rigours of a Caledonian winter. There is nothing remarkable in the hose or brogs

There is another arrangement we have seen, where the plaid is put behind the neck, but not over the head, being fastened on each shoulder behind with pins, or dealg's, and depending no lower than the kilt.

Davidson of Tulloch is one of the few chiefs who wears the Highland costume as their daily attire.

NA DRUIMAINICH—THE CLAN DRUMMOND.

THE genealogical account of the family informs us that their ancestor " is said to have been Maurice, a Hungarian, who accompanied Edgar Atheling and his sister Margaret into Scotland, and obtained from Malcolm III. the lands of Drymen, in Stirlingshire, which gave name to his posterity." For this we suspect there is no sufficient proof: the greater probability is that those inhabiting a ridge, or high ground, as Druiman signifies, would, by Celtic usage, be designated from the locality; in fact, there is a current tradition that they are sprung from one Doncha' Druimanach, about 1060. Of this family was " Gilbert de Dromund, del counte de Dunbrettan," who swore fealty to King Edward I. in 1296, and this designation, which was applied as surname to his successors, is evidence of the correctness of our etymology.

Sir Malcolm Drummond was one of the patriotic chiefs who fought with his clan at Bannockburn, and they were eminently useful to King Robert on that eventful day. It is known that, to compensate for the great inequality between the two armies, the Scottish monarch resorted to stratagem, and among the expedients adopted was that of using caltrops, which are pieces of iron, formed with four points, so that whichever way they lie, one shall be upwards; these are strewed along the ground for the purpose of defence from cavalry, the horses being lamed by treading on the sharp spikes. The duty of scattering these destructive articles would appear to have been entrusted to Sir Malcolm, from which circumstance they are introduced in the coat armour. The chief of the Drummonds fought with his kinsman, Earl Douglas, at the brilliant field of Otterburn, anno 1388, commemorated in the celebrated English song of " Chevy Chase," so beautiful in composition, but false in description. David Lord Drummond was in arms for Queen Mary, and King James VI. conferred the dignity of Earl of Perth on his grandson by patent, dated 1605. John, second Earl, and his son, were resolute in the cause of King Charles, and of much assistance to the Marquis of Montrose, and James the fourth Earl, being actively

opposed to the revolution of 1688, prepared to avoid the consequences by escape to the continent, but he was intercepted when passing down the Firth of Forth in a boat, and thrown into the prison of Kirkaldy, after having been unmercifully plundered. Here he remained until 1693, and was then released on giving bond for £5,000 that he should leave the kingdom; retiring to the court of James VII., he was there invested with the order of the garter and other honours, and was created a Duke. He died in 1716, and his eldest son being under attaint for being engaged in the rebellion of 1715, the titles in the British peerage were lost, but he had fortunately saved the estate, by having previously conveyed it to his son. Escaping to France with King James, he assumed the title of Duke, and died at Paris in 1730, leaving a son, styled Lord John Drummond, who raised a regiment for the French King, called the Royal Scots, with which he joined Prince Charles in Scotland, and after the defeat at Culloden, 1746, succeeded in reaching France, where he died next year. James, his eldest brother, continued to bear the family titles after the death of his father, and settled in Scotland, applying himself to the improvement of his estates, but he also joined Prince Charles, after whose defeat he retreated to Muidart, whence he embarked for the continent, and died on the passage in the thirty-third year of his age. He held the rank of Lieut.-General in the Highland army, and was much esteemed by both parties for his conciliatory spirit and exertions to moderate the calamities of domestic war. The lands were thus finally forfeited, but in 1784, an act was passed to enable the heirs, who would have been entitled in succession, to resume all the possessions which had fallen to the crown by forfeiture to George II. in 1715. Accordingly James Drummond, lineal descendant of John, Earl of Melfort, second son of James, third Earl of Perth, who was created 1686, made claim, and obtained a crown grant of the estate of Perth, in 1785, and was raised to the British peerage by the titles of Lord Perth and Baron Drummond, of Stobhall. Dying without male heirs,

DRUMMOND

these titles became extinct, but he had settled the estates on his daughter, Lady Clementina Sarah, who, in 1807, married the Right Hon. Peter Robert Burrel, eldest son of Lord Gwydir, with licence to take the name of Drummond, who, upon the decease of his mother, succeeded to the ancient barony of Willoughby de Eresby, and the hereditary great chamberlainship of England.

The Drummonds of Strathallan are descended from James, second son of David, the second Lord Drummond, who received a charter from his father of the lands of Culquhalzie, dated the 6th of September, 1561. He was a great favourite with King James VI., and for " the distinct and clear deposition relative to that mysterious affair," the Gowrie conspiracy, the king was pleased to erect the abbey of Inchaffray, of which he had before been commendator, into a temporal lordship, and to create him a peer, in 1609, by the title of Lord Maderty. The Hon. William Drummond suffered much for his adherence to King Charles I. and II., and as a recompence for his loyalty, he was, by the latter, created Viscount Strathallan and Lord Drummond, of Cromlics, 1686. William Lord Strathallan was " out in '15 and '45," and in the act of mounting his horse, to escape from the slaughter at Culloden, was cut down by the dragoons, and his eldest son having engaged in the same cause, was forfeited. Of this branch of the clan are descended the Drummonds who have been so long Bankers in London ; Andrew, fifth son of Sir John Drummond, of Machany, a near relative of Lord Strathallan, founded the well known establishment at Charing Cross, in the beginning of last century.

President Forbes does not think the Duke of Perth had a greater following than his Highlanders in Glenartnie and elsewhere, who might amount to 300, but his influence was much more extensive About forty of the clan swelled the body of Highlanders in attendance on George IV. at Edinburgh, in 1822, and the loyal reception of her Majesty at the ancient castle of Drummond, was worthy of a house of such noble descent on both sides.* His Lordship preserves all the usages for which Highlanders have so strong a predilection, and he is distinguished among Highland proprietors for the attention he pays to the improvement of his estates and his indulgent consideration of the interests of his tenantry.

The ARMORIAL BEARINGS for Drummond are on a shield or, three bars wavy, gules. Crest, on a ducal coronet, a slouthhound proper, collared and leashed gules. Supporters, two savages proper, wreathed about the head and middle with oak leaves, and carrying batons over their exterior shoulders, standing on a green mound in compartment, semee of caltrops, all proper. Motto, " Gang warily."

The SUAICHEANTAS, or Badge, is Lus mhic Righ Bhreatiunn,† mother of Thyme, *Thymis syrpillum.*

Spaidsearchd Dhuic Pheart, or the Duke of Perth's march, is a very fine Piobaireachd, and a Strathspey tune composed in honour of " the Lady Sarah Drummond " is very popular.

For some reason unknown to us, the Drummonds of Perth have adopted the Grant tartan. The figure is represented in breacan of that pattern, but a plaid is introduced of the set which the Seanachi's consider genuine. The shoulder plaid is ample as it was always worn in the olden time, being adapted for use—not intended merely for show. The bonnet is the broadest which the Highlanders wear, and it is ornamented with the pretty mountain shrub which forms the badge and an eagle's feather, which indicates a duineuasle, or gentleman. A tartan coat is here introduced for the first time in our series; the ingenuity displayed in its formation, cut as it is on the bias, will be hereafter shewn, in the back of a figure represented without the plaid. The shoes have buckles, which are a comparatively modern appendage, having been introduced in the lowlands only, about the year 1680. Although now considered part of the full costume, and worn by the Highland regiments, they were never much admired by those of the old school ; Donncha' Bàn, the poet, regrets that fashion led to their use while the neat shoe-tie was more becoming.

" Bucal an dunadh ar Bròg,
  'S e'm Barr-ial bu bhoiche leinn."

In the beginning of the sixteenth century a feud arose with the Murrays, who had intercepted the rents payable by the tenants of Monievaird, on which William, then chief, and Duncan Campbell, of Dunstaffnage, went against them to compel restitution, and punish them for the aggression. Not daring to meet this force, the Murrays retired to the church, and Drummond, respecting the sanctuary, gave orders to retire, but as they commenced march, a shot was unhappily fired, by which one of the Campbells was killed, when so enraged were they at this cowardly act, that they immediately returned, and not taking the trouble of storming the sacred edifice, they set fire to its heather roof and burned to death the miserable inmates. This was more particularly the crime of the Campbells, but Drummond was brought to trial for it, and, being pronounced guilty, he was executed in 1511.

Lord Drummond, of Perth, was King's forester, in Glenartnie, and about 1588 Drummondernach was his deputy, in which capacity he had occasion to punish some Mac Donalds whom he found slaying deer. These desperate poachers, smarting under their disgrace, attacked and killed Drummond, cutting off his head, which they exhibited to his distracted lady, and carried it to Balquhidder, where, placing it on the altar of the church, " they laid their hands upon the pow, and in ethnic and barbarous manner swore to defend the authors of the said murder." Some Mac Gregors had been induced to join in this vow, although generally on friendly terms with the Clan Drummond, but this deed brought on them the fiercest resentment of that tribe, who, making a descent on their territories, severely visited on this unfortunate race, the act of a party of its most lawless members.

* The beautiful Anabella, daughter of the seventh Chief, married Robert III., by whom she was mother of James I. † Literally—the plant of the son of the King of Britain !

IanMacFhearchar
a Mharbadh air blar
Chulodar's
a bhliahna
1746

FARQUHARSON

SIOL FHEARCHAR, NO FHIUNNLA'—
THE FARQUHARSONS.

This is a division of the great Clan Chattan, and they are derived by their family historians and current traditions from Shah of Rothiemurcus in Strathspey, who was lineally descended from the ancient Thanes of Fife. This Shah Macduff with his followers were of great assistance to the Mac Phersons in driving the Cummins from Badenach, and his activity recommended him to the favour of The Bruce, from whom the lands of Braigh Mhar in Aberdeenshire seem to have been first obtained, and of which he was appointed hereditary chamberlain. Fearchar, son of Shah, lived in the reigns of Robert II. and III., and married a daughter of Patrick Mac Dhoncha,' ancestor of the Robertsons of Lude, by whom he left a son Donald, who likewise married a Robertson of the Calveen family. His successor, Fearchar, left a numerous issue by a daughter of Chisholm of Strathglas, of whom several settled in the braes of Angus, and were the progenitors of many respectable families there.

From his grandson, Fiunnla,' mòr, or great Findlay, the clan has obtained the patronymic Clan Fhiunnla,' whence Mac Fhiunnla' or Mac Kinlay, a name which in low country parlance became Findlayson. It is from Fearchar that the clan receives the appelation Mac'earchar or Farquharson.

The Riachs, Lyons, Greusachs, Mac Hardys, Mac Caigs, Fergusons, and other Bræmar families, were followers of this clan.[*1]

The cadets of this clan are numerous and respectable both in the braes of Mar and in the low country, and are connected with influential families in Perthshire, two of the chiefs having intermarried with the noble house of Athol.

James Farquharson, tenth in descent from Fearchar Mac Shah, leaving no male issue, the chiefship, according to the rule of clanship, devolved on the family of Finzean, descended from Donald, second son of Fiunnla' mòr, usually designated Mac-an-Toisach, or son of the leader. The surviving daughter, Catherine, is styled Lady Invercauld, from the family seat, and marrying Captain Ross, R.N., who, by the courtesy, of Scotland, took the name of the heiress, has issue, James Farquharson, Esq., deputy-lieutenant of Aberdeenshire, representative of this ancient family.

The possessions of the clan are extensive both in Aberdeen and Perth shires, and upwards of 100,000 acres are covered with valuable woods mostly of fir, the remains of the Sylva Caledonia. The hills in the former county are celebrated for topazes, which, from a noted mountain, have come to be better known as Cairn-gorms.

In the year 1639, Donald Farquharson of Monàltrie, being opposed to the covenanters, with several hundreds of the clan, joined Lord Ludowic Gordon, who had escaped from school, and, arrayed "in Highland habite," this youth became leader of a strong band of royalists.[*2] The Farquharsons joined Montrose, in 1645, "with a great number of gallant men;" they fought at the battle of Worcester, 1651, and were equally alert in the wars of Viscount Dundee. They were first to muster on the summons of the Earl of Mar in the rising of

1715, and accompanied Brigadier Macintosh with the division which entered England, and were defeated at Preston. In 1745, they again took the field, and formed two battalions under the respective commands of Monàltrie and Balmoral, when they were mainly instrumental in the defeat of the Mac Leods at Inverury, and well supported their military renown at the battles of Falkirk and Culloden. Balmoral must, on this occasion, have given particular offence to government, for he was specially excepted from mercy, while Invercauld himself was pardoned. The estimated strength of Clan Fhiunnla' was 500 men.

The ARMORIAL BEARINGS of Farquharson of Invercauld, certified by the Lord Lyon, king-at-arms, in 1670, are quarterly: 1st and 4th or, a lion rampant, gules, armed and langued, azure; 2nd and 3rd arg. a fir tree growing from a mount in base, seeded proper. On a chief gules, the banner of Scotland displayed bendwise, from the circumstance of Findlay mòr being killed while carrying it in the field of Pinkie, 1547, and a canton of the first, charged with a hand holding a dagger point downwards, proper. Crest, a lion issuing from a wreath gules, holding a sword in his dexter paw, hilted and pomelled, or. Supporters, two wild cats proper. Motto, "Fide et fortitudine;" anciently, " We force nae friend, we fear nae foe."

There are several cadets of Invercauld, who also carry supporters to their coat armour as chieftains: thus, Finzean has on the sinister a tiger, and on the dexter a Highlander in trews, plaid and plate jack, holding a banner of St. Andrew; and Balmoral bears on the sinister a Highlander armed with claì mòr and targaid proper.

The SUAICHEANTAS, or Badge, as a branch of Clan Chattan, is Lus nam braoileag, *vaccinium vitis idea*, or red whortle berry.

The CATH-GHAIRM, or Rallying-cry, is Cairn na Chuimhne—the cairn of remembrance—an artificial heap of stones, around which the clansmen assembled, and on which the bard chanted the Brosnucha'-ca', or incentive to battle, before they departed.

The Farquharsons had a proportionable share in the feuds which so often disquieted the Highlands of Scotland; and it is a curious fact that a contract was made between the City of Aberdeen and the Laird of Invercauld, by which, for the consideration of certain " black mail," or tribute, he engaged to keep 300 men in arms for the " landward " protection of the burgesses.

Fearchar gaisgach liath, or the grey warrior, had served in the battles of the " great Montrose," when he was but a mere gillie, or lad, and had been distinguished for his heroism in 1715, as well as his sense of justice, having got into a serious squabble with a party of Lochaber

[*1] Family History, Baronage, &c.   [*2] Rothiemay MS.

men, with whom he interfered to prevent their plundering the house of a widow, on the march to England, and was wounded in the *mêlée*, before the guard arrived to quell the disturbance. The Farquharsons were very desirous of opposing the English army when it was known that the Highlanders were to be attacked, and they marched out of Preston to Ribble-bridge, with the intention of giving their enemies the first check, but they were soon after ordered to rejoin the main body. The unfortunate issue of the succeeding fight might have been averted, had they not been recalled. Fearchar sorely lamented this untoward event, and used to say that the Farquharsons were prevented from acting like the old Clan Chattan, who were always anxious to acknowledge an intended compliment, and make a suitable return for the proposed kindness *before* the debt had been incurred, a sentiment which is more expressively delivered in the native Gaëlic.

At Cullòden, Fearchar lost his only remaining son, who, like many others, was basely slain after the battle; and being now at the extreme age of 115, left dessolate and forlorn, he wandered through the country, delighting to ruminate over the graves of those who fell on Drummossie Muir, deploring his own bereavement and the loss of that cause in which his paternal clan had taken so warm an interest.

From the very old age of this veteran arose the name by which he was distinguished; and the aged Gaël is represented as he might have appeared, dressed in an ample robe of his native tartan, and retaining in his still nervous grasp the Taugh-cath, which is better known as the Lochaber axe.

FERGUS, MAC FHEARGHAS, OR FERGUSONS.

THIS name is a personal appellation, in its secondary sense, implying a hero, but, primarily, signifying a spearman, being compounded of fear, a man, and gais, or geis, a spear, the weapon carried by the Gais-gach, or heavy armed warrior, among the Highlanders. The identity of their language with that spoken by the ancient inhabitants of Gaul, will be observed in the similarity of this word to gæsum, the term which the Latin writers tell us that people applied to their spear or lance.

The name may vie with any in point of antiquity and honour, for who has not heard of the renowned Fergus, the founder of Scotland's monarchy? We shall not insist on the existence of the first of that name, whose era is placed upwards of 300 years before the advent of Christ; it is matter of no slight pride to be able to authenticate the reign of a second prince, who flourished 1300 years ago! The kinglet of Dalriada was formed in the north of Ireland, anno 210, when the Scots had been forced to abandon their native isle, and in 503, Fergus, the son of Erc, then king, came over to Argyle, and re-established their dominion in Caledonia. From him, as the first and most distinguished of his name, the Furgus-sons assert their origin, a descent in which the most noble of the land may glory!

Many respectable families of this name are found in Antrim, and the counties which formed Dalriada. In Scotland, the Fergusons are much dispersed; there are many in the south-western counties, in Athol and in Mar, but it would be difficult to determine which has the best claim to chiefship. There was a charter of several lands in Airshire granted by Robert the Bruce " Fergusio filio Fergusii," who was ancestor of the family of Kilkerran, of which Sir Charles D. Ferguson, Bart., is representative.

Thomas, Earl of Mar, grants a charter to Eugene, *i.e.* Eoghan, or Ewen Ferguson, of the lands of Uchtererne in Chromàr; or, as

expressed in the confirmation by David II., " Egoni filio Fergusii," dated apud castrum de Kyndromy (Kildrummie), 1364.

The " Fergussonis " appear in the Roll drawn up in 1587, of " the clannis that hes capitanes cheiffis and chiftanes, quhome on thay depend," and who by this act, agreeably to Highland usage, were made responsible for their followers.

It was the practice of the Highlanders, in 1745, to impress and carry along with them, every man whom they discovered to be a piper, and the music of their favourite instrument solaced them on many a weary march. Donald Ferguson, from Coire-garf, in Mar, was a cheerful volunteer in the prince's cause, and he, no doubt, officiated at all times with becoming alacrity. When Colonel Roy Stewart surprised and made prisoners a party of the king's troops at Keith, Donald was thrown in the skirmish off the bridge into the Isla, but with singular presence of mind, if it was not merely instinctive devotion to duty, he kept blowing with vigour, and the inflated bag completely sustained him until he was rescued! The danger of his situation could not repress the merriment of his companions at his peculiar drollery, but he used afterwards to say that as long as he was able to blow up his muckle pipes, he should neither die nor drown!

The ARMORIAL BEARINGS vary in several families of this name. Fergus bears argent, a lion rampant, gules. Crest, a demi lion, proper, crowned with a mural diadem, or, which is believed to denote the royal descent. The Fergusons in some instances, also, carry a lion as Craigdarach. Kilkerran and others bear azure, a buckle, argent, between three boars' heads couped, or langued, gules. Crest, on a thistle leaved and flowered proper, a bee, or. Supporters, two griffins proper, Motto, " Dulcius ex asperis."

The SUAICHEANTAS, or Badge, is Ros-greine, Little Sun Flower, *Helian thymum marifolium.*

In accordance with the plan proposed at the commencement of this work, a figure is introduced clad in one of the oldest garments peculiar to the Celts. This was called the Lein-croich, or saffron-coloured shirt, which was the habit of people of distinction, and, as its name imports, was dyed of a yellow colour from that plant. This vestment resembled a very ample belted plaid of saffron-coloured linen, being fastened round the middle, and was formed of sufficient breadth to fall below the knees when so required. The usual number of yards which it contained was twenty-four, but there was sometimes more ; the accompanying illustration was painted from a similar drapery composed of twenty-three yards.

The Scots and Irish, people of identic origin, resembled each other closely in dress and arms, as Camden observes, and the Leincroich appears to have been in every respect the same in both countries, Campion, writing in 1571, observes that " linnen shirts the rich doe weare for wantonnes and bravery, with wide hanging sleeves, playted ; thirty yards being little enough for one of them, but they have now left their saffron," &c. Martin remarks that the Highlanders had laid this antiquated dress aside about 100 years before his time, say 1600. In Ireland this habit, so costly from its profusion of cloth, was the subject of legal enactment, Henry VIII. prohibiting the people from putting more in it than seven yards. It does not appear that, among the Gaël of Ireland, the tartan pattern was ever in use; but there can be no doubt that the costume in both countries was formed in the same manner, as ancient monuments and authentic prints sufficiently prove. Derricke, who published his " Image of Ireland," in 1581, has given a series of extremely interesting wood-cuts, which represent the " wood Karne," dressed in kilts, plaited and fastened in almost the present form ; and his discription and illustrations of the " shirte," exactly suits the Lein-croich.

> " Their shirtes be verie straunge,
>   Not reaching paste the thigh,
> With pleates on pleates they pleated are,
>   As thicke as pleates may lye," &c.

It is not to be supposed by our readers, that, although here introduced, the Lein-croich was peculiar to the Fergusons- it was worn, as we see, by the Duine-uasal, or gentleman of every clan. That those who take an interest in their appropriate costume may not feel disappointed, we beg to assure them, we do not think the Ferguson tartan is inferior in the richness of its colours, and effect of their arrangement, and we shall describe it by the scale of an eighth of an inch, as laid down in " the Scottish Gaël."

$\frac{1}{2}$ green	6 green	$\frac{1}{2}$ red
6 blue	1 black	6 blue
$\frac{1}{2}$ red	6 green	1 green
6 black	6 black	6 blue

The badge of the Fergusons is fixed in the clogaid, or skull-cap. The target is from one of the very oldest pattern, composed of wood, strengthened by layers of flax, mixed with tar, the rim is bound with iron, it is ornamented with a large copan, or boss, and has but one handle. This target could not be used with a two-handed sword, for the weight of that weapon required the strong grasp of two hands to wield it aright. In fact, we see by Thibaut's work on swordsmanship, that the two-handed clai'mor was itself both " sword and shield."

The sword is painted from one in possession of Mr. Donald Mac Pherson, Pimlico, which is said to have been in the family for nearly 600 years, and the form certainly favours the tradition.

THE FORBESES.

FORBES is a Celtic word, which designates an ancient parish in the county of Aberdeen, and from this locality the appellation of the clan was undoubtedly derived. It is here where the ancestors of the chief, Lord Forbes, have been resident from the earliest period of their known history, and all the numerous families who bear the name trace their descent from this original stem.

The fertility of genealogical imagination has, nevertheless, been egregiously displayed in discussing the etymon of this word : the name, says one, was originally Bois, and a certain king, allotting lands to a follower for some extraordinary service, observed that they were " for Bois !" Another relates the story of a ferocious bear, which was destroyed by the founder of the family, the deed being commemorated by the armorial insignia. That bears have once roamed in the Caledonian forests may be readily admitted, but we suspect the period of their existence even genealogists are not able to determine. The Highlanders pronounce the word Firbis, and in Ireland there long flourished a race of celebrated Seanachai's, or antiquaries, called Mac Firbis.

In the reign of King William the Lion, which extended from 1165 to 1213, John de Forbes was in possession of the lands so called,

FERGUSON

and to his son Fergus, Alexander, the earl of Buchan, gave a charter about 1236, of possessions in the same district.

Alexander, fourth baron, took up arms to revenge the death of James III., which occurred in 1488, and marching through the northern provinces with the bloody shirt of the murdered king displayed on a spear, he summoned all loyal subjects to join his standard. The call was responded to with ardour, but hearing of the defeat of the Earl of Lennox, in the south, Lord Forbes submitted to James IV.

The Forbeses were the rivals of the Gordons, whom " they often most manfully resisted in divers hot quarrels." They stood stanchly on the side of the reformers and the king, while the Gordons as strongly contended for the interest of the unfortunate Queen Mary. Adam Gordon of Achandoun, the Earl of Huntly's brother, having defeated the Forbeses after a hard-fought battle, the Earl of Mar, then regent, gave "the Master of Forbes," his lordship's elder son, some horsemen and five companies of foot, on which it was determined to dislodge the Gordons, who had taken possession of Aberdeen; but he unfortunately fell into an ambuscade as he advanced, his troops were defeated, and he was taken prisoner. A Captain Carr, with a party of hagbuteers, or men armed with muskets, did great execution, but the victory was decided by a company of Sutherland cearnaich, or bowmen, in the service of Achandoun.

The Lords Pitsligo were descended from Sir William, second son of Lord Forbes, who flourished anno 1424, and inherited Pitsligo through his wife, who was daughter of Frazer of Philorth. The peerage was conferred in 1633. Alexander, fourth baron, was a man of very estimable character, and literary reputation. He had protested against the Act of Union, and was concerned in the rebellion of the Earl of Mar, 1715, but escaped prosecution. When he engaged in "the rising" under Prince Charles, in 1745, he was not so fortunate: on the suppression of that disastrous attempt, his lordship's title and estates were forfeited, and on the death of his only son, in 1781, the family became extinct in the direct line.

The ancestor of Sir Charles Forbes Bart., of Newe and Edinglassie, was William of Dauch and Newe, brother of Sir Alexander Forbes, of Pitsligo, who lived in the fifteenth century. Sir Charles has established his claim to the male representation of the Pitsligo branch of the clan; and, in consequence, has received a grant from the Lord Lyon, king-at-arms, of the armorial bearings and supporters of the family of Pitsligo. He was created a British baronet by George IV. in 1823. The patriotism of Sir Charles, and the unostentatious munificence with which he supports all objects of national interest require no eulogium.

Sir John Stuart Forbes, of Pitsligo and Fettercairn, is descended from a daughter of the third baron, who married John Forbes of Monymusk. The Baronetcy of Nova Scotia was conferred on his ancestor in 1626.

Sir John Forbes of Craigievar, is descended from Patrick of Corse, armour-bearer to James III. and son of James, second Lord Forbes. The title of baronet was conferred in 1639.

The family of Cullòden has attracted considerable attention from the exertions which Duncan Forbes, then president of the Court of Session, made for the suppression of the rebellion, in 1746. To his unrequited efforts to prevent the disaffected chiefs from pouring

their forces on the low country, it is believed that George II. owed the preservation of his throne. The descent is through the family of Tolquhon in Aberdeenshire, from Sir John, third son of Sir John de Forbes, who died in 1405. Duncan purchased Cullòden from the laird of Macintosh, in 1626, and although the family have not been ennobled, a Highland following of 200 men was assigned them, in the report furnished by Marshall Wade, 1715.

The power and influence of Lord Forbes, we have seen, was very great; to what extent his clan following extended, is not so apparent. The Farquharsons, whose possessions were contiguous, and some of whom dwelt on his own lands, frequently swelled his forces. Many of his name were feudal dependants on the Earls of Huntly, but, of course, they only obeyed the summons of their natural, or patriarchal, chief.

Walter, the present Lord Forbes, is the twenty-fourth baron in the family genealogy. He is premier baron of Scotland, and takes rank accordingly. The date of creation is lost in antiquity, but the title is applied in a deed of 1442.

The ARMORIAL BEARINGS are azure, three bears' heads, couped, arg. muzzled gules. Crest, a stag's head, attired, proper. Supporters, two greyhounds, arg. collared, gules. Motto, " Grace me guide."

The SUAICHEANTAS, or Badge, is Bealaidh, common Broom, *Spartium Scorparium.*

The CATH-GHAIRM, or gathering shout, is Loanach, the name of a noted hill in the district of Strathdon.

Of the PIOBAIREACHD, the urlar, or ground-work, only, seems to be preserved in the popular rallying tune, " Ca Glenernan, gather Glennochtie," the names of valleys in the same district.

The ancient residence was the strong fortalice, Druminnor; the present seat is Castle-Forbes, a modern mansion in the embattled style.

This is the first of the illustrations in which the wig, worn in the middle of the last century, is introduced. There are, also, some other minutiæ in the full court dress of a Highland gentleman of that period, about 1740; the doublet, waistcoat, ruffled sleeves and shoe buckles, are according to the fashion then prevalent in France and England. The plaid is kept down, an arrangement which allows the dirk and the pistols to be seen. The latter are stuck in the sword belt; rather an unusual mode of carrying them, but an authority is found for it in a portrait at Drummond Castle, of James, Duke of Perth, lieutenant-general in the Highland army of 1745. The bidag, or dirk and purse, are from the same picture.

FORBES

NA FRIOSALAICH, THE FRASERS.

Of the Norman descent of this clan it is asserted there can be no doubt whatever, and the Roll of Battle Abbey is cited as evidence that the knight from whom the whole Frasers are descended came over in the army of William the Conqueror, 1066. The exact period when the posterity of this warrior obtained a settlement in Scotland is not spoken of with so much confidence, but the convenient circumstance of David I. having married an English princess, is fixed upon for the establishment of her countrymen on the lands of the native Scots. No record is found, decisive of this opinion, respecting the origin of the Frasers; the name of the reputed founder of this clan, as it stands on the Norman Roll, is Frisell, and we find the Latin and Saxon chroniclers presenting the various orthographies of Frazier, Freshele, Fresale, Frizil, &c. The first, " who is supposed to be found in charters, is Gilbert de Fraser, who lived in the time of Alexander I;" and Sir Andrew, who appears about 1290, is the first who occurs as a Highland proprietor.* It is from his brother and successor Simon, that the chiefs have taken the well-known patronimic " Mac Shimi."

We have formed an opinion on the origin of this clan, as on the Siosalich, or Chisholms (No. 2), and venture to think that as the first person mentioned in Scottish record is named Fraser, it may be an appellation nowise synonymous, or related to the Norman Frisell, and that Fraser itself is possibly a corruption of the Gaëlic Friosal, of which a reasonable etymon can be given: Frith—a forest; siol, a race, the *th* being quiescent. Thus the clan inhabiting the woods with which the country was then overspread, were distinguished as " the race of the forest," and in traditions in the lower parts of the county, detailing forays by the inhabitants of the Aird, they are denominated Cearnich na coille, or warriors from the woods. This conjecture may not be held tenable, but the clan must, we should think, be pleased with an attempt to prove it an indigenous Gaëlic tribe.

Hugh Fressel is the first chief who is styled Lord of the Aird and the Lovet in an indenture, dated 1416, and he is said to have been created a lord of Parliament in 1431. The succession of the chiefs was carried on through considerable troubles until the death of the unfortunate Simon, who was beheaded at the age of eighty, on Tower Hill, 1747, for having engaged in the rebellion of the preceding year, when the estate and honours were forfeited. His eldest son, who commanded the clan in the service of Prince Charles, was subsequently pardoned, and had the estates restored; which, by the failure of direct issue, went into the possession of Thomas A. Fraser, of Strichen, who, in 1837, was created Baron Lovat by patent.

The military exploits of Clan Friosal have been numerous and brilliant, for Mac Shimi had a " good number of barons of his name in Inverness and Aberdeenshire." In 1544 was fought the battle between them and the Mac Donalds of Clan Ranald, fully related in our second Number, a conflict maintained with such obstinate resolution as to threaten the annihilation of both parties, four only of

the Frasers escaping, and seven of the Mac Donalds. When the arrows were spent, the combatants used their two-handed swords, and, stripping their upper garments, the battle, which took place on the margin of Loch Lochy, was called Blar nan lein, the battle of the shirts.

The Frasers opposed Montrose, but when King Charles arrived in Scotland, 1650, they joined his forces with 800 men; they also swelled the army of Viscount Dundee, and reinforced Prince Charles with a body of 600. When the royal troops were rashly engaged at Culloden, in the absence of so many of the clans, the Frasers effected a junction the morning of the day of battle, and having behaved with characteristic valour when the Highlanders were forced to retreat, the clan marched off with banners flying and pipes playing in the face of the enemy. Simon, the eldest son or master of Lovat, had obtained his pardon for having commanded the clan in this rising, when he entered the service of government, and raised 1800 Frasers in 1757, who covered themselves with glory in the American war.

The Aird, or country of the Frasers, lies west of Inverness, and, as the name imports, is an elevated district, stretching along the bank of Loch Ness, and bounded on the north by the firth of Beauly and river Farar. The ancient castle of Lovat was succeeded by one adjoining, which was designated Beaufort, and was rased to the ground after the battle of Culloden, but rebuilt on the same site, a beautiful position, near the river Beauly

The Armorial Bearings of Lord Lovat are quarterly, first and fourth azure, three cinquefoils, arg., second and third arg., three antique crowns, gules.

Crest, a stag's head erased, or, attired argent.

Supporters, two stags' proper.

Motto " Je suis prest," which was usually given of old in English, " I am readie," but an ancient emblazonment has " Se je puis."

The Cath-ghairm, battle shout, or rallying cry, is Caisteal Downie, the last word being Duna, a camp or fortified dwelling, anciently it was Mòrfhaich, the " great field" of meeting.

The Suaicheantas or Badge, is Iubhar, the Yew-tree, *Taxus baccata.*

The Piobaireachd Cruinneachadh, or Gathering, is Spaidsearechd Mhic, Shimi, and Cumhadh Mhic Shimi is an affecting lament for the death of Lord Simon in 1747.

* Peerage, Anderson's Hist. of the Lovat family, &c.

FRASER

The only peculiarity in this illustration is the hair: the prints in Birt's " Letters from the Highlands," 1725, represent the Gaël of that period, wearing it much in the fashion here shewn. The bonnet is called " a Glengarry ;" it is a form not more than forty years old, and has been adopted by many as an improvement, but is only an imitation of the lateral cock of a flat bonnet carried round, with a slit behind for convenience to pull it forward. The badge and two feathers denote a person of consequence :—the kilt and ample shoulder plaid have been given in former figures. The hose are knit, and gartered low, which, as a matter of taste, is generally preferred.

NA GORDONICH, THE GORDONS.

VARIOUS origins have been assigned to this clan, one of the most distinguished in Scottish annals. In Normandy is found a manor called Gourdon, whence the first settlers are said to have arrived and brought the name into Scotland, but Chalmers, the erudite author of " Caledonia," settles the point with the brevity and confidence which characterize his dicta on "English Colonization." "The progenitor of the Gordons came from England," he says, " soon after the commencement of the twelfth century, and obtained the lands of Gordon in Berwickshire, where he settled with his followers." The authority of this writer in settling family origins, is a discovery of the first charter in which he finds the name mentioned! This is a plausible derivation compared with the heraldic, which makes the common ancestor a valorous Norman knight, who *gored down* a hideous boar, and thence derived, by royal command, both the name and the boars' heads as the armorial insignia of himself and successors! Certainly, if the fact were satisfactorily established, that strangers were the founders of so great a number of the highest families in Scotland the sovereigns of that country had a very contemptible opinion of their native subjects, who must have been a despicable race to be less worthy of royal favour than Saxons, Normans, Danes, or Norwegians.

There were, however, a succession of distinguished knights of this name, whose possessions were in the south of Scotland, until Sir John de Gordoune obtained the lands of Strathbogie, in Aberdeenshire, after which they settled in these parts, and the representation devolving on Elizabeth, an only daughter, she married a son of Sir William Seton, of Seton, who, by the courtesy of Scotland, took the name of Gordon. His son, who died in 1470, was created Earl of Huntley, George, sixth of that title, became Marquis in 1599, and George, fourth Marquis, was elevated to the rank of Duke, 1684, a title which became extinct on the death of his late Grace in 1836, on which the Marquisate of Huntly reverted to the Earl of Aboyne, descended from the third son of George, second Marquis, who was raised to the peerage by Charles II. in consideration of his great and faithful services, September 10, 1660.

Charles, present Earl of Aboyne, is the sixth in descent, and married the amiable Lady Elizabeth, daughter of the Marquis of Conyngham, who died at Orton Longueville, near Peterborough, a beautiful property acquired by his mother, without issue, August 24,

1839. Aboyne castle, in Strathdee, is built in one of the finest situations being surrounded with extensive plantations, and commanding lovely views of a noble river, wooded hills, and the grandest mountain scenery in the distance. His lordship is one of the few Highland proprietors who have thought it of importance to make himself acquainted with the Gaëlic, the language of the clans and the mother tongue of many of his tenantry.

The Earl of Aberdeen represents another branch of the Gordons, of purer descent than the ducal family who preserved the name through a female heir, while his Lordship has an uninterrupted male lineage. Patrick Gordon, of Methlic, a cadet of Lord Gordon of Huntly, is the first who figures in national history ; he died, bravely fighting at the battle of Arbroath, in 1445. In 1533 the family acquired the lands of Haddo, in Aberdeenshire, whence they were so long distinguished as the Gordons of Haddo. Sir John was created a Baronet of Nova Scotia, in 1642, and his son Sir George, having embraced the legal profession, in which he distinguished himself, was appointed President of the Court of Session, or College of Justice, and in 1682 was raised to the peerage. The crest of Lord Aberdeen is two arms in the act of letting fly an arrow, with the motto " Fortuna sequatur," to commemorate the deed of his ancestor Bertrand de Gourdon, who according to tradition, slew Richard Cœur de Lion, in 1190.

Viscount Kenmure, another branch, creation of 1633, is descended from Adam de Gourdoun, of Lochinvar, who flourished about 1300, and the Earls of Sutherland themselves were of Gordon descent, Adam, second son of George, Earl of Huntly, marrying the Countess Elizabeth, in the beginning of the sixteenth century. Besides these noble families there are eight baronets of the name.

The Gordons of the north were at one time all powerful, and, single handed, were at times opposed to government. The Earl of Huntly being lieutenant over all Scotland, " except the Earl of Argyle's bounds," and having received charters of many lands which had been forfeited, the family were involved in frequent and very desperate feuds, especially with the Macintoshes, Camerons, and Murrays. Having acquired the lordship of Badenach, the Gordons received willing assistance from the Mac Phersains, but although Sir Robert Gordon calls them " his servants," the gift of superiority did not confer the right of chiefship. He had however, a Highland

GORDON

following in Strathavan and Glenlivat, which was raised for Prince Charles, by Lord Lewis, who with a force of about 1600 men, kept the northern counties in subjection while the Highland army marched southwards. The influence of duke Alexander, as chief of the Gordons, was shown when he raised, at different times, three fencible regiments, and the gallant 92nd Highlanders, who wear the clan tartan.

Mr. Gordon, minister of Alvie, was summoned before the Duke of Cumberland for harbouring the rebels. He went without hesitation, equipped with sword and loaded pistols, to his highness, in answer to whom he asked whether he was to obey the son of his heavenly or the son of his earthly king? and boldly pressed for mercy to the unfortunate Highlanders!

The old seat in Strathbogie is one of the finest castellated remains, and Gordon castle the most princely edifice in the north of Scotland.

The ARMORIAL BEARINGS for the name are azure, three boars' heads couped, or, but his late Grace quartered the arms of Seton, Fraser

and the lordship of Badenach. Crest, a buck's head affrónté couped, proper, attired or. Supporters, two deer hounds proper. Motto, above, "Bydand," and below, "Animo non astutio."

The SUAICHEANTAS, or Badge, is Eidhean na craige, Rock Ivy— *Hedera helix.*

The CATH-GHAIRM, or war cry, is said to have been the superior motto as a stimulus to stand firm; but, "a Gordon! a Gordon!" was generally used by those who lived on the border.

FAILTE and SPAIDSEARACHD NAN GORDONICH, the march and salute of the Gordons, are very fine specimens of that peculiar music called Piobaireachdan.

This figure is in the dress of a Highlander of the present day, in his ordinary occupations, and is here enjoying the sport of angling; the bonaid in which he is represented is modern, and caprice has named it the "Athol bonnet;" the hose are thick, and strongly knitted, terminating at top in a fillet of white wool. He has hooked a salmon, which gives excellent play, and carries another slung on his back, a practice we have seen in a Highlander pursuing his finny game in the roaring stream of the Awe.

NA GRAMAICH—THE GRÆMES.

THE "gallant Græmes" have acted so chivalrous and important a part in the annals of Scottish history, as to have well merited that appellation. Their traditional origin is of the highest antiquity, the ducal family of Montrose tracing its descent to the fifth century. The emperor, Antoninus, had raised a fortified wall of extraordinary strength, from sea to sea, in the vain hope that it would preserve the conquered provinces from the dread incursions of the Scots, but Græme, who commanded the confederated tribes, broke through this useless defence, which from him became afterwards known as "Græme's dyke." The name was indicative of the fierceness of the man, Gruamach or Gramach being applied to one of stern, forbidding look and manner, the term whence is derived the gothic "grim."

Any satisfactory record of the several generations who succeeded this hero, filling up the interval between him and William de Græme, who lived in the reign of David I., and is witness to the foundation of the abbey of Holy Rood, in 1128, cannot be expected, but from this ancestor they are regularly authenticated.

Amongst so many personages of this clan who have distinguished themselves, a few of the more renowned only, can be here briefly noticed. Sir John Græme, of Dundaff, with the exception of the immortal Wallace, was the most valiant of the Scottish patriots. After sharing in the glorious victories obtained over the

"southern foes," he fell in 1298, at the disastrous battle of Falkirk, and was interred in the churchyard there, where a monumental slab, with an inscription commemorative of his valour and attachment to the Guardian of Scotland, marked his narrow bed. This was opened by the Highlanders in 1746, for the reception of the body of Sir Robert Munro, as a fitting mark of respect for that chief although slain as their adversary, in the victory which they gained in the vicinity over general Hawley.

James, who was fifth Earl, and the twentieth in descent from William, before mentioned, has gained imperishable fame from the wars which he carried on, in behalf of the unfortunate king Charles I. and his undaunted deportment when he met his tragic fate. A bare enumeration of his rapid and brilliant successes is all that can be given—it will shew his bravery and energy of character, and the devotion to himself and their sovereign, of the heroic band whom he led. In 1644, having been created Marquis, he received a commission, constituting him Captain General of all forces to be raised in Scotland for his Majesty's service, and the Earl of Antrim having engaged himself to provide a strong reinforcement, Montrose made his escape from Oxford in disguise and reached the Scottish mountains, where in a common highland dress, he concealed himself until the Mac Donalds had arrived from Ulster, when he opened

GRAEME

his commission. With 3000 men hastily collected, badly armed and without cannon, he marched southwards and completely defeated the covenanters at Tippermuir, who were 6000 strong, capturing their whole artillery and baggage. Returning to the north soon afterwards, he gave a signal defeat to Lord Lewis Gordon at the bridge of Dee and took possession of the city of Aberdeen, but Argyle advancing with a powerful army, he retired, burying his artillery in a morass and crossed over the mountains to Badenach. Not resting here, he descended through Athol to Angus, and rapidly marched over the Grampians to Aberdeenshire, where he defended himself successfully against repeated attacks by Argyle, particularly at the castle of Fyvie, where prodigies of valour were displayed. Hence he made good his retreat once more to Badenach, the "country" of the friendly Mac Phersons, from which he descended on Argyleshire which he ravaged, with great severity, for upwards of six weeks, and killed or dispersed almost the entire inhabitants. Exasperated by his losses, Argyle immediately prepared for revenge by the most vigorous exertions, and marched to Inverlochai' in Lachaber, with unwonted celerity, where he was immediately attacked by Montrose, who had made an almost incredible night march over the pathless mountains in a deep snow storm, with such determination that the Campbells were speedily routed with great slaughter, no fewer, it is said, than 1500 having been slain, with but the trifling loss of three privates to the victors. Montrose marched southwards, the Grants and Gordons joining him; he carried Dundee by storm, but was obliged to abandon his acquisitions and betake himself again to the mountains. This retreat, in which he passed between two powerful armies, and marched at the rate of sixty miles a day, was pronounced by military men of the time, a more masterly operation than his most brilliant victories! Proceeding to the north, he defeated general Hurry at Aultearn, who lost 2000 men, and in a little time afterwards he overthrew general Baillie's army at Alford, in Aberdeenshire. These astonishing successes procured Montrose reinforcements from various clans, and with a body of 6000 men, he forthwith marched southwards and gave battle to the enemy at Kilsyth, who were vanquished with exceeding carnage, 5000 perishing in the field. Edinburgh and Glasgow were now in his possession, and in a little more than one year, he had almost recovered Scotland for the king whom he invited to come and take possession, lest, quoting a passage of Scripture, "it might be called by his name!" Fortune at last forsook her favourite; about a month after his last victory he was surprised when nearly 4000 of the highlanders had left his army, and routed by General Lesley at Philiphaugh. His troops were entirely dispersed and he retreated to the north, where in conjunction with Sutherland, Seaforth, and other chiefs, he prolonged a feeble warfare, until ordered by king Charles to lay down arms, when he was allowed to retire to the continent. Obtaining permission from Charles II. to raise a body of troops in Germany, he landed with them in the north highlands to renew the war, but before any thing could be accomplished, he was made prisoner by Mac Leod of Asynt, on whose fidelity he had thrown himself, when being tried and condemned, he was beheaded and quartered with circumstances of revolting cruelty.

Viscount Dundee was another Græme who, had he not fallen so early in the bright "field of his fame," might have rivalled Montrose in his military renown. He "rising" in favour of king James II. promised important results, but his lamented death at the battle of Raonruarai' which took place at the pass of Killiecrankie, 1689, when victory had been obtained, dissipated all its advantages: under an incompetent successor, the army speedily disbanded. His memory as Græme of Claverhouse is yet cherished among those highlanders who indulge in the retrospection of past glories.

The late Duke of Montrose ably seconded by Col. Archibald Fraser, son of Lord Lovat, who was beheaded for his engagement in the rebellion of 1745, procured the repeal of the Act which suppressed the use of the highland dress that the people might be rendered loyal. For this service, performed in 1782, his grace's memory is held in veneration by the Gäel, and a poem on the occasion, by the celebrated Donchai', bàn, or Duncan Mac Intyre, is exceedingly popular. He had likewise composed another piece lamenting the indignity to which his countrymen, Georgites and Jacobites, were subjected, in being disarmed and compelled to wear a dress in which they could "scarcely recognise each other, which destroyed their smart appearance and graceful carriage, and made them blush when in presence of the fair." Ducan, who had fought on the Hanoverian side, having wound up his composition with a threat that should Prince Charles return, every highlander would hasten to join his army, he was committed to prison. Thirty-two years afterwards the obnoxious Act being repealed, he had the more pleasant task to commemorate the restoration of the costume of which his countrymen are so proud, and the highlanders always drank with enthusiasm "deoch slainte Mhon' t-ros." "Many a noble current," exclaims the patriotic bard, "flows in his veins, the heir of the great Montrose!"

James, present Duke of Montrose, is the twenty-sixth chief in authentic record. His property lies chiefly in the county of Stirling, where Buchanan house on Loch Lomond side, formerly the property of the clan whose name it bears, is the family mansion, noted for the benevolence and hospitality of its illustrious owners.

The ARMORIAL BEARINGS for the name Græme or Graham are, or. on a chief sable, three escallop shells of the first. Crest, an eagle, wings displayed or, preying on a stork, on its back proper. Supporters, two storks argent, beaked and membered gules. Motto, "Ne oublie."

The SUAICHEANTAS, or Badge is Buaidh craobh, Laurel spurge, *Laureola*.

The PIOBAIREACHDAN, Salutes, Marches or Laments composed on the battles gained by a clan or the losses it has sustained, form the undoubted music appropriate to that clan. The Græmes have, therefore, the Failte or Spaidsearachd, "Blar Aultearn," 1645 and "Blar Raonruarai," 1689. On this last occasion there is also "Cumha' Chlabhers," the Lament for the loss of Claverhouse, which is composed in sufficiently doleful strains.

The figure is clad in Kilt and shoulder plaid as shepherds and travellers usually equip themselves, in a small pattern of the tartan which is held distinctive of the clan. It has, however, been objected to, and we should have been obliged had any one supplied us with a "sett" which could be proved more legitimate. The recent production of so many fanciful patterns which are introduced to the public as Clan Tartans, is much to be regretted, but it may lead those more particularly concerned to a careful examination of authorities.

The hose are ca' da' or made from cloth and the blue garters were sometimes worn from fancy; the red waistcoat was thought becoming and it is an agreeable contrast to the green plaid. The sporan or purse is a plain snap one, closing like a lady's reticule. In the plain round bonnet, which in the more lowland districts was frequently distended with a small hoop inside, is fixed the clan badge of wild Laurel. On the toes of the shoes the friochan appears, which was an additional piece of leather fancifully serrated and super-added as a protection against the friction of the heath, whence its name from Fraoch, heather.

NA GRANNTAICH—THE GRANTS.

It is a proof of the high antiquity of a clan when its origin is lost in the gloom of remote ages. Various opinions have been given respecting the Grants, and genealogists have indulged their imaginations in deriving them from Denmark, from France, and from England. The generally adopted history informs us that the founder of the clan was Gregor, second son of Malcolm, chief of the Mac Gregors, who flourished in 1160, and bearing the epithet Grannda from his unhandsome appearance; that he established himself in the north, and was the progenitor of all those who are distinguished by the name. It has never, indeed, been disputed that the Grants are a branch of the Siol Alpin, the chief division of whom is clan Gregor, but Dr. John Mac Pherson appears to have first started a derivation, the probability of which strongly recommends it for adoption. In Strathspey, the bosom of "the country of the Grants" is an extensive moor, called Griantach, otherwise Sliabh-Grianais, or the plain of the sun, which is remarkable for many Druidical remains scattered over its expanse, indicating it to have been a place consecrated to the worship of that luminary, the great object of Celtic adoration. Those engaged in the services performed on this plain, would be resident in its vicinity, and might have been distinguished by a local epithet which monkish writers expressed by "De Grant." If any proof could be drawn with confidence from the symbols of heraldry, the crest borne by Grant might be referred to as representing the Baal-teine, or fire raised in honour of this Gaëlic deity, and the tribe who conducted the ceremonials in this province being of the Alpin stock would always recollect their paternal descent.

The Grants of England, of whom there are many respectable families of ancient standing, are quite distinct from the Scottish race, and have, no doubt, taken their designation from locality, the most honourable derivation. The river Cam, which gives name to the County of Cambridge, was originally called Grant, and the city Caer Grant, the Grant ceastre of the Saxons.

The written record of the noble house of Grant commences with Gregor, who was sheriff of Inverness in the reign of Alexander II. annis 1214—1249. His son Laurin, or Laurence, appears witness in a deed of the bishop of Moray, 1258, and his grandson, Sir Iain, was a resolute adherent of the immortal Wallace. Sir Donchà, or Duncan, was the chief who flourished in 1442, and in a charter under the great seal dated that year, he is described as "Dominus de eodem et de Freuchie," being the first who receives the designation generally given to succeeding lairds from the name of the property where they fixed their residence. Sir Iain, or John, lived in the reign of James III. and joined the Earls of Huntly and Mar with his clan in support of that unfortunate monarch who lost his life in the rebellion of his son, anno 1488. The clan rose with Montrose, under James, the sixteenth chief, but his son and successor Lewis, or Ludowic, joined Col. Livingston in the opposite interest with 600 men. In 1745 there were about 800 of the clan in arms, but they took no active part against Prince Charles. The military strength of the clan was estimated at 850 men.

Sir Lewis, grandfather of the present chief, married Lady Mary Ogilvie, daughter of the Earl of Seafield and Findlater. The direct line of this family terminated in Earl James who died 1811, when the titles and estates devolved upon Sir Lewis Grant, on whose death, in 1837, the present much respected and patriotic chief succeeded.

One of the unfortunate refugees from the horrors of the French revolution, was Charles Grant, Viscount de Vaux, an amiable man, who acquired considerable literary reputation from various useful and entertaining works, among which are "Memoires de la Maison de Grant," where he enters minutely into its history, and takes occasion to compliment his chief and patron, Sir James Grant.

Sir Aluin, who lived in the beginning of the fourteenth century, was founder of the branch called from him clan Allan, the representative of which is Grant of Achernach. Sliochd Phadric is another cadency, descended from Patrick, second son of John, who died in 1508, and is represented by Grant of Tullachgorm. Duncan, third son of John, ninth chief, was founder of Clan Donchà, and John, the fourth son, was ancestor of the Grants of Glenmoriston. This last branch, although acknowledging their common chief, have long acted independently. Their seat is a picturesque valley opening to the Great Glen of Caledonia. Sir James Grant of Monimusk, in Aberdeenshire, is descended from James, eleventh chief, who flourished 1540. Sir Alexander, of Dalvey, is from John who died about 1525.

The ARMORIAL BEARINGS, are gules, three eastern or antique coronets, or. Crest, a mountain inflamed, proper. Supporters, two savages, wreathed around the head and loins, proper. Motto, " Stand fast."

The SUAICHEANTAS, or Badge, is the Giuthas or Pine, *Pinus Sylvestris.*

The CATH-GHAIRM, or battle shout, is Craig Elachai', a noted hill in Strathspey.

The PIOBAIREACHD, CRUINNEACHAI', or gathering, is a beautiful composition, usually called Craigelachai'.

Castle Grant is an imposing specimen of a Highland baronial residence, and contains many fine portraits of chiefs, and some interesting specimens of ancient armour.

The troubles in which the elder scions of the Alpin stock, the Mac Gregors, got involved, induced the Grants anxiously to desire to draw closer the natural bonds of clanship which their distant locality rendered less useful for their mutual interest. A meeting was held for this purpose in Blair of Athol in the early part of last century, and in the prospect of the reversal of the attainder and proscription, it was agreed that they should adopt the name of Mac Gregor in common; and if this should not be obtained that of Mac Alpin or Grant was to be assumed by both parties. The meeting was harmonious on these and other subjects, but the point of chiefship could not be settled. From the peculiar situation of the Mac Gregors; in disorder, and persecuted by government and vigilant enemies on all sides, compared with the Grants who were powerful, united, and at peace with their neighbours, it was contended that their name should be the general designation. Respect for Clan Alpin was too strong for this proposition, and after a conference, which lasted fourteen days, the meeting finally broke up without settling the question, but several Grants, as Ballindallach and others, adopted the patronymic Mac Alpin.

The figure adopted to shew the Grant Tartan is such a gillie, or lad, as we have frequently met in Strathspey, and who is to be seen everywhere throughout the Highlands. He is useful in herding black cattle, sheep, or goats, and is especially serviceable to the sportsman, directing him through hill and dale to the best moors for game, or streams for trout; and he skips with cheerful agility, leading the way across morasses which would be thought impassable by a stranger, and under a cumbrous load of game, as represented, he trudges gaily along side the garron, or pony. Ragged as he appears to be, he is the son of honest and, mayhap, affluent farmers, and such a youth is the embryo of many a hero who may carve out, like his fathers, an honourable fortune and military renown with his sword.

NA GRANTAICH—THE GRANTS OF GLENMORISTON.

IN the letter press, relative to the Grants of Strathspey, the origin of the name of this clan is investigated. It is there observed that the opinion of Doctor John Mac Pherson is entitled to great respect. He believes they received the appellation from Griantach, or sliabh Grianus, "the plain of the Sun," a remarkable place in Strathspey, where there are many remains which indicate the worship of that luminary in the ages of Druidism. It seems quite conjectural that the Norman "le Grand" should be the origin of this name, and scarcely more reasonable to derive it from the epithet Grandach, given to an ancestor who is said to have been distinguished from the ugliness of his countenance.

The Lairds of Grant were crown chamberlains of the lordship of Urquhart, in which Glenmoriston was comprehended, and in 1509, the barony was granted to John, elder son of the chief, but as he died without issue, it reverted to the crown, and was bestowed on Grant of Ballandallach, who sold it in 1548, to John Grant of Culcabuck, both being near cadets. The latter is thus the direct progenitor of the present Glenmoriston. Patrick, son of Culcabuck,

GRANT

by a daughter of Lord Lovat, took up his residence in this district, and it is from him that the clan derives its patronymic Mac Phatric, by which it is distinguished among the highlanders. His son, who married a daughter of " The Grant," built the castle of Glenmoriston, and hence, according to the practice of Celtic genealogists, he is distinguished as Ian nan Caisteal—John of the Castle.

John, the sixth chief, married Janet, daughter of the celebrated Sir Ewen Cameron of Lochiel, and living in troublous times he built a small house for his personal safety, on a rock at Blary, from which circumstance he was familiarly spoken of as Ian na Chreagan. He left a son, John, who, dying without issue, the honour and estates devolved on Patrick his younger brother. His son, who likewise bore the name of Patrick, married Henrietta, daughter of Grant of Rothiemurcus, and left John his successor, captain in the 42nd highlanders, who distinguished himself highly during a long service in India, and attained the rank of Lieutenant Colonel. He died at Invermoriston, in 1801, and the elder son dying in minority, his brother, James Murray, the present chief succeeded to the family estates, and, in 1821, he acquired the lands of Moy, in the county of Moray, as heir of entail to the late Colonel Hugh Grant.

This chief married his cousin Henrietta, daughter of Cameron of Glenevis, by whom he has a numerous family.

The clan joined Viscount Dundee, and were prominently engaged in the battle of Killiecrankie; they also fought under the Earl of Mar, in the rising for the Stewarts, in 1715, and displayed their wonted bravery in the extraordinary campaign of Prince Charles Edward Stewart. Glenmoriston on that occasion joined the army at Edinburgh, by a rapid march from the highlands, and an anecdote is recorded of the first interview with his Highness, which is characteristic of the two personages. Grant immediately requested an audience of the Prince to announce the addition he had brought with such alacrity to the army. He did not think that on such an urgent occasion very high etiquette was to be observed, and he had not stopped to prepare himself for the meeting. The prince acknowledged, in a becoming manner, the sense he had of the service which had been rendered; but, in a jocular manner, passing his hand over the rough chin of this ardent warrior, observed, that it must have been some time since he had shaved. "It is not beardless boys that are to do your Highness's turn," promptly exclaimed the chief, as he turned away, much offended. Prince Charles had the good sense to overlook this unsophisticated ebullition.

The estate, which had been forfeited in 1715, was restored in 1733, and although Patrick Grant of Glenmoriston was included in the first bill of attainder, 1746, the name was subsequently withdrawn. By whose influence this was done never became known, but it is supposed that the protection which had been afforded to Prince Charles, when concealed in this district, procured the favour of Lord President Forbes, whose unremitting exertions, having been so effectual in suppressing the rebellion, were afterwards sedulously applied to save those engaged in it from the penalties they had incurred.

This clan possessed a charm, by which it was believed they were rendered invulnerable. The nature of this treasure so invaluable during the existence of clanship, has not come to our knowledge; but, although the Grants were brave as their swords, it does not appear that they were much more fortunate than their neighbours.

The Duke of Cumberland, at the intercession of the Laird of Grant, offered his protection to Glenmoriston's clansmen, if they would march into Inverness and lay down their arms; but in violation of his guarantee, they were forthwith made prisoners, and about 100 of them were transported to the colonies!

The ARMORIAL BEARINGS are gules, three eastern crowns or, with the difference marking the cadetship. Crest, a mountain inflamed, proper. Motto, " Stand fast."

The SUAICHEANTAS, or Badge of recognition, is the Giuthas, Pine, *Pinus Sylvestris.*

The figure has the hair clubed, or glibed, in the manner represented in some prints of the old Black Watch, the percursors of the 42nd Highlanders. He is in the attitude of throwing the ball, at the commencement of the game of Camanachd or Shinnie, as it is named in the low country. This exhilirating amusement is very popular among the highlanders: two opposing parties endeavour by means of the camac or club, to drive a ball to a certain spot on either side, and the distance is sometimes so great, that a whole day's exertion is required to play out the game. A vigorous runner, it is obvious, has a great advantage: but agility is not the only requisite; great skill in preventing the ball being driven to the desired goal is necessary, and many awkward blows and falls take place during the contest. Different parishes frequently turn out to try their abilities at this exciting game, and no better exercise could be enjoyed in a winter day. When there is a numerous meeting, the field has much the appearance of a battle scene; there are banners flying, bagpipes pealing, and a keen mélée around the ball. Young and old, rich and poor, join in this athletic sport, and though it is usually engaged in, con amore, prizes are frequently contended for.

Note.—Glenmoriston is a corruption of Glen-mòr-esan, the valley of the great waterfall.

GRANT of GLENMORISTON

CLANN NAN GUINNAICH, OR GUNNS.

THE Gunns were in the north the counterpart of the Mac Gregors in the south. Although not numerous, they were most martial and resolute, and the appellation by which they were distinguished is very indicative of their general character. Guinneach signifies sharp, keen, fierce, and was doubtless imposed as descriptive of their known or imputed dispositions. The genealogical derivation of the clan is from Guinn, the second son of Olaus or Ollav the Black, King of Man and the Isles, who died in the year 1237.

The county of Caithness was the original seat of this hardy clan; and, notwithstanding the feuds in which they were so repeatedly engaged with their powerful neighbours, they were able to extend their possessions considerably. Through the favour of the Earls of Sutherland they obtained extensive lands in the parish of Kildonan and elsewhere, which they enjoyed for ages by the old clannish tenure of undisturbed possession, or a lease in perpetuity, for the Highland reddendum of watching, warding, hunting, and hoisting, when required by the superior.

From James, son of George, the chief who flourished in the end of the fifteenth century, is derived the patronymic Mac Iamais, by which they have been since distinguished among their countrymen, and from other chiefs of this clan are sprung the Mac Ian, the Mac Uilliam, the Mac Eanruig and the Mac Rob, or, as now more generally known in Caithness, Johnsons, Williamsons, Hendersons, and Robsons, besides several others. The Gallies also were of the Clann Guinnaich, a party of whom, settling in Rosshire, were designated as coming from Gall-'aobh, the stranger's side.

As observed, the Gunns were frequently embroiled in war, being alternately on terms with the great rival families of Mackay, ancestor of the Lord Rea, the Earls of Sutherland, and Caithness, &c., to whom they were valuable allies or implacable foes! About 1562, Alasdair the chief, whose mother was an illegitimate daughter of the Earl of Aboyne, was "a very able and strong man, and indued with sundrie good qualities;" having offended the Earl of Moray by not giving the middle of the street of Aberdeen to his Lordship and his followers, a point of honour, the contention for which often led to bloodshed, he contrived to take the haughty chief prisoner, and had him executed "under pretence of justice."

In 1616, John, another chief, was imprisoned in Edinburgh, and exposed to rigorous prosecution for having, at the instigation of the Earl of Caithness, burnt the corn-stacks of some of his opponents' tenants, a service which he long objected to execute, offering, however, to "do his best to slay William Innes," the object of this outrage! The history of the Gunns is replete with incidents which, in the present age, have more the character of romance than reality. The Keiths, or Clan Cai', a branch of the Cattans, having, by marriage with the heiress of the Cheynes of Acrigil, obtained a settlement beside the Gunns, continual quarrels arose between them, which led at last to a meeting in the chapel of St. Tair, with a view to their reconciliation; but no other means of quenching their animosity being found practicable, it was solemnly agreed it should be decided by combat in a remote part of the country, and twelve relations of each chief were the number of champions agreed upon. George Gunn was then "a great commander in Catteyness, and one of the greatest in that countrie, becaus when he flourished there was no Earle," and, holding the office of crowner, the badge of which was a large brooch or plate of silver, he was distinguished as Fear a Bhraiste mòr. The hostile bands accordingly met in a retired part of Strathmore, but the Keiths had treacherously brought two men on each horse. The Gunns then perceived that their destruction was intended, but they scorned to retreat, and the battle commencing, they fought with furious desperation until both parties were so reduced that the mortal combat ceased, the crowner and seven of his clan being killed, whilst the Keiths were scarely able to leave the field and carry off their slain and wounded. The five surviving Gunns, who were sons of the chief, retired to the bank of a stream, where Torcuil, the slightest injured, washed and dressed their wounds. Here they began to ruminate on their sad disaster, and Eanruig beag the youngest, burning with revenge and a determination to recover his father's sword, mail, and brooch of office, prevailed on two of his brothers, who alone were able to accompany him, to follow the victors, who had gone to the castle of Dalraid. On reaching this place Eanruig approached the narrow window, and observed the Keiths quaffing ale and detailing to the Sutherlands the result of the sanguinary battle, when, singling out the chief, he bent his bow and shot him through the heart, exclaiming; "Beannachd na Guinnaich do 'n Chai!"— the compliments of the Gunns to Keith. The company in alarm rushed to the door, where several were killed by their enraged enemies, but the exhausted Gunns, unable to maintain so unequal a contest, made their escape in the darkness of the night, and hastened to the place where they had left their wounded brothers, and all five got safely to their own country! This battle, called, from its site, Alt na gaun, was fought in 1478. In 1585, the clan was again involved in war, being "invaded by the Earles of Sutherland and Cateynes, becaus they wer judged to be the chief authors of troubles which wer then like to ensue; and to this effect, it was resolved that two companies should be sent by the Earles against the Clan Gunn, thereby to compass them that no place of retreat might be left unto them." They had taken up their position on the Beann-gruaine, and the Sinclairs were the first to attack the devoted clan, who, although much inferior in numbers boldly prepared for the onslaught, and, having the advantage of rising ground, they reserved themselves until the enemy had come close up to their line, when they poured a flight of arrows on the Sinclairs, and, rushing down, their commander, with 120 of his men, were killed, and the survivors pursued until darkness covered their precipitate retreat! The party of the Earl of Sutherland immediately followed the Gunns, who

GUNN

fled to Lochbroom in the height of Ross, where they were brought to an engagement and defeated, with the loss of thirty-two men slain, and their captain, George, wounded and taken prisoner!

The COAT ARMOUR is arg., a galley of three masts, sails furled and oars in action, sab., displaying at the mast-head, flags, gu., within a bordure, az. On a chief of the third, a bear's head of the first, muzzled of the second, between two mullets of the field. Crest, a dexter arm wielding a broadsword, proper. Motto, "Aut pax aut bellum."

The SUAICHEANTAS, or badge, is Craobh Aitean, *juniperis communis*, juniper bush.

The most ancient seat of the chief was Hallburg, a fortress then deemed impregnable; latterly they inhabited the castle of Kilearnan, which was unfortunately destroyed by fire in the year 1690. George Gunn, Esq., of Rhives, Sutherland, descended from a second son of the fifth Mac Iamais, is now chief of the clan.

The Gunn tartan will be seen from the figure to be of a fine dark pattern which, like that worn by the clansmen of Roderic dubh, served so well to conceal an ambuscade among the sombre-coloured and luxurant heath and mountain herbage. The coat is madar, a colour produced by a native vegetable dye.

CLANN ULRIC—THE KENNEDYS.

OF the origin of the illustrious house of Carrick, represented by the Marquis of Ailsa, we are told that all historians agree that they came originally from Ireland. Upon what satisfactory authority are we to believe that all the old highland, and many of the lowland, gentry of Scotland emanated from this "Officina gentium?"

It was long the practice to repeat in every genealogy, this absurd tradition, derived from the legends of what has been called the corrupted age of bardism. In the course of this work, several of these extractions have been shown to be quite untenable, and, in the present case, we do not see any valid reason to withdraw our scepticism. Nisbet, the famous Scottish herald, says he finds this "to be a groundless conjecture;" at the same time it is to be observed that the O'Kennedies of Ireland were of considerable note.

Duncan de Carrick, so called from a district in Ayrshire, lived in the end of the twelfth century, and in 1220, we find his son Nicol, actuated by the piety of the age, granting the church of Maybole to the nuns of North Berwick.

Nial, or Nigel, Earl of Carrick, executes a deed of confirmation and acknowledgment to Roland, son of the above Nicol, in which he is styled "caput tocius progeniei suæ," having right to the Calps, a term explained in a former number, and whatever else belonged to the "Kinkenoll," that is, the chiefship of his clan, he being Ceanncinnidh, or head of his race.

At this time the patronymics coming into use, the name of Kennedy became the common appellation given to this tribe, the etymology of which has been given as Ceann na tigh, signifying the head of a house, but such designation is applied to those who are cadets only of the chief house. The more probable derivation, and the most consonant with the Celtic practice, is from personal appearance, and it is very likely it was from the black headed Roland, "Ceann dubh," that the name Kennedy arose. Certain it is that Carrick and Kennedy were used for the same person in many charters. It is to be observed, however, that there are lands called Kennedy mentioned in the family deeds as early as 1290.

The territorial appellation began to be laid entirely aside towards the end of the thirteenth century, and Alexander Kennedy, who was chancellor in the time of Baliol, 1295, is the first of the name who appears in written record. In the succeeding year we find Dominus Alexander Kennedy, with John and Hugh, signing Ragman's Roll, that bond of allegiance forced on the Scots by Edward the First, and about this time there occurs in the Lennox chartulary another individual, called Fergus Kennedy.

As Carrick was, until even the time of Buchanan, a Celtic district, in other words a part of the country in which Gaëlic was the language; Gaëlic customs prevailed and surnames in that language are there abundant to this day. The above acknowledgment of Kinkenoll, that important hereditary right, was confirmed by a charter of Alexander III., dated 1275, and it is ratified by two others, granted by Robert II., in 1375, and in Robertson's Index to the Missing Records: there is a "carta to James Kennedy and his heirs-male, of the capitanship, head and commandment of his kin." There had been previously a deed executed by David II., "anent the clan of Muntercasduff, and John Mac Kennedy captain thereof."

The name of this people has puzzled antiquaries; but a knowledge of the Gaëlic would have enabled them easily to resolve it. It is simply the people of the black feet; and this appellation seems to have been acquired from their practice of wearing Cuarans of a different character from those in general use among the highlanders

KENNEDY

of former ages, which being made of deer's-skin with the hair outwards, gave rise to the term "redshanks," by which they were distinguished among their lowland countrymen.

Ulric Kennedy went from Carrick at an early period and settled in Lochaber, from whom and his followers are descended the Mac Ulrics of that county, who put themselves under the leading of the Camerons. They were accounted rather a lawless race, and a song composed by one of this clan, when in prison for cattle-stealing, is very popular in the Highlands.

The ARMORIAL BEARINGS are, on a field argent, a chevron gules, between three cross croslets, fitchee, sable, all within a double tressure, flory, counterflory fleur-de-lis, of the second. Crest, a dolphin naiant, proper. Supporters, two swans, proper, beaked and membered, gules. Motto, "Avise la fin." These are borne by the Marquis of Ailsa, but we have seen the seal of a Mac Ulric in which the lymphad or galley appeared in base, and the crest was a hand grasping a dagger.

It is to be observed, that the tressure was borne previous to the alliance of this house with the royal family of Robert III., as by the seal appended to a deed, executed in 1285, thus showing that it was not granted or assumed in consequence of that marriage.

The illustration is given from a rare print of William, Earl of Sutherland, who in 1759 raised a Fencible regiment, 1100 strong, in

nine days, and the men were so tall that there was no light company, nearly 300 being upwards of five feet eleven inches in height. The portrait was painted by Allan Ramsay, son of the celebrated Scots poet, and the figure seems to verify the above fact. This is the authority for the costume, which is that of the regiment which this nobleman had raised; the tartan is adapted for the clan here illustrated, and is taken from a plaid in possession of Dr. Kennedy, Fort William. The old artists made sad blunders in depicting this costume; even here the plaid is represented as being fastened on the back in such a manner as we never saw, nor can well understand. The old military hose were of the pattern here shown, as may be seen in portraits of the Black Watch, Lord Loudoun's Highlander's, &c. The ostrich feather was at this time occasionally worn.

After the last unfortunate rising for the house of Stewart in 1745, the Highlanders were treated with the utmost severity. Their dress was proscribed, and acts were passed which put them in the position of outlaws; cases actually occurred in which those guilty of murder got acquitted on its being proved that the man who had been slain was clad in the Highland garb, which the wisdom of the British Legislature pronounced to be the badge of rebellion, and endeavoured to make the people loyal by its entire suppression! We shall mention one fact, among others which could be cited, that a trial for the murder of a man in Glenprosan, took place in 1751, when the delinquent was "asoilzied simpliciter," the man who was killed having been in the Highland dress. The great Chatham perceived the value of that portion of the northern population and brought them into the public service, legalising their fondly cherished costume when worn in the British army, before the act of proscription was repealed, and the wisdom of so doing was amply approven. Fifty Highland battalions have been embodied from 1740 to 1800.

CLANN LAOMAINN—THE LAMONDS.

THE Lamonds were the original proprietors of Cowal in Argyleshire: the Campbells, Mac Lachlans, and others having obtained their possessions in that district by intermarriage with these old lords of the soil. There are also a series of feudal charters by which they held their property in latter times, and several deeds are extant conveying portions of their lands to various religious establishments. There is one granted in the middle of the thirteenth century by "Laumanus filius Malcolmi, nepos Duncani, filius Fearchar," and another, dated 1295, by "Malcolmus filius et hæres domini quondam Laumani." It is from Lauman that succeeding chiefs have received the name, and by modern usage are styled Mac Laomainn, but at an earlier period they were distinguished from another ancestor, as Mac'erachars, or sons of Farquhar, at which time it would appear they were intimately connected with the

Clan Dugal, Craignish, an ancient branch of the Campbells. That clan contrived eventually to get possession of a large portion of Cowal, by which the power of the Lamonds was greatly reduced, but the imposing ruins of many castles attest their former greatness.

In the ancient churchyard of Kilmun an inscription is, or was, to be seen, which gives a curious indication of superiority:

"Is mise Mac Laomainn mor Choail gu h-uile,
A thug iasad do Bharon dubh Lochau,
De uaigh lic tiolaig a mhic' us e' na airc".

That is, "I am he, the great Mac Lamond of all Cowal, who *lent* to the Black Baron of Lochau, a grave and a slab for his son when he himself was in distress."

LAMOND

The sacred observance of the rites of hospitality was a remarkable trait in the character of the Highlanders, and it was exemplified in an affecting manner towards one of this clan. A young man from Cowal, travelling through the Mac Gregor's country, went into a Tigh osda, or Inn, to pass the night. A company of others had met there, and in the course of the evening a quarrel having arisen, dirks were drawn, and Lamond unfortunately killed his opponent, who was no other than son of Mac Gregor of Glenstræ, who was then head of the clan. The young man fled with the speed of a deer, and reached a house at the door of which stood its proprietor, looking out, as the practice was, before retiring to rest, for passing strangers, and to him Lamond exclaimed, "I have slain a man, save me from the death which now pursues me!" "Whoever you are," says the old chief, "enter my house and you are safe." In a few minutes the pursuers were at the door impatiently inquiring whether the fugitive had been seen, for said they, with great emotion, "he has slain your son, and we burn for revenge!" Alas! alas! my beloved son," cried Glenstræ, bursting into a flood of bitter tears, "the stranger has besought my protection and received it—my promise cannot be forfeited even for this dreadful deed—as I live he shall here be safe." The generous but sorrowing Mac Gregor, true to his word, not only shielded him from the vengeance of his clansmen, but conveyed him under a strong guard to his native place, and, on parting, clasped his hand and thus addressed him : "Mac Lamond, you are now in safety, but take care that you meet not hereafter with my followers, for I no longer can or will protect you, farewell!"

Sometime after this when the Mac Gregors were visited with the dire and relentless persecution, by which they were so long afflicted, old Alastair, of Glenstræ, obliged to conceal himself from his enemies, was received with becoming hospitality and treated with the greatest respect and kindness by this Lamond, who blessed God for affording him the opportunity of so far repaying the deep debt of gratitude which he owed to his now unfortunate friend.

It was a maxim with the Highlanders that they should not ask the name of a stranger who might be forced to seek the shelter of their roof, lest they might discover that he was an enemy, and nothing could be thought more shamefully dishonourable than taking any advantage of those who might sojourn with them "under trust," as it was expressed. This virtue of hospitality, exercised with so high a sense of honour, led, no doubt, to occasional imposition, and induced the generous to indulge in an expenditure more profuse than prudence would have warranted; it may, indeed, be believed that the desire to supply a diminished store sometimes impelled a chief to foray on his inimical countrymen.

A gentleman of this clan, who held a captaincy in the 42nd, or Royal Highlanders, inherited, in an eminent degree, the warlike spirit of his ancestors. He was so much attached to the service in his national corps that he would never quit it, nor revisit his estate in Argyle, and refused to accept promotion in another regiment. An infectious fever having broken out among the men while lying at Winchester, Captain Lamond could not be restrained from his attendance on the sick, and fell a victim to his humanity, being seized with the fatal complaint. Finding himself dying he passionately expressed his regret that he should leave the world like a manufacturer or tradesman, quietly expiring in his bed, when he might so often have died in the field like a soldier!

The publication of Ossian's poems led to an investigation into the use of the harp in the Highlands, and Mr. Gunn published an elaborate work on that interesting subject, in which the "harps of Lude," so long in possession of the Robertsons, were described and illustrated. One of these had belonged to Queen Mary, the other was acquired about 1640, by marriage with a lady of the house of Lamond, where it had been preserved for some centuries previous.

The chiefs of this clan resided at Dunoon until the time of Charles I. when Sir James Lamond having stood by the fortunes of his unfortunate sovereign, his castle of Towart was destroyed by the Marquis of Argyle. Other buildings fell a prey to the ravages of war at the same time. Ascog, the residence of a cadet, who also distinguished himself as a royalist, was burned, and the picturesque ruins still remain. The present seat of the chief is at Ard Lamond, in a rich and beautiful flat, commanding a fine view of the Clyde and the distant shores.

The ARMORIAL BEARINGS were anciently an imperial mond, an heraldic pun on the name, but the bearing most usual at present is a lion rampant, arg., in a field, azure. Crest, a hand couped at the wrist, proper. Motto, "Ne pereas nec spernas."

The SUAICHEANTAS is Luibheann, Dryas, *Octopetala*.

The figure is that of a lady dressed in the fashion prevalent towards the end of last century; the hair is powdered, curled, and made up in that style, and in the blue snood is fixed the Clan badge. We see the rich brocade gown and silk quilted petticoat, while the plaid, so characteristic and becoming a portion of the dress of a Highland lady, is thrown over the shoulders in the graceful mode, usual among gentlewomen at this time, and for many years previously, not only in the Highlands but in the Low Country.

It will be observed that the Tartan in this figure is almost the same as the pattern appropriate to the Forbeses. This coincidence might happen with two clans who lived distant from each other, but it could not lead to material confusion.

Air son Eachdraidh
nanGael nah Alba
le Jaimais Logan
is airidh e air
Cuimhneachan buan

LOGAN

SIOL LOGANICH—THE LOGANS.

IT is accounted most honourable to be distinguished by a local appellation, as it is an indication that the property from which it is derived was in possession of the founder of the tribe or family. Logan and Lagan signify a low lying, or flat tract of country, and these terms occur in various parts of Scotland; in some cases giving name to a parish, as Logan in Ayr, and Laggan in Inverness-shire.

When an individual receives a crown charter, it is evident that he must have been a person of some consideration—it is not to be supposed that he was the first who bore the appropriate name, although in this manner, the erudite Chalmers, in his elaborate " Caledonia," derives the most distinguished families in Scotland!

Guillim, the celebrated writer on English heraldry, gives this account of the origin of the name: a certain John Logan, serving with the English forces in Ireland, whom the historian Barbour calls one of the lords of that country having, upon the defeat of the army which had invaded the island under the command of Edward Bruce in 1316, taken prisoner Sir Allan Stewart, that nobleman gave his daughter, with several lands, to his conqueror's son, and from this union, our genealogist says, came the Logans of Scotland, who were then represented by those of Idbury in Oxfordshire! Unfortunately for the accuracy of this derivation, we find various individuals of the name in Scotland, witnessing royal grants, and giving charters themselves, one hundred and fifty years before this period. In the former capacity, Robertus de Logan appears frequently in the time of William the Lyon, who reigned from 1165, to 1214. As a Gaëlic cognomen, Logan was found equally in Ireland, and many notices of persons so called, particularly in the northern province, are found in the Irish records, and there seems good reason to believe that these were emigrants from Scotland.

The signatures of Walter, Andrew, Thurbrand, John, and Phillip de Logan, are found among those attached to the celebrated " Ragman's Roll," a bond of fealty exacted by Edward I. of England, in 1296. The Scottish chiefs, whom that crafty monarch suspected of being too much imbued with the principles of liberty to be safely trusted at home, he compelled to serve during his wars in Guienne, and John Cumin, Lord of Badenach, and Allan Logan, a knight, " manu et consilio promptum," were thus disposed of.

In 1306, Dominus Walterus Logan, with many others, having been taken prisoner, was hanged at Durham, in presence of Edward of Carnarvon, the King's son.

In 1329, a remarkable occurrence took place in Scottish history. Robert the Bruce, had made a vow of pilgrimage to the city of Jerusalem; but the continued wars, and unsettled state of the kingdom, rendered it impossible for him to carry his long cherished intention into effect, and on finding death approach, he willed, that the heart, which had so long panted to view the scene of his Saviour's sufferings, should be taken there, and deposited in the church of the holy sepulchre. For this purpose, preparations were made on a scale very magnificent for the age, and a choice band of the most chivalrous Scottish nobility were selected as a becoming escort for the princely relic. To " the good Sir James Douglas" was assigned the command, and Sir Robert and Walter Logan, are particularly noticed, as being among the most distinguished of his companions in the pious embassy, which was unhaply fated to abortion. Passing by Spain, the gallant Scotsmen learned that the Saracens had devastated that country, and were then employed in the siege of Grenada, when it was at once resolved, that as the Moors were bitter enemies of the Cross, the duty of the expedition was to land and fight against them. In the heat of the attack that speedily followed the debarkation, Douglas, taking from his breast the silver casket which contained the precious charge, threw it into the thickest rank of the foe, exclaiming, " there, go thou valiant heart as thou were wont to lead us," when the heroic troop dashed after it with a fury irresistible. The casket was regained, but in attempting the rescue of their friend Lord Sinclair, both Sir Robert and Sir Walter Logan were slain.

In 1364-5, Henry Logan obtains a salvus conductus to pass through England to Flanders and return, with six companions on horseback, and others of the name obtained similar passports for different purposes in subsequent years.

The Logans of Lastalrig, were chiefs of the name in the south of Scotland, and this property, with other lands near Berwick, they held prior to the thirteenth century. In the time of Malcolm IV., who reigned from 1153, to 1165, " Edwardus de Lastalrick," gave to God, Saint Mary, and Saint Ebbe, and to Herbert, and the monks of Coldinghame, two tofts of land in Eiemouth, and one in Leith, " reddendo annuatim pro recognitione, tres terses de Lano serico," to be paid at the feast of Pentecost, wherever it might be demanded. By another deed, he grants to the convent of the blessed Mary, Newbottle, a considerable piece of ground at Leith, and the monks of North Berwick were treated with equal generosity, by his son and successor, Thomas. *Coll. in Mus. Advoc. Edinb.*

The preceptory of Saint Anthony, the picturesque ruins of which are to be seen on a small level in the precipitous ascent of Arthur's seat, beside Edinburgh, was founded in 1430, by Sir Robert Logan of Lastalrig, and it was the only establishment of this order in Scotland. The collegiate church of Lastalrig, a fine Gothic structure, now restored and made the parish kirk of South Leith, is mentioned as early as 1170. If it was not founded by the Logans, whose castle was closely adjoining, they were great benefactors thereto, and were patrons of the valuable living.

The lairds of Lastalrig, which has been generally spelt Restalrig, although always pronounced Lasterrick, were barons of considerable note, most of them having received knighthood for national services. Some of them, also, were sheriffs of the county, and others held the dignity of Lord Provost of Edinburgh. Sir Robert Logan of Lastalrig, married a daughter of King Robert II., by his wife Euphemia Ross; and a successor of the same name, was one of the hostages given for the ransom of James I.

Leith is the flourishing sea-port of the Scottish metropolis; the land on which it is built, and the harbour itself, belonged to the Lairds of Lastalrig, and in 1398, Sir Robert Logan granted a charter, conferring on the city of Edinburgh, free liberty and license, for "augmenting, enlarging, and bigging the Harbory of Leith," and that all ships coming there, might "lay ther ankers and towes upon his grounde, and grants for him and his airs all his wawes, roades, and traunses whatsomever, by the land of the barony of Restalrig, to be holden as freely as any other King's streets within the kingdom is holden of the King. And gif any of his successors quarrel thir libertyes, he obliges him and them in a penalty of two hundred pound sterling, to the Burgesses for damndage and skaith, and in a hundred pound sterling to the fabric of the kirk of Saint Andrews, before the entry to the plea." In 1413, he gave an additional grant of land, on which to build a free quay, and both of these charters were afterwards ratified and extended by the crown.

It was the misfortune of the barons of Lastalrig, that they possessed property so near to Edinburgh, and held the superiority of lands, the improvement of which was so necessary for the rising prosperity of the capital. The corporation and the Logans began to live on disagreeable terms; quarrels arose between their retainers and the burgesses; brawls and bloodshed took place in the streets of Edinburgh, and one of the lairds was clapt in jail, under the vague charge of being "a turbulent and implacable neighbour, and had put certain indignities upon the Edinburghers." Finally, that mysterious affair, the Gowrie conspiracy, "afforded an opportune occasion for the citizens to get rid of their superiors, and the crafty James VI., to gratify his own revenge, for the raid of Ruthven, and his grasping favourites with the forfeited estates."

A series of letters addressed to the Earl of Gowrie were produced, alleged to have been "written everie word and subscribed by" him, in which he is implicated as a zealous partisan in the alleged treasonable plot. Logan had been dead nine years, but as by the Scottish law, a traitor was required to be present at his own trial, the mouldering remains were exhumed and produced in court! An infamous fellow had sworn that the letters, which were not originals, and had appeared in different forms and numbers, during the trial, were purloined, and preserved by him. He afterwards recanted, declaring that "he had no wish to live," but being urged by the authorities and a promise being made that his wife and family should be well provided for, he adhered to his first deposition, when, for surety's sake, he was forthwith hanged. The Lords of the Articles were, notwithstanding, prepared to bring in a verdict of acquittal, but the Earl of Dunbar, who got most of Logan's estates, "travelled so earnestly to overcome their hard opinions of the process," that they at last acknowledged themselves convinced! The forfeiture was accompanied by proscription, so that, as in the case of the Clan Gregor, it was illegal for any one to bear the name of Logan.

The effect of these astounding proceedings was, that many families were obliged to abandon, with the loss of their name,

their ancient possessions, and adopt other designations, whence great confusion in families and property arose.

These transactions relative to the house of Lastalrig, have been dwelt upon rather lengthily; but they show in what manner the power and influence of tribes have been reduced, in the unsettled ages of society, and their possessions seized, by the tyranny of monarchs and the unbridled cupidity of courtiers.

The Logans of Lastalrig had ample lands, either in their own possession or as superiors, in the counties of Ayr, Renfrew, Perth, Lanark, Aberdeen, and even so far north as Moray, where they held the barony of Abernethie, in Strathspey.

There was another clan in the north, who, like the Chisholms, appear to have retained no remembrance of any connection they might have had with those of the same name in the south. They have distinguished themselves from an early period in the transactions of the country, and from this tribe most of the Logans, north of the Grampians, hold themselves descended.

It seems impossible to arrive at anything satisfactory respecting the history of the Ceann-cinnidh, or head of this race, previous to Colan Logan, heiress of Druimanairig, who married Eachuin Beirach, a son of the baron of Kintail, who died at Eadarachaolis, about 1350, leaving a son, Eanruig, from whom are derived the sliochd Harich, or those of the race in the island of Harris. Although by the "courtesy of Scotland" a person marrying an heiress takes her name, yet the celtic law, or patriarchal rule, does not give him the chiefship, which, like the salique law which prevailed in France, excludes the "regimen of women." It would therefore appear that the Logans left wester, and moved towards easter Ross, the chief settling in Ard-meinach, since called Ellan dubh, or the Black Isle, and although they have always been highly respected and enterprising in farming and commercial pursuits, they afford an instance of the loss of a considerable landed inheritance, and in a great measure of the original strength of patriarchal influence.

One of these chiefs, who was called Gilliegorm, from his dark complexion, was renowned for his warlike prowess. He married a relative of the Lord Lovat, but he fell into an unfortunate misunder-standing with the Frasers, arising from some claim which is not, now precisely known, but which he endeavoured to make good by force of arms. Hugh, the second Lord Lovat, determined to settle the matter of dispute, summoned to his assistance, 24 gentlemen of his name from the south, and being joined by some Mac Ra's and others, he marched with his clan from the Aird, against Gilliegorm, who had mustered his forces, and was fully prepared to meet his enemies. Some overtures for a peaceable settlement of differences being rejected, a sanguinary battle took place on the muir above Kessock, where Logan was slain with most part of his clansmen. Lovat plundered the lands and carried off the wife of Gilliegorm, who was then with child; but the barbarous resolution was formed, that, if it were a male, it should be maimed or destroyed, lest, when grown up, the son might revenge his father's death. The child proved a male, but humanity prevailed, and he was suffered to live, there being the less to be apprehended from his sickly and naturally deformed ap-pearance, from which he received the appellation "Crotach," or hump-backed. He was educated by the monks of Beauly, entered holy orders, and travelled through the Highlands, founding the churches of Kilmôr in Skye, and Kilichrinan in Glenelg. He seems to have had a dispensation to marry, for he left several children, one of whom, according to a common practice, became a devotee of Finan, a popular Highland saint; and hence he was called Gillie Fhinan, his descendants being Mac Ghillie Fhinans. The Fh being aspirated, the pronunciation is Ghilli'inan, which has now become Mac Lennan.

Dempster, the biographer of Scottish ecclesiastics, mentions, under 1511, Josias Logan, a devotee, who "Europam omnem, Asiam universam, totam Africam incredibile labore lustravit."

There have been several distinguished individuals of this clan, who have lived in more recent times. James Logan was the coadjutor of Penn the founder of Pennsylvania, and from him a county has received its name. His chair is yet preserved, which is occupied by the President of the anniversary meeting, instituted to commemorate this venerable colonizer. Dr. George Logan, another emigrant, was founder of the celebrated Loganian Library, Philadelphia. The Rev. George Logan, of Edinburgh, maintained a literary controversy of no slight description with the learned Ruddiman; and the various works of the Rev. John Logan, another presbyterian clergyman, are well known to the public. The late Logan of Logan, in Ayrshire, who was the last of his name, having left only a daughter, who married a Mr. Campbell, was celebrated for his wit, and a considerable degree of eccentricity; but the amusing publication which was brought out under his name is a compilation of drolleries, a small portion of which only could emanate from him.

Several remarkable instances of longevity in persons of this name have occurred—"Old Logan" served as a soldier fifty years, and died at Halifax, aged 105, about twenty years ago; another in Westminster, about forty years ago, also considerably above a hundred, &c.

The castle of Lesteric, some remains of which still exist, was the usual dwelling of the lairds of that title, but they also possessed the strong and picturesque Fastcastle, with those of Fleurs, Gunsgreen, &c. The residence of the northern Logans is situated on a height called originally Druim-na-clavan, but, after the above described battle, the name was changed to Druim-an-deur, "the ridge of tears." Robert Logan, Esq., banker, London, is representative of this ancient family, and possessor of the property, which is now called Drumdeur-fait.

A wooden figure of Gilliegorm, whose cairn was lately to be seen on the muir, among others of lesser size, was long preserved at Druim deur fait, with great care, "until after the battle of Dunblane, in 1715, when a party of Sutherlands and Munros, under pretence of the public good, having found this relick, charged the Logans with popery and the worship of this figure, which, after plundering the place, they destroyed."

The ARMORIAL BEARINGS are allusive to the expedition with

the Bruce's heart to the Holy Land, being or, three passion-nails conjoined in point, sable, piercing a man's heart, gules. Crest, a heart, gules, pierced by a passion-nail, proper. Motto, "Hoc majorum virtus." The Logans of England have not the piles conjoined, nor the heart, but carry a lion passant, in nombril. After the above mission the piles were conjoined, and termed passion-nails, as symbolical of the three nails wherewith the Saviour's feet and hands were nailed to the cross. In the manuscript collections of Sir James Balfour is a drawing of the "Sigillum Roberti Logan de Restalrik," 1279, in which the piles are simply conjoined in base. The Douglases bear, in commemoration of the mission of their renowned ancestor, a heart ensigned with an imperial crown, proper.

For some of these particulars I am obliged to Mr. Logan of Druimdeurfait, who kindly gave me the use of an old manuscript account of the family.

The SUAICHEANTAS is Conis, whin or furse, *Ulex Europeus.*

The CATH-GHAIRM, or battle shout, in the south was "Lesteric lowe," and in the north, "Druim an deur."

The figure is dressed in the Breacan Loganich, or Logan tartan, and the large plaid is worn, which is found so convenient in cold or rainy weather. In the bonnet is the badge, a sprig of whin in bloom, and the white cockade, which distinguished the adherents of the Stewarts. The sporan, or purse, is from one in possession of the Earl of Eglinton. It is an old and rather curious specimen, formed of badger skin, and closed with a silver snap. The figure resembles an "Old Mortality" among the tombs, conning over some curious legend relative to some of the silent tenants of the grassy mound. In the inscription on the stone the artist has paid a flattering compliment to the author, which he is proud to think may pass for an epitaph. As there has not hitherto been any Gaëlic presented in the ancient character, still most carefully cherished by the Irish, but long disused by the Highlanders, it has been thought well to introduce it in giving the above inscription, as somewhat interesting to those who have not before seen the "Litir Eireinich," or "Irish letter, as it is now called. Although not used in Highland literature, there are many gentlemen who can both read and write it. It is mentioned in the "Scottish Gaël" that Rorie mòr Mac Leod, of Dunvegan, chief of his clan, who died 1626, was the last person who continued the use of the ancient character in correspondence.

Air son Eachdraidh nan Gael na h-Alba le Jamais Logan
Is airidh e air Cuimhneachan buan.

On the box: J. Macalister Passenger Canada

MAC ALLASTER

CLANN ALASDAIR—THE MAC ALLASTERS.

MAC ALASDAIR, the patronymic of this clan signifies "the son of Alexander," and the personage from whom it is derived, according to the Seanachai's, or highland genealogists, was a son of Angus mòr, Lord of the Isles, who flourished in 1263.

This branch of the Mac Donalds settled in South Knapdale, in Ceantire, where the chief was in the situation of Ceann-tigh, or the simple "head of a house," during the independence of the Hebudean princes. After their forfeiture, the Mac Allasters attached themselves to the powerful division of Clan Donald, called Ian-mhòr from John the Great its founder, who lived in 1400, but they soon became independent, and under their chief, Loup, they maintained a respectable position, among surrounding tribes, until they were reduced by the rising power of the Campbells who, at different times, broke up so many others. In the statistical account of the parish, furnished to the late Right Hon. Sir John Sinclair, in 1796, it is said that not an acre then remained in the possession of a Mac Allaster.

In 1493, Ian du', then chief, was a person of some note: his son was named Angus, and his grandson was Alasdair Mac Alasdair, who flourished in the sixteenth century.

A notable stroke of policy was made by King James VI., in 1587, who passed an act called "The General Band," the object of which was to make the chiefs accountable to government for the peaceable behaviour of their clansmen, and the "broken men," who lived on their lands. It was, indeed, only adopting a well-known Celtic practice which the highlanders observed among themselves with excellent effect. In the long roll of those who were thus held responsible, appears "the Laird of Loup."

In 1605, all the principal chiefs in the Isles and west highlands were summoned to make their personal appearance at Kilkerran, now Campbelton, in Argyleshire, before Lord Scone, Comptroller of Scotland, and there exhibit the title deeds to their lands— acknowledge obedience to his majesty, and give sureties for their future allegiance. Non-compliance with this mandate was to be considered an act of rebellion, for which the usual penalty was immediate attack by fire and sword. To enforce the compliance of the highlanders on this occassion, all the fencible men of the western counties and burghs were ordered to muster at Kilkerran, with forty day's provisions; and, that none might escape the threatened vengeance, all boats were to be put in possession of Lord Scone. These severe measures had, however, very little of the desired effect.

The principal seat of the chiefs was formerly at Ard Phadriuc, on the south side of Loch Tarbet; latterly they resided at Loup, whence they received their usual designation. Sommerville Mac Allaster, of Kennox, is the representative of the old chiefs. The nearest cadet was Mac Alasdair, of Tarbet, and this family were constables of the castle of that name, situated on Loch Fine, and built by Robert the Bruce: a place which appears to have been of great strength, but is now in complete ruin. The clan held other posts of honour and responsibility, for, in 1481, we find Charles Mac Allaster was steward of Cean-tire.

The ARMORIAL BEARINGS of Mac Allaster of Loup are— an eagle displayed gules, beak and legs sable, in dexter chief point, a galley, sails furled, oars in action of the last, and in sinister chief point, a cross croslet fitchee, of the first, on a field argent, all within a bordure ingrailed of the second. Crest, a dexter-hand, holding a dirk in pale, both proper, motto "Fortiter."

Mac Allaster of Glen-Barr, carries his insignia differently.

The SUAICHEANTAS, is that borne by all branches of Clan Donald—Fraoch gorm, common heath, *Erica vulgaris*.

The figure represents an emigrant about to bid farewell to his native hills, and he appears sufficiently doleful, as one in such a situation might well be. Much sympathy has been excited by the clearing out of the highland tenantry, and undoubtedly great injustice and cruelty have been shewn towards them by many unfeeling landlords and factors in the process of ejection; at the same time, it is easy to believe that when the abolition of the patriarchal system, in 1748, dissolved the ties of clanship, and compelled the lairds to live in other society, and support their rank by other means, the tenants found themselves in a new and uncomfortable position. Their natural protectors were gone—military duty and local servitudes were no longer accepted in lieu of money rent, and the dispirited highlanders, unsuited for their altered circumstances, and resenting treatment by which they often found themselves in less estimation than sheep, in many cases, voluntarily left a country in which they could not again find the same delight, and emigration agents found it an advantageous pursuit to foster the spirit of discontent.

In saying thus much, we must not be understood as approving either of the system of removing the native tenantry or the mode in which their expulsion was, in many instances, so lamentably effected; for we agree in opinion with the late Sir John Sinclair, President of the Board of Agriculture, that sheep might have been introduced without any necessity for driving out the people.

There is nothing peculiar about the dress: it is such as the people fifty or sixty years ago.

We are always pleased to see the highland gentlemen wearing the dress of their country, for which it is so well adapted, not merely from an antiquarian predilection for the ancient garb, honoured as it is. We view it as encouraging a tasteful and economical manufacture which the highlanders have every facility for producing without extraneous aid. The wool can be had in abundance, and the hills and valleys abound with herbs and shrubs, from which they have the ability to extract dyes of beautiful variety, whilst the abundance of water power is a recommendation of no slight weight, for the establishment of so excellent a branch of national industry. The propriety of encouraging so suitable a manufacture among a pastoral and agricultural people is so obvious, that it is matter of surprise the object has been overlooked. A kilt will wear so long, that a committee of the Highland Society, which originated with the Chisholm, is now making exertions to excite the highlanders to adopt a plan, by which so great a saving to the poorer classes would accrue.

Keith, Mac Donald Mac Allaster, of Inistrynich, Esq., is one of those who wears the costume of his fathers, and encourages others to do so likewise, and he otherwise displays those feelings and practice which constitute the virtue of patriotism.

CLANN ARTAIR—THE MAC ARTHURS.

THE condition of clans has, in many cases, fluctuated very considerably. Some originally of little note have attained an important position among their countrymen, whilst others, who at one time lorded it over extensive districts and a numerous people, have become reduced to a state of comparative obscurity, or have been finally merged in the race of their more powerful neighbours. Different circumstances operated to effect these changes; the more usual were the fortunes of war, and internal misunderstanding. The system of clanship was well suited to the preservation of a balance of power, or a degree of equality among the different tribes; but a continuation of feuds would weaken a clan and render it an easy prey to the ambitious.

It was the policy of the Scottish government, too weak to enforce its laws on a fiercely independent people, to engage one clan to subdue another by granting a commission of fire and sword, that is, a licence to attack the obnoxious party, slay them in the field, burn their houses, and harry their cattle—taking their lands as a reward for the service! The effect of such proceedings will be easily perceived:—they account for the reverses in the circumstances of many clans.

The Mac Arthurs are a branch of the great Clan Campbell, and trace their descent from the original stock. They, indeed long disputed the seniority with the powerful family of Argyle.

In the reign of Alexander III., 1249—86, the Campbells presented two great divisions: those of Mac Chaillain mòr and Mac Artair, and the latter maintained their right to the chiefship, and were, in fact, at the head of the clan; a position which they retained until the time of James I., who ascended the throne in the year 1406.

Mac Artair espoused the cause of Robert the Bruce, and was rewarded by ample gifts of the forfeited estates of Mac Dugal. The chief was also appointed captain of the castle of Dunstaffnage, and the clan was in possession of such an extensive district as to rival that powerful house, which had so fearlessly opposed the royal champion of Scotland's independence.

John Mac Artair was beheaded by James I., and his lands were forfeited, since which time the Mac Chaillain mòr branch have held the chiefship, and gradually acquired the vast importance which they formerly held and still possess. The above John is described as being a great prince and leader of a thousand men.

In 1275, Cheristine, only daughter of Allan Mac Ruarai' granted a charter, " Arthuro filio domini Arthuro Campbell militis de terris de Mudewarde, Ariseg et Mordower, et insulis de Egge et Rumme." At subsequent periods the Mac Arthurs obtained Stra' chur in Cowal, from which they are designated, and they also held portions of Glenfalloch and Glendochart.

The ARMORIAL BEARINGS appropriate to this clan must anciently have been that carried by the Campbells; but they have long borne insignia peculiar to themselves, viz. azure a cross moline, argent between three antique or eastern crowns, or. Crest, two laurel branches in orle, proper.

The SUAICHEANTAS, also, must have been the same as that borne by the Campbells, which is given in Part I. and XIII.

Mac Arthur of Miltoun and Ascog bore different arms, which are quarterly; first and fourth azure, a cross moline between three antique crowns or; second and third, or, a fesse checky azure, and argent within a bordure sable, charged with eight mascles of the third. Crest, a greyhound couchant, within two branches of bay tree, proper. Motto, " Fide et opera." The coat armour of the Mac Arthurs of England deviates very considerably from these, whence it would appear that they are not of the same race.

The seat of the Mac Arthurs of Stra' chur, is on the side of Loch Awe. Many of this name are still to be found about Dunstaffnage, who have long been merely tenants to the Campbells.

The figure wears the ancient yellow or saffron colour garment, in which a former figure has been pourtrayed. This was the peculiar distinction of the Gaëlic grandees, and, indeed, when it is considered that it was formed of linen, and contained twenty-four, or perhaps, thirty yards, it will be seen that it could not have been a common article of dress.

In a MS. History of the Gordons, preserved in the Library of the Advocates, at Edinburgh, there is a curious passage, which shows that it was well-known as the dress of the Daoine-uasal, or gentlemen in the north, in the end of the sixteenth century, about which time Martin, in his description of the western islands, 1698, says it had been laid aside : — "Angus, the son of Lauchlan Mackintosh; Chief of the Clan Chatten, with a great party, attempts to surprise the castle of Ruthven, in Badenoch, belonging to Huntly (Earl of), in which there was but a small garison; and finding this attempt could neither by force nor fraude have successe, he retires a little to consult how to compasse his intent. In the meantime one creeps out under the shelter of some olde ruins, and levels with his piece at one of the Clan Chattan, cloathed in a yellow war-coate, which among them is the badge of the chieftains or heads of clans, and piercing his bodie with a bullet, strikes him to the grounde, and retires with gladness into the castle. The man killed was Angus himselfe, whom his people carrie away, and conceills his deathe for manie yeires, pretending he was gone beyond the seas."

All trades and professions, by the rule of Celtic society, went from father to son and a long line of hereditary pipers to the Mac Donalds of the Isles were Mac Arthurs, of whom several amusing anecdotes are given in the interesting work on the piobaireachd music, by Mr. Angus Mac Kay, piper to her Most Gracious Majesty Queen Victoria. The last of the race, who composed many pieces highly esteemed by judges of these national melodies, died in London, having been long piper to the Highland Society.

MAC AULAIDH—THE MAC AULAYS.

THIS Clan has been derived from the ancient Earls of Lennox, of whose family in the thirteenth century, was Aulay, brother of Maol-duin, then Earl, whose son, also called Aulay, signed the Ragman's Roll, that unjust and abortive bond of fealty, to Edward I. of England, who claimed to be Lord paramount of Scotland, 1296. Although this has, "upon good grounds been presumed to be" the correct descent, it has not met with invariable belief; but, on the contrary, the Mac Aulays have been pretty satisfactorily proved to be descended of the clan Gregor. In 1591, a bond of manrent, or deed of friendship, was executed between the chiefs of these two clans, in which Mac Aulay acknowledged being a cadet of the Mac Gregors, and agrees, in that character, to pay Mac Gregor of Glenstrae, the Calp, which was a tribute of cattle given in acknowledgment of superiority; and in 1694, a similar bond was given to Sir Duncan Campbell of Achanbreac, where, with other subordinate tribes, they again professed themselves Mac Gregors. They are thus seen to be a branch of the wide-spread Clan Alpin.

Aulai' seems to be identical with the Norse name Olla, or Olaus, personal appellations being anciently, in many instances, common to the continental nations, and the Celtic race in Britain and Ireland. We have, however, heard it suggested, that Ollamh, the term applied to a learned person, and equivalent to doctor, might be the proper etymology. Be this as it may, the clan were settled in the Lennox at a very early period, their chief being from his place of residence, designated as of "Ardincapil," and among the deeds in the Lennox chartulary, the Mac Aulays repeatedly occur. This, no doubt, led at first to the supposition of their being descendants of that distinguished line, who would appear to have afforded them protection, sufficient to shield them from the consequences of participation in the feuds by which the unfortunate Mac Gregors where at last overwhelmed.

The Mac Aulays were pretty numerous in different parts. About one hundred and fifty years ago, a considerable number were located in Caithness and Sutherland, who traced themselves to the chief, and a number of Mac Pheideirans in Argyle also acknowledged their descent from the Mac Aulays. In Ireland there were several who had emigrated to that country, of whom the ceann tigh, or chief, held the estate of Glenerm in the county of Antrim. George Mac Aulay, a native of Uig in the county of Ross, who died in the end of the last century, was a much respected Alderman of London. Of the Hon. T. B. Mac Aulay, M.P., the distinguished statesman and writer, this clan may be justly proud.

Dun Ollai, the fortress of Olla, is a very picturesque ruin on the coast of Argyle. The castle of Ardincapil, is in the county of Dumbarton, on the north side of the firth of Clyde, opposite Greenock.

The ARMORIAL BEARINGS are gules, two arrows in saltire, argent, surmounted of a fess checky of the first and second, between

MAC ARTHUR

three buckles, or. Crest, an antique boot, couped at the ankle, with a spur thereon, proper. Motto, "Dulce periculum."

The SUAICHEANTAS, or badge, is that of the Siol Alpinich Giuthas, Pine, *Pinus sylvestris.*

The figure is that of an old man journeying in a snow-storm, when the advantage of the ample plaid, in which he is inwrapt, is obvious. The motion, in a quick and extended walk, prevents any unpleasant sensation of cold in the limbs.

CLANN BHEANN—THE MAC BEANS.

ON the etymology of this patronimic, as many different opinions exist, as there are various orthographies of it. It is commonly pronounced Bane, and being aspirated in the genitive, it becomes Mac Bhean. While some are of opinion that the appellation was given from the fair complexion of the founder of the clan; others believe that the term simply arose from the circumstance of living in a high country; Beann being the gaelic name for a mountain. The derivation from complexion seems exceedingly probable, as that is the most usual mode of personal distinction among the Gaël; and hence it will account for many of the name being found in disconnected parts of the highlands. One of the ancient Scottish Kings, is Donald Bàn, and all those called Bain or Bayne, must have obtained the name from a "fair featured" ancestor.

There is an opinion among several of this clan, that they are a branch from the Camerons, and a division of the Mac Beans fought with Locheil, as their kinsman, in 1745. But, although some few might have been his followers, unvarying tradition ranks the clan as one of the many tribes comprehended under the generic appellation of Clan Chattan, and it is certain that the Mac Beans, with the above exception, in all general expeditions, and other transactions, ranked under the banner of the Mac Intosh, as their superior.

The Mac Beans must have, at one time, been numerous and united, having an acknowledged chief with an independent following. He was distinguished in the highland fashion as Kinchoil, from the name of his property. He could bring somewhat more than a hundred men into the field, and in the rising with Prince Charles Stewart in 1745, he held the rank of Major in the Mac Intosh battalion. His son was likewise engaged in that attempt, but escaped, and afterwards obtained a commission in Lord Drumlanricks regiment, a better fate than awaited his gallant father on "Culloden's awful morning." When the Argyle militia broke down a wall which enabled them to attack the highlanders in flank, Major Gillies Mac Bean, who stood six feet four inches and a quarter in height, stationed himself at the gap, and as the assailants passed through he cut them down by the irresistible strokes of his broadsword. No fewer than thirteen, including Lord Robert Ker, were thus slain when the enraged enemy closed around him in numbers, that they might bring down so formidable an opponent, on which Mac Bean, placing his back to the wall, bravely defended himself for some time against

the fierce assault. An officer, observing his heroism, rode up, calling on the soldiers to "save that brave man!" but at that moment, the heroic Gillies fell, with many bayonet wounds, his head dreadfully cut by a sword, and his thigh bone broken. A pathetic elegy, entitled, "Mo run geal oig" or, my fair young beloved, is said to have been composed by his disconsolate widow. Another composition in the English language on the same subject, said to have been one of Byron's early effusions, appeared in a northern periodical.

" The clouds may pour down on Culloden's red plain,
    But their waters shall flow o'er its crimson in vain,
    For their drops shall seem few to the tears for the slain,
    But mine are for thee, my brave Gillies Mac Bain !

" Though thy cause was the cause of the injured and brave ;
    Though thy death was the hero's and glorious thy grave,
    With thy dead foes around thee, piled high on the plain,
    My sad heart bleeds o'er thee, my Gillies Mac Bain !

" How the horse and the horsemen thy single hand slew !
    But what could the mightiest single arm do ?
    A hundred like thee might the battle regain ;
    But cold are thy hand and heart, Gillies Mac Bain !

" With thy back to the wall, and thy breast to the targe,
    Full flashed thy claymore in the face of their charge ;
    The blood of their boldest that barren turf stain,
    But, alas ! thine is reddest there, Gillies Mac Bain !

" Hewn down, but still battling, thou sunk'st on the ground—
    Thy plaid was one gore, and thy breast was one wound ;
    Thirteen of thy foes by thy right hand lay slain—
    Oh ! would they were thousands for Gillies Mac Bain !

" Oh ! loud and long heard shall thy coronach be,
    And high o'er the heather thy cairn we shall see ;
    And deep in all bosoms thy name shall remain—
    But deepest in mine, dearest Gillies Mac Bain !

" And daily the eyes of thy brave boy before
    Shall thy plaid be unfolded, unsheathed the claymore ;
    And the white rose shall bloom on his bonnet again
    Should he prove the true son of my Gillies Mac Bain ! "

MAC AULAY

There was another of the same name and of no less daring, who fought in this battle-field under the banner of Cameron of Locheil. This was Gillies of Free, formerly of Fàlie, whom some considered the elder male branch. Locheil being wounded at Culloden in both ankles, was carried out of the field by two near relatives, when it would seem that this Mac Bean undertook to convey him to a hiding place whence he might get safely to Lochaber. Upon crossing the river Nairn at Craigie, they met with a party of Cumberland's soldiers with whom they were obliged to fight; but killing some of them, the others made off. The wife of Gillies paid every attention to the wounded fugitives, and with a pair of scissors extracted two bullets from the leg of her husband, who lived long afterwards, and is commemorated by an altar, or, table monument, in the churchyard of Moy, with a suitable inscription in the Gäelic language.

There was a gentleman of this clan, called Æneas, father of the Rev. Mr. Mac Bean of the Secession Church, Inverness, who, escaping from the field of Culloden, was closely pursued by two dragoons, from whom he fortunately saved himself by an extraordinary effort of strength and agility. Reaching a brook, when about to be cut down, he leaped across, followed by his foes; but having broken his sword blade, to fly before them was a vain attempt at escape: he quickly recrossed and ran along the margin, but the soldiers, also leaping their horses, pursued the agile highlander, who, as they reached him, again bounded over the stream. Nerved by the dread of impending slaughter, these arduous evolutions were repeated until, baffled by the singular and dextrous tactics, the dragoons gave up the unsuccessful chase.

We knew an old highlander of this clan who shared in the "fearful skaith," which the right wing suffered in the furious onset which was made on the left of the Duke of Cumberland's army at the above disastrous battle. One cheek bore the mark of having been entirely slashed down by the cut of a horseman's sword. Poor John Mac Bean's cattle were carried off, his cottage rifled and burned, and he was obliged to skulk long among the hills, haunted by a fearful dread of again meeting with the Duke's dragoons. The fire of loyalty and attachment to Tearlach ban òg, as the Prince was styled, seemed unquenchable amongst his unfortunate followers; and it was amusing to see Mac Bean, under the weight of five score and one years, along with Ian beag Gordon, who had also been "out," averring, with animation, as the veterans flourished the staves which then assisted their feeble steps, that they were still ready to fight for the "auld Stewarts back again."

The Bains or Baynes of Tullach, an old and respectable family in Ross-shire, like several other highland septs, never prefixed Mac to their name; but they must be accounted members of this clan, and although we have not discovered their military strength; but they possessed considerable influence in the county, which a short notice of a transaction in which they were engaged may exemplify, as well as present a picture of the state of society in the good olden time.

At the Candlemas market, held at Logieree, on the bank of the Conan in 1597, Ian Mac Leoid Mhic Ghillichallum, brother to the Laird of Rasa, a Cearnach, who traversed the country with a retinue of six or eight men, having refused payment for some wares, and assaulted a merchant and his wife, Ian Bain, brother of Tullach, remonstrated with Mac Leod against the injustice of his proceedings. His reasoning, however, had no effect, and the dispute grew so hot that a fight took place, when Bain slew his adversary, with three wounds, and assisted by Donald Fraser, mac Alasdair, his foster brother and only second, two others of Mac Leod's party were likewise slain. The Mac Kenzies then interfered on the side of the Mac Leods, and the Munros took the part of Mac Bain, when several were killed on both sides, and a running fight was kept up as far down as Mulchaich; but Bain and his friend escaped unhurt, and took shelter with Lord Lovat at Beaulie, who afforded them protection, and sending his kinsman Fraser of Phopachie to represent the matter at court, a remission was given to Bain, and legal proceedings were ordered to be taken against their assailants.

The ARMORIAL BEARINGS, are quarterly, 1st, or, a lion rampant, gules; 2d, argent, a dexter hand apaumee, gules; 3d, argent, a dagger in pale proper; 4th, a galley, with sails furled, sable, all within a bordure of the last. Crest, a demi cat, gules. Motto, "Touch not the cat bot a glove."

The SUAICHEANTAS, or badge of distinction, is that of the great race, of which they are a portion. Lus nam Braoileag, red whortle berry, *vaccinium vitis idœa.*

The figure is intended to represent the undaunted Gillies, dealing out his deadly blows on those who successively advanced through the breach in the wall. Those who witness the parade of troops on review, the music playing, and the columns going through the various evolutions with mechanical precision, amid the swelling notes of martial music, every individual being so clean and neatly dressed, are apt to believe that in the field of battle it is much the same. On these deadly occasions, however, there is often no time for nicety, and as in this case, the army having been the previous night occupied in a harassing march to surprise the royal camp, we may well believe that the highlanders in general did not present a very smart appearance. In the turmoil of battle, caps and bonnets, arms and accoutrements, are scattered about, and the combatants are only intent on achieving a triumph. The figure is painted in the tartan of the Mac Intoshes, which as major of that battalion Mac Bean would appropriately wear.

The highlanders were fond of ornament, and solicitous to have rich lace, silver buckles and buttons, &c., that should they fall in battle, or die at a distance from home, there might be sufficient value in their clothing to defray the expense of a respectable funeral.

MAC BEAN

CLANN CHOLLA—THE MAC COLLS.

THIS clan must be descended from the Mac Donalds, among whom Coll is a favourite name.

It is rather an idle pursuit to seek for an etymology of a proper name, especially when it is a simple vocable. Epithets were no doubt, applied originally from caprice, and they might have been in some way significant at first, as applicable to the individual; the appellation would be given to the descendants as the proper means of recognition. Of this clan there have been many celebrated characters; Coll Ciotach Mac Dhonuill, the trusty companion of the gallant Marquis of Montrose, was of the Mac Donalds of the county of Antrim, in Ulster, who acknowledge their descent from the Mac Donalds of the Isles.

The Mac Colls were settled from a very early period in the County of Argyle, chiefly around Loch Fine, but like many other of the smaller clans in that district, they did little to distinguish themselves as an independent tribe, being merged in the great race of Clann Dhiarmid an Tuirc, or the Campbells.

When the Mac Gregors got involved in the unfortunate feuds which at last overwhelmed them, the Mac Colls were brought into collision with them; but they seem to have been forced into that position by the Colquhouns, Buchanans, and others, for their own locality was too remote to have permitted personal misunderstanding or quarrel. Clann Ghriogair, finding themselves so hard pressed, that it was necessary for their self-preservation to take up arms, intimated their perilous situation to their friends, and the Clann Mhurich, or Mac Phersons, who, although living very remotely, were so well disposed to the unfortunate Siol Alpin, that with great alacrity, they sent fifty picked men to their assistance. Meantime, however, the Mac Gregors had fought the battle of Glenfreon, in which they gave so signal a defeat to their enemies, the Colquhouns and their allies the Buchanans. The Mac Phersons were apprised of this when they reached Blair in Athol, on which they retraced their steps, and in passing the dreary ridge of Drum Uachder, they encountered a large body of Mac Colls, returning with a creach, or spoil, of cattle from Ross or Sutherland. Having a quarrel of their own to settle with the Mac Colls, as well as taking on themselves the cause of the Mac Gregors, the Mac Phersons struck off by Loch Garry, on the side of which the battle took place. The traditional account represents it as having been very sanguinary—the Mac Phersons were victorious with trifling loss; but the Clann Cholla suffered very severely, losing their commander and most of the men.

On this occasion, Aongas bàn Mac Coll, displayed great strength and dexterity, and having met, hand to hand, with one of the Mac Phersons, a mortal combat took place, which continued until the Mac Colls were driven off the field, when he leaped backwards over a chasm and effected his escape. The width of this is so great, that to leap across by a forward jump would be accounted an amazing effort for the most agile!

The earliest covering adopted by mankind is a skin, or piece of other material, wrapped around the loins, and this is undoubtedly the origin of the kilt or feile beag.

This light form of garment, which left the limbs at freedom, was common to all the European nations; but none have retained the primitive costume save the Highlanders of Scotland. The Saxons dressed with a tunic which reached to the knee; but it was one of plain colour, and it would seem that the Franks abandoned the intermixture of hues to which the ancient Gauls were so partial. The figure selected as the illustration of this clan, is from the mosaic of Charlemagne, the renowned Emperor of Germany, as formed in the church of St. Susan, by order of Pope Leo. III., and it serves as a proof of the change which had begun to take place in the national attire, from the emperor's example. Eginhart tells us that Charlemagne, adhering to the ancient manners, for many of which he seems to have had a great veneration, wore the short tunic; and from Windichind's description of an ancient Saxon, we find him closely resembling a Caledonian! So universal was this habit.

The Celtic nations have been remarkable in all periods of their history for a partiality to gaudy colours. Tartan, the national manufacture, distinguishes the Highlander of the present day, and the same variegated garments were equally characteristic of the Gauls in the most early ages. They are described by Diodoros, Varro, and others, as delighting in clothes in which were blended various colours, and although the former seems to say that they were "flowered," the simplicity of warp and weft must point out the striping and checkering in the loom as the natural and primitive method of producing the required patterns. Indeed late writers, who viewed the Gaëlic warriors at a distance, as Beague, who described them in the time of the great civil war, said their dresses were painted! Aldhelm, Bishop of Sherborne, writing in 970, plainly describes the manufacture of tartan, so untrue is Pinkerton's assertion that it is a late invention. Equally mistaken was this prejudiced Anti-Celt when he prophesied that this fabric, sometimes so beautiful, would never come into general or fashionable use!

The Gauls obtained the dyes, which produced the rich effect of their garments, from native productions, chiefly plants, for which Pliny very highly commends them, as turning their own productions into such excellent use. In this respect the Gaël, their descendants, bear to them a close resemblance, having from time immemorial produced a variety of beautiful and permanent colours from different vegetable substances. The description of the robes woven by the Caledonian women, as given in one of the Ossianic poems is highly beautiful, at the same time that it proves the exist-

MAC COLL

ence of the manufacture at a very early period : they were, we are told, " like the bow of the shower."

The subject of clan and family tartans has given rise to much discussion. It must be admitted that improvements in chemistry, &c., has led to the production of patterns greatly superior to the old clan tartans. These, however, like coat armour, must be retained without alteration ; but the propensity of manufacturers and tradesmen to supply spurious " setts" to customers, either from ignorance or the desire to dispose of their commodities, has had an effect much to be regretted. It is hoped that the present work, where so many of the patterns are displayed, drawn from sources of undeniable authority, will have the merit of settling much of the doubt which has recently been cast on the " Science of Tartan Heraldry." It has been mentioned in the introduction to this work, that the tartans are those which have been ever acknowledged by chiefs and their clansmen.

The ARMORIAL BEARINGS for the name of Mac Coll are— Argent, in chief, two spur rowels, gules, and in base a phæon azure. Crest, a star between the horns of a crescent, gules. Motto, " Cole Deum serva Regem."

As Mac Donalds, this clan carry for SUAICHEANTAS, or badge, the Fraoch gorm, common heath, *erica vulgaris.*

Evan Mac Coll, Esq., has lately published a volume of poems of considerable merit, under the appropriate title of " Clarsach nam Beann," or the Mountain Harp.

SIOL CHRUIMEINN—THE MAC CRUIMINS.

THE Mac Cruimins were not distinguished as chiefs of their clan, nor, although they possessed the national military ardour, were they particularly renowned in war. They were, however, the most celebrated pipers in the Highlands, and ranked deservedly high as musicians, while the ancient manners still existed.

It is known to all who have made themselves acquainted with the history of the Celtic nations, that all trades and professions were hereditary among them, and they must also be aware that there were a number of persons attached to the establishment of a chief, who, for the performance of their duties, had certain privileges and allowances for their proper maintenance. One of the most important of these personages was the piper, who seems, in latter ages, to have succeeded the harper, cheering the company at banquets, and inspiriting the clans during battle with his spirit-stirring notes. The Mac Cruimins were the hereditary pipers of Mac Leod of Mac Leod, and they held a good farm in virtue of their office. This possession, called Boreraig, which, during the continuance of clanship, was a sort of freehold, now supports eighteen families, who pay a considerable rent. Here they kept a seminary for the instruction of students in that music peculiar to the Highland performers on the great pipe ; and here still exists the house, called Oil-thigh, and dignified with the name of college, wherein they resided.

No tradition exists as to the time when the Mac Cruimins became the professional attendants of Mac Leod, but the first of whom there is any account was called Ian Odhar, or dun-coloured John, who lived about 1600 ; but it is evident, from their compositions, that these pipers must have been long previously established

in their vocation. On the suppression of clanship, by Statute, 1748, called the Abolition of Heritable Jurisdictions Act, the Highland proprietors were obliged to dispense with their retinue of armed followers ; and, in relinquishing this usage, they resumed possession of the lands which were held by the less objectionable class of bards and musicians. The Mac Cruimins shared the common fate, and Donull Dubh, the last of these hereditary professors of pipe music, died in 1822, at the advanced age of 91.

Many professional and other anecdotes are given of Mac Leod's pipers. Patrick Mòr, who lived in the middle of the seventeenth century, was frequently accompanied to kirk and market by eight grown up sons, seven of whom died within one twelve months ; on which the sorrowing parent composed the affecting piobaireachd, called " Cumhadh na Cloinne," or, Lament for the Children.

This man's father, Donald Mòr, went through a series of romantic adventures, and made some narrow escapes in attempting to revenge the death of a brother who had been slain in Kintail by the Mac Kenzies. In prosecution of this object, he was at one time surprised in the house where he had been concealed, by a party sent out by Lord Kintail, under the leading of his son, for Donald's apprehension. The day was very rainy, and the woman of the house, with great presence of mind, very obligingly hung the wet plaids of the Mackenzies over ropes placed opposite the recess in which Mac Cruimin was hid, who, under their cover, got safely away. Next night, when they were asleep, he returned, and, taking their arms, he placed them across each other by the side of the bed where the commander of the party lay ; on

MAC CRUIMIN

observing which in the morning, and rightly believing it was the work of Mac Cruimin, he sought an interview with the fugitive, who having thus spared his life when he might have taken it, he procured a pardon, and Donald Mòr returned to Skye without molestation.

Donald Bàn was piper to Mac Leod in 1745, and accompanied his chief, who was opposed to Prince Charles. In conjunction with the Munros, this clan marched southwards to dislodge Lord Lewis Gordon from Aberdeen, but they were attacked at Inverurie and quickly routed, when the piper of Mac Leod was taken prisoner. Next morning, Lord Lewis and his officers were much surprised that the pipers did not play as usual, and inquiry was made to ascertain the reason of conduct apparently so inexplicable. They were then told that Mac Cruimin was prisoner, and, while he was captive among them, their pipes would be silent. This explanation procured his immediate release, but he was shortly afterwards killed in the night attempt to capture the Prince, who was with Lady Mac Intosh, at Moyhall, near Inverness.

The pieces composed by those musicians are numerous, and chiefly in reference to the Macleods, but several, of great merit, relate to incidents in their own history. There is a salute to the above-mentioned Patrick Mòr, and also a lament for him by his brother. Another affecting cu'a' is for the Donull Bàn, who was killed 1746, and an affecting lamentation was made on the departure of the last of these pipers, who had proceeded to Greenock with the intention of emigrating to Canada. "Tha til, tha til, tha til Mhic Chruimin," Mac Cruimin shall never, shall never return,— is a melting melody to those who have a taste for bagpipe music.

The Highlanders did not pay a great deal of attention to the armorial marks of distinction—their own peculiar coat armour was the clothing of the clan Tartan. The crest of the Mac Cruimins is a hand holding a pipe chanter, with the motto "Cogadh no sith" —Peace or war, a composition of their own. The bearings are on a field argent, a chevron azure, charged with a lion passant, or, between three cross croslets fitchee, gules.

The figure represents one of these celebrated pipers in the act of saluting his chief, who is supposed to be approaching in his biorlin, or galley. It was, however, more usual to accompany the laird on his expeditions, the piper being indeed one of the chief members composing the Luchdtachd, or personal attendants, who amounted to ten, each having his proper office. As the last characteristic remains of a primitive state of society, pipers are still cherished by the Scottish gentry. The late Dukes of Kent and Sussex employed these functionaries, and her gracious Majesty has added to the royal establishment one of the best qualified of the profession.

The effect produced at a banquet by one or more of these musicians in full dress, is well known, and their influence on the military ardour of the Gaël has been exemplified on many occasions. There is a piece of music composed by the piper of Clunie Mac Pherson, where he laments that he had not three arms, that so he might wield his sword while he inspirited his clansmen. Doctor Johnson expresses his admiration of Mac Lean of Coll's piper; and Lettice, in his Tour, 1794, was equally struck with Duncan Stewart, then in the service of the Marquis of Bute.

One of the objects of the Highland Society of London is to preserve the ancient piobaireachd, or pipe music, and triennial competitions are given in Edinburgh, when various prizes are distributed to the performers, who assemble from all quarters. These entertainments are very attractive, the theatre being always full; and, agreeably to Scottish fashion, national dances are introduced in the intervals of musical performance.

CLANN RAONUIL, OR MAC DONALDS OF CLAN RANALD.

THIS branch of Clan Donald anciently held extensive insular possessions and other territories. In 1745 they inhabited the islands of Benbecula, Rum, and Uist, and the districts of Arisaig, Muidart, and South Morar, on the western coast of Invernesshire, a tract so rugged and mountainous that it was distinguished as the very highlands of the Highlands. "The people of these horrid parts could never believe they were accessible, till the king's forces penetrated their fastnesses after the battle of Culloden, which was a prodigious surprise to the inhabitants." The writer of these remarks confesses

that, notwithstanding their local disadvantages and "barbarous" manners, they bred amazing numbers of cattle, and a "sort of wild horses," the sale of which brought them much money; had plenty of venison, and were in better circumstances than most other clans, the rental being £1100. a year, "well paid,"[*] an income then reckoned large, even for so great a chief as Clan Ranald!

The descent of this clan is from John, Lord of the Isles, who married Ami, daughter and heiress of Ruarai' (Rory or Roderic) of the Isles, a collateral branch of the Mac Donalds, about 1337. From

[*] MS. in the King's Library, Brit. Mus., 104. 272. B.

MAC DONALD of CLAN RANALD

Raonal, the issue of this marriage, arose the generic appellation, Clan Ranald, and from Aluinn (beautiful), his son, is derived the patronymic of the chief, Mac Mhic Allan.

From the time of Ruarai', who was chief in the early part of the fifteenth century, the clan became distinguished in the transactions of the country, and arose in importance, as the elder branch, from a series of reverses, consequent on their collisions with government, were depressed, until at last they were so reduced, that Clan Ranald, as the nearest branch, was, by a modification of the Tanist law, acknowledged chief about 1530; and the abilities of his successors enabled them long to contend for possession of the dignity, when the others has acquired means to resume their former position. The hereditary honour of Captain of Clan Ranald could never be disputed, which not only referred to his own dependants, but denoted his rank among all who claimed descent from Ranald of the Isles.

A remarkable event in the history of this clan illustrates the state of Celtic society in the days of independence. Outrageous as may appear the attendant circumstances, considering the practice of the Scottish kings, to keep one clan in check by the other, fomenting rancorous feuds and bloodshed, we can well believe the unsuspecting Gaël were goaded into acts of desperate policy, of which the anticipated advantage was so often taken with promptitude and severity.

Dughall, who became chief in 1513, was of a froward, overbearing spirit, incompatible with the control which the sean'ir, or elders of a clan claimed privilege to exercise over their patriarchal head; he consequently became greatly disliked; and, having committed several acts of cruelty and oppression, he was at last put to death; and, by common consent, Alastair, his uncle, was declared chief, and the sons of Dughall, then children, excluded. Alastair dying in 1530, Iain Muidartach, or John Muidart, usually designated of Ellan Tirim, his natural son, but subsequently legitimized, a man of great ability, had the address to obtain the chiefship and the estates. Meantime, Dughall's son, Ranald, according to a usual Highland practice, was fostered by his uncle, Lord Lovat, and on arriving at manhood, the Frasers determined to put him in possession of his hereditary lands and title. James V. having seized and imprisoned John Muidart, a revocation of the charters which had been granted to him was obtained in favour of Ranald, who thereupon assumed his honours. Unfortunately, having been brought up with habits of economy unsuitable to the notions which his clansmen entertained of the liberality and profusion which ought to characterize a chief, he was very unpopular, and coming from a distant part of the country, of which the rougher Clan Ranald had rather a contemptuous opinion, he was sneeringly designated as Gallda, or from the low country. In this temper, it was to be expected that, upon the escape of John Muidart from prison, the clan should again hail him as their congenial chief, and compel Gallda and his party to retire, an outrage for which they could only look for a severe retaliation. Lovat immediately prepared to avenge the insult, and, applying to the king, the Earl of Huntly was ordered to assist in reducing the audacious rebels. The Clan Ranald, however, with their active leader, did not wait for the attack, but, under the command of Sir Ewen Cameron of Lochiel, and assisted by Ranald glas Mac Donald of Keppach, they quickly overran Abertarf, and Stratheric, and took possession of the strong

castle of Urquhart. Huntly, and the Laird of Grant, having joined Lovat with a strong force, commenced operations, when the Mac Donalds retreated, and, considering that they had been effectually dispersed, the confederated army thought proper to separate: Huntly retired southward up Gleanspean, and Lovat, with Ranald Gallda, their friends and followers, amounting to 400, went along the south side of Loch Lochai', on their way homewards to the Aird. Scarcely had they commenced their march, when the Mac Donalds appeared descending from the heights in front and flank, moving in seven columns, with flying banners. Retreat was impossible, and a desperate engagement ensued, equally fatal to the victorious and the vanquished: the Frasers were so cut up that one gentleman alone remained alive, and he sorely wounded, with four common men; whilst of the Mac Donalds only eight survived the sanguinary conflict! This battle was fought in 1544, and was contested with unparalleled determination: the day, being in July, was warm, and the eager combatants stripped off their clothes, from which circumstance it was called Blar-Leine, the Battle of the Shirts, and many traditions of extraordinary deeds performed on this fatal field are still current.*

The flower of the Fraser youth being slain, that clan would have been long in abeyance, but from a providential circumstance which Sir Robert Gordon relates with great simplicity, yet with a little stretch, we suspect, of credulity. " It happenit, by the singular benefite of God, that they left ther wyffs with child when they went to the feight, by which means that familie was afterwards raised and restored."

John of Muidart was an extraordinary man, and led a troublous life, but he transmitted the chiefship in his own line. His fame is recorded in many a surviving tradition, and his skull was long preserved with veneration in the chapel of Ionain Island.

The Captain of Clan Ranald was slain in the battle of Sherramuir, 1715. In 1745, the chief brought 700 to the Highland army; the MS. before quoted says, they numbered 800 " good men." For a levy of Highlanders to assist Queen Elizabeth in Ireland, in 1602, Clan Ranald's proportion was " tua," and Glengarry's " ane hundreth men."† It was in " the country of Clan Ranald " that Prince Charles landed, August, 1745, and the house of Mac Donald, of Ceannlochmuidart, first received the daring adventurer, a grand Piobaireachd being composed on the occasion. In Glenfinan he unfurled the Bratach bàn, or white standard; and on the spot where it was then displayed, previously marked by a cairn of stones, the late Alexander Mac Donald, Esq., of Glenáladale, erected a column fifty feet in height, on the pedestal of which are inscriptions, in Gaëlic, English, and Latin, commemorative of this interesting event.

The COAT ARMOUR is quarterly, 1st arg., a lion rampant gules, armed or; 2nd or, a dexter hand coupée fesswise, holding a cross

* Gregory's History of the Highlands, &c., &c.   † Collectanea reb. Albanicis.

crosslet fitchee, gu.; 3rd or, a lymphad or galley, oars in saltire, sable, and in base a salmon naiant proper, in sea, vert; 4th arg., an oak tree, vert, surmounted by an eagle displayed, or. Crest, on a castle triple-towered, an arm holding a sword, proper. Motto, " My hope is constant in thee." Supporters, two bears, each pierced by two arrows in saltire, proper.

The BREACAN, or Tartan, differs from that of Glengarry in the arrangement of the white stripes. Mac Donald, of Boisdale, has a family tartan of a red pattern, with several colours agreeably varied.

The SUAICHEANTAS, or Badge, is Fraoch gorm, *Erica vulgaris*, common Heath, the recognisance of all the Mac Donalds.

The CATH-GHAIRM, or War-shout, is the proud defiance, " Dhaindheoin cotheir-aidh e."— In spite of all opposition.

The PIOBAIREACHDAN are Failte Clann Raonuil, the Salute to the Chief, and the Cruinneachadh, or Gathering, sometimes called the Spaidsearachd, or March, composed in the war of 1715. Boisdale has his own appropriate Salute.

The BARDS of the family were Mac Mhuirichs (Vuirichs), a race distinguished in the poetical annals of the Highlands, who, according to Celtic usage, were hereditary, and held a good farm, on the tenure of preserving the oral history of the clan, and the compositions of the most renowned poets. The Mac Mhuirichs were not illiterate, but so far departed from the Druidic injunction, that they committed a great deal to writing; and one of their MSS. was lent by command of Clan Ranald, to Mac Pherson, the translator of Ossian, for the purpose of extracting some of that bard's compositions, a circumstance particularly referred to in the controversy as to their authenticity. Niall, then bard and seanachai', or historian, who was perfectly ignorant of the English language, reckoned his descent through eighteen unbroken generations.* The poem of Lachlan, poured forth to animate the clan during the great battle of Harlaw, 1411, is one of the most extraordinary of Gaëlic compositions, for its stirring energy and singular alliteration. There have been various other non-official bards of this clan whose works are very popular.

The principal seat was Castle Tirim, the ruins of which, on a prominence in Loch Muidart, insulated at high water, attest its former strength; latterly the family has resided at Arisaig House.

The figure is dressed in the Breacan an f heile, or belted plaid, of which this is a front view, the figure of Mac Gillivray, in the former number, showing its form behind, thus giving a perfect idea of the mode in which this picturesque, but now almost disused garment, is arranged. In a succeeding figure will be shown its advantage in bad weather, or a bivouac. Its amplitude is striking, and we are surprised that it should be neglected, especially by shepherds and drovers. Pipers might be so arrayed with much propriety and effect. The coat is lachdan, or the natural colour of the fleece, in which state cloth was frequently worn. The brogs are of the most primitive form, cut from a deer skin, worn with the hairy side outwards, and laced with a thong of the same material, a covering which stood the friction in walking the heath much better than its simplicity might lead one to suppose. The target is given from an old specimen, but is not otherwise peculiar than from the blade, twelve inches long, which is made to screw into the centre, thus forming a most formidable weapon for offence as well as protection. The bidag, or dirk, is of the fashion usual in the olden time.

* Evidence taken by a Committee of the Highland Society.

SIOL MAC MHIC RAONUILL—THE MAC DONALDS OF GARAGACH AND KEPPACH.

IN the letter-press accompanying the illustrations of the Mac-Donalds, Lords of the Isles, the Glengarry, the Clan Ranald, and Glenco branches of this numerous and distinguished race, their origin and descent has been given. It is from John, who swayed his princely power over the west highlanders in the end of the fourteenth century, and who married Margaret, daughter of Robert II. that the house of Keppach is descended. The youngest son, Alasdair who in a deed of 1398, is styled "Magnificus vir et potens," became Lord of Lochaber, and from him the clan is designated Sliochd Alasdair Carraich. It was Colla Mac Gillieaspuig, who lived in the end of the seventeenth century, who first changed the orthography of the name to Mac Donell, by the persuasion of Glengarry, Lord Aros.

The clan assisted their kinsman, Donald Ballach, in the formidable descent he made on Inverlochai', where he defeated the royal forces, anno 1431, in consequence of which the lordship of Lochaber was forfeited and bestowed on Mac Intosh, Captain of Clan Chattan, who had strenuously opposed the ambitious attempts of the Lords of the Isles. The Mac Donalds of Keppach, however, neither moved from Lochaber nor acknowledged a feudal grant of superiority, which was incompatible with the patriarchal rule, but with Celtic tenacity maintained their territorial right. A feud was, therefore, kindled, which burned with more or less ardour, during nearly three centuries, the Mac Donalds at times submitting as tenants, but more frequently defending their possessions by force of arms. Had not Mac Intosh proceeded with too much severity in the exaction of rent, the friendship of "kindly tenantry" might have subsisted with advantage to both clans; but, irritated by the denial of his authority, in 1688, he determined to compel the stubborn Lochabrians to submit to his demands or leave the country. In pursuance of this resolution he took the field with his clan, and to insure success as well as invest his operations with a legal character, he procured a company of regular troops, under the command of Mackenzie of Suddie. With this armament he proceeded to Brae Lochaber, where he encamped on the height of Maol rua', near the residence of Keppach. They were speedily attacked by the Mac Donalds, who after a resolute contention, gained a decisive victory—Suddie being slain, and the Mac Intosh taken prisoner! The chief was soon after liberated, chiefly, it is said, through the influence of the Mac Phersons, who had marched to the scene of action, although too late to take part in the battle; but he suffered a deep mortification in being taken captive by his own tenants, and owing his freedom to a clan with whom he was then on disagreeable terms. It may occasion surprise to read of settling private disputes by levying open war, so late as the reign of William III.; but it appears this is the last instance of a clan conflict of any importance having taken place.

These Mac Donalds joined Ian Muidartaich, and were present in the celebrated battle of Blar leinne, 1544, and they naturally took part with those of their own race in frequent warlike operations.

The signal defeat of the Earl of Argyle, in 1645, took place at Inverlochai', in the neighbourhood of Keppach, and Ian Lòm, a celebrated poet of this clan acted as guide to the Marquis of Montrose in his march to the triumphant attack on the Campbells. This man was a remarkable character and is highly celebrated in highland tradition. There was a tribe of Mac Dugals, who were followers of Keppach, and seem to have possessed great ferocity of character. Having, from some cause, imbibed a spirit of deep hostility to their chief, Alasdair Mac Dhonuill ghlas, they barbarously murdered him, and no one seemed to have any inclination to bring the daring miscreants to justice, when Ian Lòm determined that so barbarous and afflictive a deed should not be unrevenged. With this object he travelled far and wide, in order to rouse some of the chiefs to take the task in hand; but it was only after great exertions that he could prevail on Sir James Mac Donald of the Isles to do so, who sent a body of men to Brae Lochaber, who attacked the Mac Dugals in their dwellings, and after a desperate struggle slew nine of the murderous band. Their heads were forthwith cut off and sent to the Privy Council, as evidence of their fate; and as the party who conveyed the ghastly charge was passing along the great glen of Caledonia they washed the bloody trophies in a little fountain, which has ever since been called, "The Well of the Heads." Over it the late Glengarry had a monument erected, on which are inscriptions in different languages, commemorative of this revolting transaction, which it might have been in better taste to leave untold.

The first powder spent in the cause of king James, in 1745, was at Drochait Ard, in Keppach's country, by Mac Donald, of Tierndrish, a gentleman of the clan, who began the war at his own discretion, by intercepting two companies of the Royals, whom he disarmed with eleven men only, and marched them as prisoners to Glenfinan, where he joined Prince Charles before his standard had been unfurled! This flag, distinguished from its colour as the Brattach bhàn, or white banner, was brought to the field by Sir Thomas Sheridan, one of the Prince's favourite councillors, who gave it to Donald, Keppach's brother. This respected ensign was carried by the clans alternately, and the day before the victory of Falkirk, 17 January, 1746, he had again the honour of bearing it, on which occasion, the Prince being near him during the fatigue of a review, Mac Donald presented him with an apple, which was graciously accepted.

Alasdair Mac Coll was the chief who commanded the clan in this ill-fated expedition. He had been an officer in the service of France, and, as "he joined the French skill to the highland intrepidity and fierceness," he was esteemed one of the best officers in the army. He and his clan well supported their acquired renown in many arduous positions throughout the insurrection. At Culloden the chief was slain, and the depositions of his clansmen given to prove that he was killed before the act of retainder was passed, are evidence that, contrary to the general opinion which represents the Mac Donalds, in resentment of the indignity of having been placed on the left wing, as determinately refusing to fight; the Keppach regiment did attack with characteristic ardour, when its chivalrous Colonel fell by a shot through the right breast. In this unfortunate battle, sections of some other clans were under his banner, there was a company of Mac Gregors, some Mac Intoshes and Mac Nab of Iniseo'an.

The houses, corn-stacks, woods, &c. were meantime burnt, and the cattle driven away; some of the scorched trunks of trees still remaining impressive mementos of the unhappy '46; and it will show the wanton barbarity with which the highlanders were treated after their discomfiture, to state that two of this clan, who went to Fort William to deliver up their arms expecting to obtain the offered pardon and protection, were unceremoniously hanged, on a spot still pointed out near the mill!

Raonull òg, in 1752, petitioned for a restitution of his property, and compensation for losses, proving, as above, the death of his father; he subsequently entered the army, and served in the Fraser Fencibles, each company of which was commanded by a chief, and he distinguished himself very highly at the siege of Quebec, where he was wounded. The respectable family now residing in Keppach, are nearly related to the line of chiefs, but the representative is now in America.

The present house is not on the site of the old castle which stood on a point of land, steeply shelving to the impetuous Roy on one side, and the equally rapid Spean on the other. In the hollow beneath we have seen the trees loaded with apples, pears, and other fruit, delicious as those of more southern climates.

Among the more celebrated individuals of this clan, is Shela Mac Donald, daughter of Gillieaspuig Mac Alasdair buidh, sixteenth chief, who became wife of Gordon of Baldornie in Aberdeenshire. She was a poetess of great merit, and an elegant performer on the harp, so long disused by the highlanders, and tradition assigns to her the improvisatorial gift.

The force which Keppach could bring to the field was estimated by Lord President Forbes at 300.

MAC DONALD of GARAGACH and KEPPACH

The ARMORIAL BEARINGS are those appropriate to the Mac Donalds, as given in previous numbers, with the requisite difference or mark of cadency.

The SUAICHEANTAS, or Badge is likewise the same—Fraoch gorm, common Heath, *Erica vulgaris.*

The PIOBAIREACHD composed on the murder of the chief, is an affecting lament, called "Ceapach na fasaich," or the desolation of Keppach. Another called " Blar Mhaol rua'." composed on the defeat of Mac Intosh, is, of course, a Failté or Salute,

The figure which illustrates this tribe of " Siol Chuinn" is dressed, with the exception of the Glengarry bonnet, in good style for a modern highlander. The coat was painted from one in the possession of Mr. Angus Mac Donald of Inch, a genuine Celt of stalwart stature, and a worthy member of this clan, whose thighs are unaccustomed to the restraint of inexpressibles. It belonged to a relation of his, who lived fifty or sixty years ago. The tartan is from a fragment in this gentleman's possession likewise, which was cut from a plaid, formerly preserved in Moyhall, the seat of the chief of Mac Intosh. It was left there by Prince Charles, to whom it had been given by the Keppach of '45, so that it is accounted the true sett, appropriate to these Mac Donalds.

There was a celebrated Cearnach of this clan, a sort of Rob Roy in his way, of whom several anecdotes are preserved, one of which it may be amusing to relate. He was called Ranald, and was distinguished by the epithet mòr, from his great strength and stature. He had excited the wrath of the Camerons, by the slaughter of some of that tribe, and he betook himself for safety to an island in Loch Laggan. On one occasion, Locheil, passing along the margin of the lake, with a creach or prey of cattle, the product of a Morayshire foray, Ranald, being much in want of provisions, let fly an arrow, which brought down one of the drove. Locheil's retainers, burning with resentment of so daring an outrage, begged he would allow them to make a curach, or wicker boat of the dun cow's hide, in which they might get to the island and bring off the rascal's head. " No, no," said Lochiel; "no such thing, if Ranald had so wished, he could have shot me as easily as the dun cow, we will leave him and her too," and so he proceeded homewards with his men, leaving Mac Donald to feast on the supply which had so fortunately come in his way.

CLANN MHIC IAIN, GHLINNE COMHANN—THE MAC DONALDS OF GLENCO.

THESE Mac Donalds are descendants from Iain Fraoch, brother of John, Lord of the Isles, who flourished in 1346, and is said to have acquired Glenco in right of his wife, daughter of one Dugal Mac Eanruig. From the circumstance of one of the chiefs having been fostered in Lochaber this branch were often distinguished by the term Abarach, and although little comparatively is recorded of their early history, they held a high rank among the clans, and were sometimes designated " of the Isles." They are not to be confounded with the Mac Iains of Ardnamurchan, whose ancestor was Iain Sprangaich Mac Aonghais Mor, contemporary with Robert the Bruce. In the time of James VI. this division of Clan Donald were in a state of violent insurrection, and betook themselves to piracy, in which they became the terror of the whole western coast of Scotland, but it does not appear that the Glenco people had any share in their desperate conduct, although from the similarity of name it is to be suspected they have been charged with participation in the misdeeds of others.

The vengeance which was wreaked upon the inhabitants of Glenco in 1692, was an act of the most shocking barbarity which could disgrace a government. It could not have been possible for the enemies of King William III. to have exaggerated the atrocity of this "massacre," as the brutal transaction was justly termed. It was enough to estrange for ever the loyalty of a people less resentful of perfidy than the Highlanders, and the direful visitation, which fell like a thunderbolt on a confiding unarmed clan, roused, more than any other circumstance perhaps, the determined opposition which was given to the revolution settlement in the subsequent gallant risings for the restoration of the Stewarts.

This transaction is too lamentably important in the history of the clan to be passed over without a more particular detail. After the dispersion of the army, which had fought with Lord Dundee at Killicrankie, a proclamation was issued, inviting the Highlanders to lay down arms, when they would receive an act of indemnity for all

Mar Chuimhneachan air
Clann Dòmuill Ghlinne Comhann
a mhurtadh anns an oidhche 13
de an Fhaoilteach 1692 a rèir
òrdugh Rìgh Uilliam III air
am beil cuimhne bheannaichte

MAC DONALD of GLENCOE

previous offences, if they took the required oath to government before the first day of January, 1692.

This proposition was agreed to, Glenco and other chiefs meeting the Earl of Braidalban on the subject, and undertaking to live in peaceable submission to the Prince of Orange, on assurance of the promised pardon. Glenco had postponed taking the required oath until the stipulated time had nearly elapsed, and when he set out for that purpose he was unfortunately detained on his journey by the severity of the weather, which, before the formation of regular roads, very frequently prevented travelling across the Highlands. Having reached Fort William, a few days before the expiration of December, he found that Colonel Hill, the governor, was not empowered to administer the oath, but he furnished him with a letter to Sir Colin Campbell, of Ardkinlas, sheriff depute of Argyle, and hurried him off that as little time as possible might be lost. The weather still retarded his journey, and was, indeed, so severe that the sheriff was detained three days before he could meet Glenco at Inverary, on whose earnest solicitation he gave the oath, the old chief undertaking to bring in all his people, and if any of them refused they were to be "imprisoned or sent to Flanders," and having sworn allegiance and received his indemnity he returned home, believing himself and clansmen were now in safety, but his fate was sealed. Dalrymple, Master of Stair, then secretary for Scotland, had been arranging the plan for extirpating the Mac Iains of Glenco a month before the period for granting the indemnity had elapsed, and expressed himself, by letter to Sir Thomas Livingstone, as rejoiced that Glenco had not taken the oath, giving instructions that he and his people should be cut off, and congratulating himself that, as it was a winter of great severity none could escape if the passes were well guarded, or be able to carry their wives and children to the mountains! His orders were also not to trouble the government with prisoners, and his only regret was that all the Mac Donalds were not in the same situation!

Could Stair's conduct be the result of an inplacable spirit of personal revenge? or could he feel, for a moment, that murdering the inhabitants of a whole district unarmed, "and under trust," with letters of protection in their pocket, was "a proper vindication of public justice?"

His Majesty's warrant for the atrocious deed removes much of the infamy which would otherwise attach to his secretary, signed as it was in an unusual manner, both at top and bottom, as if to relieve Dalrymple from the full weight of so horrifying a charge. Here is the royal mandate for the perpetration of the horrid tragedy.

"William Rex.—As for Mac Ian of Glenco, and that tribe, if they can well be distinguished from the rest of the Highlanders, it will be proper for the vindication of publick justice to extirpate that sett of thieves. W. R."

In pursuance of this diabolical order, and that it might "be quietly done, otherwise they "would" make shift for both themselves and cattle," Campbell of Glenlyon, with 120 of Argyle's regiment, were sent to Glenco under pretence of quartering there in friendship, and they were treated with great hospitality and kindness for about two weeks. At last the day on which the barbarous slaughter was to take place arrived; on the 12th of February Lieut.-Colonel Hamilton and Major Duncanson were ordered to march with 400

men each to this lonely glen, and planting guards wherever there appeared possibility of escape, they were then to join the others, and fall on the devoted clan at an early hour next morning. Providence, however, by stormy weather prevented the greater part from reaching their destination at the appointed time, so that they merely finished the tragedy by burning the houses and carrying off the spoil — upwards of a thousand sheep and cattle.

Glenlyon had spent the evening with Mac Iain's sons, one of whom had married his niece, and next day he was invited to dine with the old chief, but about four or five o'clock in the morning, one of the lieutenant's, with a party of the soldiers, having got admittance on some friendly pretence, shot Glenco as he arose from bed, with several of his household. His two sons, through the vigilance of a servant made their escape to the mountains with others, where it is believed many perished amid the storm. About thirty-six fell on this fatal morning, some being slain with circumstances of incredible barbarity. A boy, of about twelve years of age, who had clung to Glenlyon's knee, imploring his protection, was shot by Captain Drummond's order. One man wishing to die in the open air obtained that indulgence from Serjeant Barber, "for his meat that he had eaten," but when the Highlander came out where the soldiers stood ready to discharge their bullets in his heart, he suddenly flung his plaid, which was loose, over their faces, and made his escape.

Glenco was a man of gigantic and muscular frame, and his bones are yet to be seen in an open niche of the ruined chapel of St. Munn, the size of which are evidence of the fact. We would suggest the propriety of having the relics placed in a more becoming receptacle.

This tragical event made a great noise, both here and on the continent, and a commission was appointed to investigate the circumstances, but it was illusory; no one was punished, and the most active in the massacre even received promotion!

The Mac Iains of Glenco, with whom no other method of successfully contending was deemed practicable, could bring no more than about 200 men into the field, and, although, thus doomed to extirpation, a remnant continued to occupy their ancient possessions. The late Ewen who died some years ago, was the representative of the long unbroken line of chiefs, but his lands were left to a daughter, and Alexander his nephew, son of the late Captain Ranald Mac Donald, the youth, now sixteen years of age, on whom the chiefship devolves, has no property.

The valley occupied by this clan is otherwise remarkable as being accounted the residence of Ossian who hence received the poetical appellation, "the voice of Co'ana."

The ARMORIAL BEARINGS were appropriate to cadets of the Island Kings and are usually blazoned, arg. an eagle displayed, gules, surmounted of a lymphad (Long-fada or galley), sable. In the dexter chief a hand proper, holding a croslet, fitchee, azure. Crest and motto as the Mac Donalds of the Isles.

The Suicheantas, or badge, is also the same, *i. e.* Fraoch gorm or common heath. A letter in the Woodrow MS. Advoc. Lib. dated Feb. 1, 1678, gives an account of the Highland host, which was brought down to curb the covenanters, and we find "among the ensigns, besides other singularities, the Glencow men were verie remarkable who had for their ensigne a faire bush of heath, wel spred and displayed on the head of a staff, such as might have affrighted a Roman eagle."

Among the latest instances of the use of bows and arrows, by the Highlanders, general Stewart gives the following. A party of the Mac Donalds of Glenco when returning from a foray in the low country, " attempted to pass through Breadalbane without giving due notice or paying the accustomed compliment to the Earl, who, a short time previously, had been raised to that rank. A number of his lordship's followers and a great many others who were assembled at the castle of Finlarig to celebrate the marriage of a daughter of the family, enraged at this insult, instantly rushed to arms and following the Mac Donalds, with more ardour than prudence, attacked them on the top of a hill, north from the village of Killin, where they had taken post to defend their cattle. The assailants were driven back with great loss, principally caused by the arrows of the Lochaber men. Colonel Menzies, of Culdairs, who had been an active partizan under the Marquis of Argyle and the covenanters, had nine arrow wounds in his thighs. It is said that nineteen young gentlemen of the name of Campbell, immediate descendants of the family, fell on that day."

The figure illustrative of this clan represents a young man plunged in deep and afflictive emotion, beside the sad memorial of the death of his ancestors. In a plain round bonnet he wears an eagle's feather, and the appropriate badge of his tribe. The jacket is of Lachdan or undyed cloth, and the sporan or purse is of the olden fashion. There is nothing more particularly deserving to be pointed out in the dress, which was usually worn in the beginning of last century.

CLANN DONUILL NAN EILLEAN, THE
MAC DONALDS OF THE ISLES.

The Somerleds, those famous warriors who ruled the destinies of the West Highlands and Isles in the early ages of Scottish history, are the progenitors of this renowned clan.

The patronymic is derived from Donald, son of Ranald, or Reginald, who flourished in the beginning of the thirteenth century. The ancient form in which it appears is Domhnail, of which Latin writers made Donaldus, but it is now Donull which may be the true orthography, and would signify "brown eye."

The Lords of the Isles were not subject to the Scottish kings, whom they supported or opposed as best suited their interest. They acted in all respects as independent princes, entering into diplomatic engagements offensive and defensive with other powers; thus in 1338 Donald formed a treaty with King Richard II. of England, and in 1460 John executed a formal commission to his trusty and well-beloved cousins, Ranald of the Isles and Duncan, archdeacon, to confer at Westminster with the English deputies, the object being nothing less than the conquest of Scotland! So late as 1544 we find Donald Du', with advice and consent of his barons and councillors, seventeen of whom are enumerated, all chiefs or persons of distinction, granted a warrant for two commissioners to treat with the English king respecting an invasion of Scotland, and in prosecution of the object he went to Ireland with 4000 men in 180 galleys, leaving 4000 men in the isles well armed for service. His troops were described as " very tall men, clothed, for the most part, in habergeons of mail, with long swords and bows, but with few guns."

It is evident that a power so great and so independent would give frequent trouble to the government. Donald having married Mary, only daughter of Euphemia, the widowed Countess of Ross, through her he laid claim to that great earldom, but his suit being refused, he raised an army of 10,000 men to enforce it, with which he not only took possession of the disputed territory, but advanced southward with great rapidity until within a day's march of Aberdeen, with the intention, it is believed, of subverting the monarchy itself. The sanguinary but indecisive battle of the Gariach, or Harlaw, stemmed the hostile torrent, and Donald, abondoning his advantages, returned to the isles.

Alexander, Donald's successor, landed an army, equal in number to the last, on the mainland, and ravaging the country down to

Inverness, he razed that town to the ground. James I., with characteristic spirit and bravery, immediately went against the insurgents, who were routed and dispersed as they retreated through Lochaber, Mac Donald was eventually reduced to the greatest straits, and determined on performing an act which must have been the most humiliating to so haughty a chief. In the midst of a high solemnity, at Holyrood, he presented himself before the king and his court, dressed only in his shirt and trews, when throwing himself on his knees, and holding his naked sword by the point, he implored the royal clemency. His life was spared, but he was committed prisoner to the castle at Tantallon.

The system of clanship was not deranged by the absence of a chief, and the imprisonment of Mac Donald only served to irritate his followers. Donald Ballach, chief of Clan Ranald, broke out into fierce hostilities, and in 1431 he gave a complete rout to the royal troops, under the Earls of Caithness and Mar, who had been left at Inverlochy to suppress the desire for further rebellion, when the latter was killed and the former desperately wounded.

It was a rebellion by Aonghais òg, son of John, who lived 1480, that led to the dissolution of the ancient and powerful kingdom of the isles. Three different expeditions were sent against this indomitable chief, two of which ended in their defeat, and the last was abortive, but Aonghais, in prosecution of his hostile designs, was assassinated in the county of the Mac Kenzies by an Irish harper.

In the parliament of 1493, John, last Lord of the Isles, was forfeited; by his grandson, Donald Du', escaping from imprisonment in the castle of Inchconnal, burst into Badenach, 1503, which he ravaged with fire and sword. The insurrection at last became so alarming that the whole military array north of the Forth and Clyde was levied for its suppression. Donald again becoming prisoner, remained in captivity no less than forty years, when he made a second escape, and found his clan devoted as ever to his interest.

Sir James Mac Donald, who lived in the beginning of the seventeenth century, was one of the most active and enterprising of chiefs. He was extremely popular from having given a triumphant defeat to the Mac Leans at Lochgruinart, and the government had thought it well to treat with him on measures for staunching the feuds in the Highlands; but he was, at last, imprisoned in the castle of Blackness, from which he would have made his escape, by assistance of his clansmen, had he not been betrayed by one of the garrison. Being removed to Edinburgh castle, he attempted his escape from thence, in which he was again frustrated, and laid in irons for better security, yet shortly afterwards he planned with Lord Maxwell, his fellow prisoner, a bold and well executed scheme for escape, by which his lordship got safely off, but Sir James, injuring his ankle by leaping from the wall, was recaptured at the west port while encumbered with his fetters. Sir James had made several proposals for securing the peace of the western islands and his own release, which his majesty James VI. approved of, and which this influential chief could, no doubt, have accomplished, but it was now thought proper to bring so daring and restless a prisoner to trial when he was convicted of "maist high and manifest treason," and condemned to be beheaded. It must have been from a sense of the impolicy of irritating more highly the already excited Clan Donald, that the sentence was not

executed; for six years he was suffered to linger in his dungeon, but in 1615 he at last effected his liberation, and after the narrowest escapes from his pursuers, reached the isles, where he was received with enthusiasm by his clansmen. Standing with Alastair Mac Ranald of Keppach and others who had accompanied him in his flight, Coll Mac Gilliespuig marched the Mac Donalds around the party several times firing volleys of musketry, and then every individual cordially shook hands with their undaunted chief, their hearts burning with devotion to retrieve his injured cause.

The Mac Donalds had striven, with characteristic heroism and perseverance, to re-establish the kingdom of the isles in their own line, but they had been so severely crushed and disorganized that they could not place their natural chief in possession of his inheritance. The direct line of the ancient lords became extinct in the middle of the sixteenth century, in the person of the above Donald Du', and disputes arose as to which branch the chiefship of the race, "jure sanguinis," or by clan law, had devolved upon. Several cadets had raised themselves to independence during the protracted disturbances in which all Clan Donald was involved, but those of Sleibhte, or Sleit, as descended from Aoidh, or Hugh, son of John, last Lord of the Isles, and Earl of Ross, were acknowledged the representatives of that nobleman. From the name of their ancestor they are designated Clan Aosdan, or Huisdan, and the male representative of the island kings is the present Lord Mac Donald, who with his ancestors have been always designated Mac Dhonuil nan Eillean, or of the isles to distinguish them from the other divisions of the clan.

Donald who took arms for King Charles I., was created a baronet of Nova Scotia in 1625, with a special clause of precedence to all except Gordon of Gordonstoun.

Sir Alexander Mac Donald of the Isles was raised to the peerage of Ireland, in 1776, by the title of Baron Mac Donald, of Slate, county of Antrim. He married Elizabeth Diana, daughter of Godfrey Bosville, Esq., of Gunthwaite, in Yorkshire, and died in 1795, being succeeded by his eldest son, Alexander Wentworth, who died unmarried, leaving his estates and honours to his next brother, Godfrey, who died in 1832, when his son, Godfrey William Wentworth, succeeding.

The military strength of the united Mac Donalds was 10,000 and upwards; when they became divided, their individual power declined, and although Mac Donald of the Isles was accounted the true representative of the ancient lords, and chief paramount, his following only amounted to 1000 men in 1715, and 700 in 1745.

The ARMORIAL BEARINGS of the Lords of the Isles were, of old, quarterly, 1st and 4th, sable, three battle axes, or; 2nd and 3rd,

MAC DONALD of the ISLES

gules, three biorlins, or large Highland boots of antique construction, or. Mac Donald of the Isles carries, or, an eagles displayed gules, surmounted of a lymphad sable, and in the dexter chief point a hand gules, holding a crosslet fitchee. Supporters, two bears with arrows stuck in their bodies proper. Crest, a raven sable on a rock azure.

The SUAICHEANTAS, or Badge, is Fraoch gorm, common Heath, *Erica vulgaris.*

The PIOBAIREACHDAN, or military music, is interesting from its antiquity. There is the general salute to the chief, and others to Sir James Mac Donald and his wife, Lady Margaret. The piobaireachd Dhonuill Dhui' was composed on his invasion of the North Highlands in 1503, and Donald Balloch's march to Inverlochy is of the date 1431.

The figure represents one of the Lords of the Isles sitting in judgment on the Tom Moid, or law hill, in Eillean Comairlich, with his barons around him. He wears the Habergeon, or shirt of mail which an old writer describes as being " side almost to the heels."[*] This was the usual defensive armour of the Highlanders, who continued its use until a late period. It is called Lurich, and it is observable, as an entymological fact, that the *Lorica* of the Romans, a similar body armour, is said by Varro to have been derived from the Gauls! Underneath, the sleeves of a leather doublet are seen, and the legs and arms exhibit the appropriate Breacon of Lord Mac Donald. The Clogaid, or skull cap, is of the form worn by the old Gaël, and seen in their effigies at the sacred isle of Columbia and elsewhere. It is fastened under the chin with a cord of twisted leathern thong, for which there is authority in a rare French work on costume. As a regal headpiece, it is ornamented with a circlet of Cairngorm stones, or topazes, and the " eagle's wing," which Ossian tells us distinguished a chief, is fixed on the apex amid the badge of lovely heather. The sword represents the old Claidheamh of the Highlander, and is drawn from the specimen used in a former number.   [*] *Certayne matters concerning Scotland, 1597.*

CLAN DHONUILL, GLEANN-NA-GARRAIDH, OR THE MAC DONELLS OF GLENGARRY.

THE MAC DONALDS are the most numerous and wide-spread of the clans, and are divided into several tribes, all of whom have singularly distinguished themselves. A Norwegian origin for this powerful race is claimed by writers on the subject, but the traditions of the clan invariably represent it as sprung from the aboriginal inhabitants—the far-famed Pictish division of the Gaël; and those whose ancestors were independent kings may well refer with pride to their noble descent.

The early history of Clan Donald is involved in the cloudy shades of antiquity, which, like their native mountain-wreathing mists, afford but unsatisfactory glimpses of the reality. The bare enumeration of the chiefs of a long descent, however illustrious, affords but little gratification; suffice it, then, to say, that Sorle, or Somerled, King of the Isles and Thane of Argyle, is the progenitor of the chiefs of Glengarry, and from Donald, his grandson, who flourished in 1337, the clan has derived its generic name.

This is not a work in which it is desirable to touch on the subject of dispute for precedency which has so long agitated the two great houses of Glengarry and Muidart, or Clan Ranald. In clanship each chief is independent among his own people, although there may be a superior of the whole race. Angus, then ennobled, was ordained, by the Privy Council, 1672, as Chief of the Mac Donalds, to find caution, according to the laws and acts of Parliament, for "the whole name and clan." This was a legal acknowledgment of a right, which, at the same time, his lordship, it could hardly be supposed, would attempt rigidly to enforce.

The Mac Donalds, who were always eager to take on themselves " the first press and dint of the battle," received from King Robert Bruce, at Bannockburn, the honour of taking position on the right of the army, and they were ever most jealous of this privilege, alleging that no engagement could be successful if it were overlooked, and they adduce the defeats at Harlaw and Culloden (1411 and 1746) as striking instances of this truth. Holding this position in the Scottish armies they have performed prodigies of valour.

The Mac Donald of Glengarry and Knoidart is one of the most notable personages, on occasion of passing the act, 1587, by which all the independent chiefs, carefully enumerated in a copious roll, are bound, according to the old clan maxim, for the peaceable and loyal deportment of their followers.

The chiefs of this clan were usually selected as representatives of all the others, in negotiations which concerned their general interest, as when Alastair Mac Ranald met the Earl of Mar at Inver, in Strathdee, where the royal standard was first displayed in 1715, to ascertain his lordship's plans of operation, and let him know what

MAC DONELL of GLENGARRY

the Highlanders were prepared to do for King James. This rebellion was hastened by the rejection of the address of 102 chiefs and heritors to George I., to which Glengarry was the first to attach his signature.

In 1660, Angus, then chief, was created Lord MAC DONELL and AROS, but, dying without issue in 1682, the title was lost; a warrant, however, from James VIII., is in the family charter chest for its restoration: he was succeeded by his cousin-german, Ranald of Scotas. From the above title, the Glengarry branch have continued the orthography of their name.

At the castle of Aros the Lords of the Isles held their parliament, and passed the regal decrees, which distant tribes were bound to respect. The simple form in which important rights were conveyed by these princes may be illustrated by the following brief but binding charter, which loses in translation from the original Gaëlic: "I, Donald, the chief of the Mac Donalds, sitting on the hill of Dun Donald, give thee, Mac Aodh, a full right to Kilmahomag from this day till to-morrow, and so on for ever." A lesson was afforded by one of these lords, which might greatly benefit some sticklers for precedency. He had, at a banquet, been placed by mistake at the bottom of the table, on perceiving which considerable emotion arose among the company, who dreaded the consequence of the supposed indignity; but the great Ceann-cinnidh (head of his race) speedily allayed their apprehensions by exclaiming, emphatically, "Where the Mac Donald sits, know ye, gentlemen, that is the head of the table!"

Those of the name who have distinguished themselves are truly far "too numerous to mention." As military men they have ever supported their high renown, and none have been more nobly distinguished than Sir James Mac Donell, brother of the late chief. In the bardic science, so important in Celtic society, the clan has produced many individuals of lasting celebrity. The most celebrated is Ian Lom, who lived in the reigns of Kings Charles I. and II., and by his stirring compositions so materially promoted the success of Montrose's wars.

At the battle of Inverlochy he placed himself at the top of the castle, to stimulate the combatants, and witness the prowess which he was afterwards to celebrate. The perseverance with which, for years, he laboured to bring the murderers of the children of Keppach to justice is unparalleled. He travelled throughout the country to stir up some party strong enough to accomplish the object, and even went to Edinburgh to entreat the interference of government. At last he succeeded by the assistance of Sir James Mac Donald, and a monument commemorates the fate of nine of these desperadoes, who defended themselves to death. It was erected by the late Glengarry, with inscriptions in Gaëlic, Latin, French, and English, over the well where the heads of the criminals were washed previous to their being sent to the Lords of Council: ever since, this little fountain has been distinguished as Tobar nan Ceann—"The Well of the Heads."

The ARMORIAL BEARINGS are, or, an eagle displayed gu., surmounted by a galley (Biorlin) sab., sails furled, proper; in dexter chief a hand coupé in fess of the 2nd; sinister a cross, croslet fitchee

of the 3rd. Crest, a raven proper, perched on a rock az. Supporters, two bears, each pierced with an arrow in bend proper. Motto, over the escutcheon, "Craig an fhithich"—the raven's rock: on a compartment below, "Per mare et terras." The patronymic, Mac Mhic Alastair, is derived from Alexander, son of Ranald of the Isles, who flourished about 1400.

The SUAICHEANTAS, is Fraoch gorm, *erica vulgaris*, common heath.

The BREACAN is of that class called uaine, green, to distinguish it from those patterns in which red predominates.

The CATH-GHAIRM, of the Glengarry Mac Donells, is Craig an fhithich, the name of a rock in the vicinity of the castle.

The PIOBAIREACHDAN of this clan are fuller than in most others. There is the Failte Mhic Alastair, and the Cumhadh or Lament Cille chriosd commemorates a fearful occurrence: and Blar Sròn preserves the memory of a desperate conflict with the Mac Kenzies at a place so called in western Ross.

Mac Mhic Alastair had several castles in different parts of his wide-spread lands. Aros was the ancient regal residence. Sròn, or Loch Carron, now lies in scattered fragments of Cyclopean walls, and others have yielded to a similar fate. The principal dwelling has for many centuries been at Invergarry, in Glen mòr a na h-Alban, the great valley of Caledonia, thirty-eight miles westward of Inverness, where a modern mansion succeeded the ancient castle, which still stands a stately ruin in a most picturesque situation on the north bank of the loch.

It was said by the enemies of this powerful race, that they boasted there were more reivers among the Mac Donalds than honest men in others. Glengarry's clan in 1715 was 800 strong; in 1745, 700. Throughout the campaigns of Montrose they were one of the main springs which kept up the astonishing movements of the chivalrous enterprise. Donald Gorm, brother to the chief, commanded the clan at Blar Raon-ruaradh (Killicrankie), in the war of Viscount Dundee, and he there fell: in his target were found twelve spear or pike heads, he having severed the poles with his broadsword. Angus, who was colonel in the army of Prince Charles, was killed by the accidental discharge of a musket at Falkirk, which so discouraged the clan that they did not regain their native spirit. Scotas, however, who was reckoned the bravest man of all the Mac Donalds in the prince's army, had fifty men under his command at Culloden, where he fell, with his lieutenant, ensign, sergeant, corporal, and eighteen privates!

The late Glengarry took up a body of his clansmen, on occasion of the visit of George IV. to Edinburgh. This chief kept up the dress and style of living which characterized his ancestors. He travelled with the luchd-crios, or body-guard, and when at Inverness or other towns, these were posted, with military regularity, as sentinels, at the door of the house where he might reside. He was an enthusiastic promoter of the athletic sports of the Highlanders, and gave annual prizes at Inverness and Fort William to those who excelled. His melancholy death, in escaping from a steamer which had gone ashore, will be recollected. His funeral was impressive: borne by his devoted clansmen, and preceded by the piper pealing forth the plaintive cu' a', the mournful cavalcade passed straight along to the place of rest, dashing through the deep and rapid mountain streams wherever they crossed the path.

A stranger now possesses the lands of this family; and the present chief, with 500 or 600 of his clan, has established himself in a distant colony. The hospitable feelings and generosity of his father left incumbrances on the estate, which led to an alienation of the property; and the son, with the characteristic feeling of a scion of Glengarry, has sought for greater independence on a foreign shore. The nobleman who now ranks the remaining followers as his own, seems not less a Highlander in heart. Lord Ward promotes the music, the sports, the education, and improvement of his tenantry with all the fervour of a chief of native lineage.

The figure is dressed according to the now generally adopted arrangement, but Mr. Mc Ian must be exonerated from any acquiescence in its propriety. The form of bonnet, which has received the name of a "Glengarry," is not of more than about forty years' standing, and, in the opinion of many, it is in no way an improvement on the original shape. The absurdity of the sword belt being carried over the plaid will be observed: the object of the wearer, by this arrangement, is to display the rich buckles and other ornaments, with which it is often very needlessly loaded; but it is evident that the plaid in such case must be worn even at dinner, or in the ball-room—an egregious impropriety.

MAC DHUBHICH, OR MAC DUFFS.

THIS surname is one of the most ancient in Scotland, and the chief was among the first of those nobles who became distinguished by the Saxon title of Earl.

Dubh, the *bh* having the sound of *f* or *v*, is the term in Gaëlic descriptive of a black or dark coloured man, and all those who are of this clan refer to Mac Duff, the powerful Thane of Fife, who overthrew Mac Beth in 1056, as their common ancestor; but the first Thane was created anno 838.* Several other tribes in different parts, who have long been distinguished and independent clans, are also sprung from these great Celtic dignitaries, as the family of Mac Intosh and the noble house of Weems, who took the name from Eoin mòr na-h-Uamh, great John of the Cave, who flourished 1140.

The title Thane, which has been thought, by some writers, to come immediately from the Saxon, is a contraction of the Gaëlic *Tain*-istair, a designation given to the governor or lord who acted as the representative of his king or chief in directing military operations and collecting the revenues then paid in cattle, under the name of *Tain*. The Thanes of Fife appear with high distinction in Scottish history, acting a prominent part in public transactions; and for the services rendered by the above Mac Duff, King Malcolm III, conferred on him and his posterity singular privileges. 1. They were on all occasions, when the royal standard was unfurled, to have the leading of the van of the Scottish army. 2. They had the right of placing the crown on the heads of the kings at their coronation; and 3. If they, or any of their kindred within the ninth degree, should chance to commit a slaughter, they should possess a special claim of girth or sanctuary, and obtain a free remission for the crime, on payment of an eric or atonement to the relations of those slain, which, in Scottish law, was called kinbot. This was settled at "nyne kye, and ane colpindach or young kow" for a gentleman which after the introduction of money, was commuted for twenty-four silver merks, and twelve for a common person. In order to obtain the advantage of this immunity, the party claiming it was obliged to satisfy a court appointed to be held a Cupar;* and Buchannan says, the custom was retained in the days of his fathers. The cross of Mac Duff in Fifeshire marked this sanctuary, and it bore a very curious inscription, in which Pictish, Gothic, and Latin are intermixed.† Exercising the high privilege of her family, Isabell, who had married the Earl of Buchan, performed with becoming dignity and spirit the office which devolved on her by crowning King Robert the Bruce in 1306. Duncan the Thane had married Mary Monthermer, neice to Edward I., and took the side of the English and was governor of Perth; but, falling into the hands of the Scottish king, he and his lady were imprisoned in the castle of Kildrummy in Aberdeenshire, where he died, anno 1336. In Isabell, who was the only daughter of Duncan, the twelfth Earl of Fife, who was killed in 1353, terminated the direct line of the Fife Mac Duffs; and she dying without issue, in virtue of an entail made by her father, constituted, by deed of indenture, Robert, third son of King Robert II., her heir, both to the property and title, but the Earldom at last became extinct through the forfeiture of Murdach, Duke

*Father Weems, quoted by Mann, in the Spalding Club Transactions.

* Wintoun's Chronicle.　　† Sibbald's History of Fife and Kinross, 1710.

of Albany, in 1425. The family being thus broken, the clan was dispersed, and the Duffs of the north arose, a succession of whom were respectable burgesses of Aberdeen, and other branches obtained lands throughout these parts.

William Duff of Dipple, in the county of Banff, was created a peer of Ireland by the title of Baron Braco of Kilbride, 1735, and being descended from the ancient Thanes of that title, he was created Earl of Fife and Viscount Mac Duff, also in the Irish peerage, by patent, April 26th, 1759. James, now Earl of Fife, was raised to the dignity of a peer of the United Kingdom by George IV., April 27, 1827, and is the fourth in the revived peerage. His lordship is amply imbued with the spirit of his ancestors, his benevolence and affability being the theme of praise and gratitude in the north. He served with great distinction as major-general in the army of the Spanish patriots, and was wounded at Talavera, and at the sanguinary siege and storming of Fort Matagorda, where he was a volunteer. He has long abandoned the gaieties of courtly life, and resides unostentatiously at his princely mansion of Duffhouse, in the vicinity of Banff, where his beneficence is widely felt.

The COAT ARMOUR borne by his lordship is quarterly, 1st and 4th or, a lion rampant gules, armed and langued azure, for Mac Duff; 2nd and 3rd vert, a fesse dancette ermine between a hart's head cabossed in chief, and two escallop shells in base, or, for Duff of Braco. Crest, a demi-lion rampant gules, holding in the dexter paw a broadsword, proper, hilted and pomelled, or. He also carries a horse in full gallop, arg., covered with a mantling gules, strewed with inescutcheons, or, charged with a lion rampant, of the second; on his back a knight in full armour, with his sword drawn, proper, bearing a shield charged as the inescutcheons: on the helmet a wreath of the colours, and thereon a demi-lion rampant gules. Supporters, two savages wreathed about the head and loins with laurel, holding over their shoulders branches of trees, all proper. Motto over the first crest, "Deus juvat;" and over the second, "Deo juvante;" below the shield, "Virtute et opera."

The SUAICHEANTAS carried by the Mac Duffs is Lus nam breoileag, *vaccinium vitis idea*, red whortle berry.

The PIOBAIREACHD, Cù'a' Mhic Dhu', is a fine lament for one of this clan.

There were many of this surname in the north of Ireland, where there is Baile Iamais dubh, or James Duff's-town.

Rothiemay, Balvenie, Dalgettie castles, Innes and Duff-houses, are seats of the Earl of Fife, and Mar Lodge is his beautiful residence in the Highlands of Aberdeenshire. On occasion of the visit of King George IV. to Scotland, Lord Fife attracted much notice by his Highland followers, a number of fine fellows who attended him in the olden way as Gillean ruith, or running footmen, preceding and surrounding his carriage and keeping up their speed to wherever his lordship might drive.

The flourishing town and harbour near Banff were formed by the Lords Fife, and named Mac Duff; and near the handsome church, which they also erected, is raised a cross in imitation of the original obelisk which marked the place of sanctuary, and so long remained an evidence of their former greatness.

The figure is not only a Mac Duff, but he is Duff himself, as is observable those of this clan, agreeably to their designation, usually are. He wears mogans, or knit stockings, without feet, by no means an uncommon covering, which is used more for the purpose of protecting the legs from the prickly shrubs, than as appurtenances of dress, and he appears furiously breasting up a hill, in pursuit of some one with whom he has " a reckoning to clear."

CLANN MHIC DHUGHIL—THE MAC DUGALS.

The Mac Dugals of Lorn are descended from the ancient princes of Argyle and the Isles. The patronymic is derived from Dugal, son of the famous Somerled, who held sovereign power in these parts during a great portion of the twelfth century. The name signifies the dark-complexioned stranger, and would thus seem to point to the Dalriadic settlement in 503 as the period when such an appellation was imposed.

Duncan de Lorn witnesses a charter of the Earl of Athol in the middle of the thirteenth century, and after the unfortunate death of Alexander III., which produced so calamitous an interregnum, Alexander de Ergadia, or of Argyle, appears among the barons in the great national assembly which declared the Maiden of Norway heiress of the Scottish crown.

Among those who opposed the claim of Bruce was this Alexander, chief of the clan, who was one of the royal aspirant's most determined and formidable enemies, and almost ruined the Bruce's cause. His implacable hostility arose from the murder by Bruce, of John, the red Cumin, whose daughter Lorn had married, an act of slaughter which nothing could palliate but the desperate state of the king's affairs, and the general turbulence of society.

MAC DUFF

When Bruce was defeated at Methven, in 1306, he retreated through Perthshire towards Argyle, with about 300 followers, but he was met by Mac Dugal with a force said to have been 1,000 strong, and, after a strenuous contention, he was completely defeated, in his flight most narrowly escaping capture or death. He was keenly pursued by three of the most determined Mac Dugals, said to have been brothers, who made a simultaneous attack, and so closely did they grapple him that had not the brooch which fastened his plaid given way, he would have been taken prisoner. In proof of this circumstance, a brooch was long preserved, and is, perhaps, still to be seen at Dunolla, asserted to be the identical jewel of which Bruce was thus roughly despoiled. It is of silver, richly ornamented with precious stones, and was latterly known as the brooch of Glenlion, from having been acquired by that family through marriage. An engraving of this relic is given in " Pennant's Tour," and we are in possession of an original coloured drawing of it.

After this unfortunate discomfiture the Bruce was tracked by Mac Dugal with bloodhounds, and it was only by almost incredible exertion and personal bravery that he preserved his life.

When he was at last established on the throne, he directed his first attention to crush those who had so fiercely opposed him, and he determined to expel the Mac Dugals and take possession of Lorn. In advancing for this purpose, he found John son of the chief, posted with his clan in the narrow pass between Bencruachan and Lochaw, a position which seemed to preclude the possibility of any farther march, but the superior ability of Bruce, who ordered part of his army to mount the steep, which was supposed inaccessible, and make an attack in the rear, quickly put the enemy to flight, and in the confinement of the pass they suffered great slaughter.

The castle of Dunstaffnage was then taken, and the country was so severely ravaged, that old Alastair prudently submitted to mercy, but his son John, who could not expect pardon, fled to England, where he was gladly received, and was appointed admiral of the fleet intended to co-operate with the land forces in that mighty expedition which was so signally frustrated at Bannockburn. After that battle the king again went forward, determined to annihilate the power of the Mac Dugals, and attacking John, who had carried his fleet round to the Isles, he completely defeated and took him prisoner, 1318. He was immediately committed to close custody in the castle of Dunbarton, and thence transferred to Lochleven, where he remained until King Robert's death, when he was released, with a free restoration of all his possessions, and married a grand-daughter of his late sovereign !

John Stewart, of Invermeath, and his brother Robert married the two daughters and co-heiresses of Ewen, last Lord of Lorn ; John acquired all the lordship, except the castle of Dunolla and its dependent lands, which went to the next male branch of the family.

The Mac Dugals, of Donolla, on whom the chiefship then devolved, were descended from Allan, son of John, and brother of Ewen, of Lorn, the last lord of this ancient line.

In 1715, Mac Dugal joined the Earl of Mar, and the estate was forfeited, but it was restored just before the " rising" for Prince Charles, and he, consequently, did not " go out " on that occasion.

Captain D. N. Mac Dougal, R.N., is the present representative of this ancient and distinguished house. The principal cadet was Rara, a very early branch of the Lords of Lorn and the Isles, the representative of which is supposed to be Mac Dugal of Ardincaple. Other cadets are the families of Gallanach and Soraba.

The ancient residences were the castles of Dunstaffnage and Dunolla, the latter a fortress of extreme antiquity. Near this picturesque ruin is the pleasant mansion of Captain Mac Dougal.

The strength of this clan, in 1704, was 500, but by President Forbes's report it was reduced, in 1745, to 200.

The ARMORIAL BEARINGS are quarterly, 1st and 4th in a field, azure, a lion rampant, arg. for Mac Dugal. 2nd and 3rd, or, a lymphad, representing the ancient biorlin or galley, sable, with flames issuing from the topmast, proper, for the Lordship of Lorn.

The SUAICHEANTAS, is Fraoch dearg, Bell-heath, *Tetralix.*

The illustrative figure is clothed in a flannel shirt and a simple feile-beag, a scanty covering, but such as the hardy Gaël of former years often appeared in, and found well suited to athletic exercises. The small sporan was quite sufficient to contain a snaoisin, or snuff horn, almost the only necessary he required. He is provided with a genuine Clai' mòr, drawn from one formerly the property of James Stewart, of Ardvoirlich ; the prototype of Sir Walter Scott's Allan Mac Auley, now in possession of his descendant, Robert Stewart, Esq., of Ardvoirlich ; it is five feet eight inches long, and the pomel is heavily laden with lead, counterpoising the weight of the blade, and rendering it easy to be wielded. He carries also a curious dirk, the original of which is in Mr. Mc Ian's possession. The hair is " clubbed," or tied, a fashion very common a century ago, an example of which is given in " The Scottish Gaël."

MAC DUGAL

CLAN GILLIBHREAC, OR MAC GILLIVRAY.

It is said that, about 1263, one Gabrai placed himself under the protection of the Mac Intosh, and was progenitor of the clan Gillivray.[1] It could not, however, be from this person that the patronymic is derived. Mac Gillivray, the Mac Gilli-bhreac of Gaëlic orthography, signifies the sons of the freckled lad, and is a name of considerable importance is different parts of the Highlands.

The principal branch has long resided in Inverness-shire, and the chief was designated, from his property, Duu-mac-glas, the fort of the grey man's son. When Lady Mac Intosh raised her clansmen in the cause of Prince Charles, he was made colonel, and it was his battalion which made that furious attack at Culloden, that almost annihilated the left wing of the Duke of Cumberland's army, but cost the life of Mac Gillivray, who fell, with four officers of his clan. This brave soldier encountered the commander of Barrel's regiment, and struck off some of the English colonel's fingers with his broad-sword. After the conflict was over, Mac Gillivray was stripped, and his waistcoat, doubtless handsomely embroidered, was appropriated by a private soldier. Walking along the streets of Inverness in this garment, he was met by the colonel, who indignantly stopped the man, and ordered him immediately to take it off. "I recognise that waistcoat," said the generous warrior; "I met on the field of battle the brave man who wore it, and it shall not now be thus degraded." It does not appear, however, to have been long retained by the colonel, for it was afterwards exposed for sale in the window of a tailor in Inverness.[2]

Mac Gillivray's immediate followers were about eighty. He had abjured King James in May, 1745, and took up arms in August following, which, it is absurdly alleged, he did to procure for Iain Shah, merchant in Inverness, and "a prime councillor of Lady Mac Intosh, the post of collector of the land tax," under the restored dynasty![†]

There is a very respectable branch of the Mac Gillivrays in the island of Mull, designated from the residence of the Ceann-tigh, or head of the house, as of Beinn-na-gall, the mountain of the stranger. They are probably descended from those in Lochaber and Morvern, who were dispersed on the discomfiture of Somerled by Alexander II., and seem to have been otherwise called Mac Aonghais, or Mac Innes; but it is a verbal perversion to make the name synonymous with Mac Gilli-Brid, the son of St. Bridget's follower.[‡] We took down their pedigree from an old seanachai', or antiquary, which may serve as a specimen of the traditional records of Highland society. Alastair Mac Eoghan, mhic (vic) Alastair, mhic Iain, mhic Dhonuil, mhic Mhaoil Challuim, mhic Mhaoil Challuim ghuirm, mhic Mhaistar Mhartin, mhic Fhearchar liath. Alexander, son of Ewen, son of Alexander, son of John, son of Donald, son of Malcolm, son of dark Malcolm, son of Martin the clergyman, son of grey Farquhar.

The above Mr. Martin Mac Gillivray, who lived about 1640, retained the practice of carrying a sword; and, calling on Allan,

second son of Mac Lean of Lochbuie, for his proportion of stipend, he refused to pay, asking the parson, with a sneer, if he meant to enforce his demand by the sword? "Rather than lose what is my due," replied the sturdy clergyman, "I do mean to use my weapon." "Well," says Mac Lean, "I have no objection to take a turn with you." "Tha mi deonach a chall ma chuireas tu mo dhruim ri balla:" "I am content, then, to lose if you are able to put my back to the wall," was the prompt return of Mac Gillivray; and he quickly brought his antagonist to the ground, who gave in, and paid the amount, with the observation that he liked well to see a man who could maintain his living by the sword.

From an intelligent gentleman, in Mull, of this name, we were told the following anecdote. The Laird of Beinn-na-gall fought in the battle of Sherramuir, 1715, and, happening to stumble, a gentleman standing near, believing he was shot, exclaimed, with great concern, "God preserve you, Mac Gillivray!" "God preserve yourself," was the ready reply, "I have, at present, no need of his aid."

The COAT ARMOUR is party per pale arg. and az.; in the dexter chief a hand fesswise coupée, holding a dagger in pale; in the sinister a cross crosslet fitchee arg. Crest, a cat sejant, proper. Supporters, two armed Highlanders, with steel caps, tartan jackets, and feilebeags, and bearing targets on their exterior arms, all proper. Motto, Touch not the cat bot (without) a glove.

The BADGE, as a branch of Clan Chattan, is Lus nam braoileag (*vaccinium vitis idea*), red whortle berry.

The rallying cry was Loch moy, that of the Mac Intoshes, but we have heard it said that their own cath-ghairm was Dunma'glas.

The position of this figure is intended to display the Breacan an fheile, or belted plaid, the original dress, so called from being fastened around the body by a belt. This ample robe, which contained ten or twelve square yards, was peculiarly useful, answering the purpose of a garment by day, a comfortable cloak in bad weather, and bedding by night; for by unfastening the belt the whole was disengaged.

The target is from the collection of Colonel Mac Lean, of Coll, preserved at his seat, Druim Fhinn, Fingal's Ridge, in Mull.

The sword is the usual claymore, with plain, strong, steel basket-

[1] History of the Mac Intoshes.
[2] Angus Mac Donald, who fought at Culloden.—Author's MS. Collections.
[†] MS. Account of the Clans, 1748, in British Museum.
[‡] Coll. rebus Albanicis, and Skene's History of the Highlanders.

MAC GILLIVRAY

hilt. The jacket is dyed of a light shade with the native crotal, which produces a colour of which the Highlanders are very fond. The hose are ca' da', a thick stuff of the same pattern as the plaid, not knit but sewed, similar to those still worn by the Highland regiments.

The brogs are of deer's skin, the hairy side outwards, of the common form; the bonnet, also, is of the shape at one period prevailing throughout the Highlands, and the white cockade, worn by the adherents of the Stuarts, is conspicuous on the left side.

SIOL ALPIN NO NA GRIOGARAICH--THE MAC GREGORS.

"Is Rioghal mo dhream," *i.e.*, my race is royal, is the proud boast of this indomitable clan, and the descent is traced to Griogar, third son of Alpin Mac Achài', king of Scotland, who commenced his reign in 787. Donngheal, the elder son, gave the patronymic Mac Gregor to his posterity, and his brother, Guarai', was founder of the clan, since distinguished as Mac Quarrie.

Malcolm, who died about the year 1164, appears to have been the first who is designated of Gleann Urchài'. Malcolm, who lived in the time of Bruce, supported his interest with the utmost power of the clan, and fought bravely at Bannockburn; he also accompanied Edward, the king's brother, in the invasion of Ireland, and having been severely wounded at Dundalk, he was afterwards alluded to as being "am Mor'ear bacach," the lame lord.

Campbell of Lochaw, in the fifteenth century, incited the Mac Nabs to quarrel with the Mac Gregors, who meeting their enemies in battle at Crinlarach, cut them off almost to a man. Lochaw thereupon received a commission to proceed by martial law against both, when they made common cause, but, after repeated skirmishes, with different success, they were forced about 1500 to obtain peace by ceding a considerable part of their lands to their too powerful neighbour.

Alastair, of Glenstrae, was celebrated for his martial prowess, and signally avenged a galling quarrel with the Colquhons, who had attacked him by surprise, at the battle of Glenfruin, in 1602. The vanquished, excessively mortified, accused the Mac Gregors of having stained their laurels by the commission of acts of atrocious cruelty. Colquhon endeavoured to "entrap and ensnare" the unfortunate victors "within compass of law," which he effectually did by a grievous complaint to the Lords of Council, when the whole clan were denounced rebels, and the Earl of Argyle was ordered to fall on them with fire and sword, a process by which, if successful, the Mac Gregors' lands would be his reward; various collisions consequently took place.

Argyle at last succeeded in persuading the chief that he could procure his pardon if he would accompany him to the court in England, engaging to conduct Mac Gregor, who was outlawed, safely into that country. The latter part of the agreement he truly performed, for he conveyed his charge across the Tweed, but by an act of gross perfidy, he had old Alastair immediately seized

and carried back to Edinburgh, where he was executed with thirty of his followers![*] On his death, without lawful issue, the clan, then in a state of disorder, elected a chief; but the head of the collateral branch reversed this arrangement very unceremoniously, by dragging the expectant of the honour from his inaugural chair in the kirk of Strath Fillan, and placing therein a more acceptable ruler in the person of Gregor, natural son of the late chief.

The severity of the laws under which the Mac Gregors were at this time suffering, is unparalleled. Those who might kill a Mac Gregor, were not only held "scaithless," but were actually rewarded by a free gift of their "haill moveable goods and gear!" In 1603 they were commanded to change their name under pain of death, and prohibited from carrying any arms, except a pointless knife to use at their meals: subsequently, no greater number than four of the clan was permitted to meet together. It is even alleged that bloodhounds were employed to track them in their retreats, and had their countrymen been as hostile as the law required, the Mac Gregors had been speedily exterminated. The Camerons, being stirred up to this service, agreed to attack the Mac Gregors, who, reinforced by a party of their friends, the Macphersons, marched northward, and gave battle in Brae Lochabar to their enemies, who met a signal defeat.

The loyaly of this clan was remarkable, for, although suffering from a proscription so severe, they took the field under Montrose with their whole strength. That general did, indeed, assure them that when his majesty's affairs were settled, all their grievances should be redressed, and on the restoration, Charles II., in reward for their inflexible fidelity, annulled the statute which prohibited them from bearing the name Mac Gregor, and restored them to all rights and privileges, but the advantage of this act they unfortunately did not long enjoy, for it was insidiously rescinded by William III.

John, who was chief in 1715, adopted the name of Murray. Like his ancestors he maintained the claim of the Stewarts, but he did not deem it prudent to appear publicly in arms. The famous Rob Roy took the field, a hero of the Dugal Ciar branch of the clan, but he posted himself in sight of the field of battle at Dunblane, and, believing victory secure, he did not advance, remarking to a messenger sent from the Earl of Mar, with pressing orders to charge, that if

---

[*]He left an affecting declaration of the base purposes for which Argyle had sought to employ him, and for which he had met so sad a reward.—*Pitcairn's Crim. Trials.*

MAC GREGOR

he could not gain without the Mac Gregors, he could not gain with them.

Robert, the succeeding chief, was so zealous a partizan of the exiled family, that he mortgaged his whole estate to support it, and commanded his clan in the Prince's army, 1745. When they were in the north, the Duke of Cumberland employed Mr. Gordon, minister of Alva, in Strathspey, to treat with them to lay down arms, offering restoration of their name, and other considerations, to which they replied that they could not desert the cause, but chose rather to risk all and die with the characters of honest men, than live in infamy, and disgrace their posterity. When the war was determined on the moor of Culloden, the clan marched off the field with banners flying, and dispersed in their own country, which was thoroughly ravaged by the victorious army. The chief was long confined in Edinburgh Castle: and on his death, in 1758, the honour devolved on his brother Evan, who held a commission in the 41st regiment.

John of Lanrick, who also bore the name of Murray, was created Baronet, in 1795. When the act which proscribed the Mac Gregors was repealed, he resumed the family name. On which occasion 826 clansmen of mature age, subscribed a judicial deed, acknowledging him to be chief, an honour which is disputed by Mac Gregor of Glengyle, of the "sliochd Gregor, a chroic," who are descended from the twelfth chief who died about 1413.

Sir John died in 1822, and was succeeded by the late distinguished officer and warm patriot, Sir Evan Murray Mac Gregor, who died in 1840, leaving as his successor Sir John Bannatyne Mac Gregor, who died in 1851.

The military power of the Mac Gregors, in 1645, was 1000, and 700 when last mustered in their national independence, 1745. Colonel Alexander Mac Gregor Murray, in 1799, raised the first battalion of Clan Alpin Fencibles, 765 strong, and a second battalion was embodied making together 1230 men.

The old ARMORIAL BEARINGS are, arg. a sword in bend dexter, and fir tree eradicated in bend sinister, proper, in chief a crown, gules.* Crest, a lion's head crowned with an antique diadem. Motto, " E'en do bot spair nocht." The dexter supporter is a unicorn denoting the royal descent, arg. crowned and horned, or ; the sinister a deer proper, tyned azure.

The SUAICHEANTAS, or Badge of the Clan Alpin, is Guithas, Pine, *Pinus Sylvestris*.

The CATH-GHAIRM, Ard-choille, the wood on the height.

The PIOBAIREACHDAN, are the Mac Gregor's salute, and the battle of Glenfruin.—Gleann Bhraoin, the Valley of Grief.

The hereditary standard bearers were a family of the clan Mhurich, or Mac Phersons, and when the late Sir Evan mustered a body of his clansmen to swell the pomp of George the Fourth's visit to Edinburgh, the charge of the Brattach Griogaraich was assigned to two gentlemen of that name.

The practice of swearing on the dirk, the most solemn oath of the Highlanders, is shown in this figure. The place is supposed to be the old kirk-yard of Balquhidder, where, beside the tombstone of one of those murdered under the sanction of " Letters of fire and sword," the vengeful clansman vows unceasing enmity to the oppressors—the deceitful sons of Diarmid. He wears the short jacket and long waistcoat, woollen shirt, belted plaid, ca' da' hose and cuarrans The sporan is from a rare specimen in Mr. Mac Ian's possession, and is curious from showing the primitive use of the thongs and tassels for closing the purse ; in his bonnet is placed the clan badge.

James Mac Gregor, the son of the famous Rob, who served as major in the Highland army, escaped to France, where his urgent applications to Prince Charles and his chief being unavailing, he was reduced to extreme destitution. An offer of pardon was made to him by government, and a lucrative situation provided if he would secure Allan breac Stewart who had murdered Campbell, of Glenure, factor over the confiscated estate of Ardsheil. This he willingly undertook to do for his pardon, but respectfully declined the appointment, as he " was born in the character of a gentleman, and never intended to accept of that which would be a disgrace to his family as well as a scourge to his country." In this he affords an example of that honour and independence which so strongly characterised the old Highlanders, and we regret that men of such high principle should have been subjected to a fate so hard. Shortly afterwards this unhappy member of a proscribed clan died at Paris in utter want !

The practice of levying " Black mail," a tribute exacted for protection afforded by the Highlanders, has been repeatedly denounced as a most tyrannous and oppressive exaction, but when the unwarlike inhabitants of open districts found that they could not defend themselves, the assistance of the Highlanders was solicited, and bonds of agreement were entered into between the parties. Thus to protect the city of Aberdeen from " landward assaults," the magistrates engaged the chief of the Farquharsons who agreed to keep 300 men in arms for that purpose. The lawfulness of this obligation to the Mac Gregors was acknowledged by an act of council in 1658, charging the inhabitants of several parishes to pay up arrears, and holding them bound in future, except they should give regular intimation that they no longer required protection.

The cruel treatment which this loyal clan so long experienced aroused a feeling of respect and sympathy throughout the Highlands, and, to this day, " Clann na Griogar" is frequently given as a spontaneous and cordially received toast.

It is to be observed that the Glengyle branch of the clan wears a peculiar old *sett* of Tartan, which, with every other pattern, can be readily procured at Mr. Donald Mac Dougal's Clan Tartan Warehouse, Inverness.

*The tree in Sir John's arms and some others, is oak. With the Baronetcy several honorary augmentations were conferred, viz., a chief embattled gules, charged with an eastern crown surmounted of a flag, argent ; there were also added as mottos, " Ard choille " and " is Rioghal mo dhream." The motto, I suspect, is correctly, " In debate (or contention) spare not."

MAC INNES

CLANN AONGHAIS—MAC INNES.

ANGUS is one of the oldest names in the Gaëlic language, occurring frequently in Scottish and Pictish history.

The Gaëlic orthography is Aongas, but, as in the genitive, the g is aspirated by the following h, the word is pronounced Aon'es, and hence Innes. There can be no doubt but many of the latter name, and those who are called Mac Innes, are properly of the Mac Aon'ais clan; but it is probable also, that many families bear this name as a local appellation. Innis signifies an islet, and those whose residence was in such a situation, would be designated from that circumstance, as in the instances, Aird, Glen, Ballach, Blair, Ross, &c., originally designations applied as descriptive of locality. Innes of Innes, and other families of antiquity in the county of Moray, acquired their name from lands so called, but no history or tradition derives them from the Mac Aon'ais's.

Morven, that district of Argyleshire celebrated in the poems of Ossian, as the territory of the great Fingal, was the chief seat of this clan; and in a romantic situation, at the confluence of a rapid stream, with a salt water loch, stands the ruined and romantic castle of Ceann-loch-aluin, long the residence of the Mac Aon'ais's. It is a massy square tower, or keep, built to the top with stones of a remarkably large size, and was reared by a lady named Du'ghall, which would imply the dark-complexioned stranger. The tradition respecting its erection is, that it cost this lady the worth of a quantity of butter equal to its own size, and certainly, if as much is meant, as the bulk of the outer walls, and the interior space, it was rather a costly edifice. It underwent at one time a very sharp siege, during which the Clan Aon'ais bravely stood out until a breach was made in the wall. This was probably when it was taken and garrisoned by Montrose's Irish auxiliaries, in 1645. In the burial ground of Kilcolumkil, at a short distance, are several monuments of the old possessors of the adjoining lands. They are chiefly slab stones, beau-tifully sculptured in intricate foliage and tracery designs, a style prevalent throughout the Highlands until late years; but in few cases have there been inscriptions, and where they were introduced, time and the injuries of the weather have defaced them.

There is a common saying, "Mac Aonghais an Dun's Mac Dhughil an Laorn," the origin of which is not very clearly understood, even by the natives with whom we have conversed.

The hereditary bowmen to the chiefs of Mac Kinnon were of the Clan Aon'ais, and many characteristic anecdotes are related of their exploits. Besides carrying a bow and arrows for their own, or Mac Kinnon's use, these officials were required to instruct the clansmen in the management of this favourite weapon, and for their services they enjoyed a hereditary farm, called Dal na Saighdear, or "the field of the archer."

The ARMORIAL BEARINGS are, azure, on a chief, argent, three stars of six points, of the first. Crest, a thistle, proper, and thereon a bee sucking the flower! Motto, "E labore dulcedo."

The figure represents a warrior assailed by archers, the shower of whose deadly missiles he wards off by the dexterous use of his target. The Highland archers were excellent marksmen; and it has been observed in a former number that the Celtic practice was to draw the arrow to the breast. A bowman was termed saighdear, from saighead, an arrow and fear a man, a word which appears to be the origin of "soldier."

CLANN MHIC AN T-SAOIR—THE MAC INTIRES.

THE Mac an t-Soars are a branch of the great Clan Donald, from whom so many of the Highland families are descended. They are the posterity of an individual, whose skill in wooden work seems to have been the reason for applying to him the appellation of the Saor, or Carpenter; and there is a traditional account of the circumstance which procured him the designation, which savours a little of other legendary relations. It bears that a Mac Donald being at sea, when his boat sprung a leak, probably by starting a treenail, and finding it impossible to keep her long afloat, forced his thumb into the hole and cut it off, so that he might be able to carry the vessel to land. From this action, he was ever afterwards called An t-Saor.

To those who are unacquainted with the Gaëlic language, it may be well to explain that, in certain cases, the article an meeting the letter s in a masculine genitive, aspirates, or renders it quiescent by the interjection of t, gratia euphoniæ: thus Mac an t-Saoir is pronounced very nearly like Mac Intire.

This clan were never able to rise to great eminence among

MAC INTIRE

their brother tribes; they were unable to maintain their separate independence, and became amalgamated with their more powerful neighbours, of whom they accepted the holding of their lands, and were content to array themselves under their banners; in which capacity however, they were amiable auxiliaries.

There was one Paul, a man of great power in Sutherland, who lived in the end of the thirteenth century, and it is highly probable if he had no surname before, he acquired it from a family qualification in the building line. He is said to have built Don Creich, in that county, which is a vitrified fort, one of those very singular remains, constructed by such means as antiquaries have not yet been able to determine. As professions were hereditary among the Celts, there is no doubt but the father imparted to the son his own knowledge in that now lost style of architecture.

The Mac an t-Saoirs of Rannach were a race of famous musicians, a profession held in so much esteem by the Gaël; and, since the year 1680, they have been pipers to Menzies of Weems, chief of Clan Meinanich, for whom they composed the appropriate salute. Iain Mac Dhonuill mòr, who then officiated, was the author of "Cath Sliabh an t-Siorra," a fine piobaireachd, which commemorates the battle of Sheriffmuir, or Dunblain, fought in 1715.

Celebrated as this family was in the musical profession, one of the clan has immortalised himself in the kindred walk of poetry. The productions of Duncan Mac Intire are so highly estimated in the Highlands, that they have " obtained for him a comparison with Ossian himself." He is known among his countrymen as " Fair Duncan of the Songs," which possess an unrivalled originality of conception, with the most mellifluous flow of language, yet this unassuming man was perfectly illiterate !

Duncan fought against Prince Charles at the battle of Falkirk, and composed a humorous song on the defeat of his party; and when the act which proscribed wearing the national dress was passed, he poured forth his sorrow in a poem, wherein he boldly assails the Government for having passed a law which was equally obnoxious to the friendly clans as to those who were hostile; and if he was hearty in his loyalty previous to this measure, he could no longer suppress his feelings when he found his countrymen deprived of their dearly-prized breacan, or tartan, their dirks, swords, guns, pistols, and cross belts ! " We are made the Saxons' jest," he exclaims; " to us victory has proved an evil. Should Charles return, we are ready to stand by him: then up with the carmine plaid !— then up with the rifle ! "

For this animated burst of patriotic indignation, honest Duncan was committed to prison; but by the interest of his numerous friends he was saved from a long confinement, or any other punishment.

When the Bill introduced by the late Duke of Montrose and General Fraser passed into law in 1782, by which the Act against wearing the Highland dress was repealed, this worthy Highlander gave vent to his feelings in a joyous strain, which was as popular with his countrymen as the former had been. We have no wish to give undue prominence to Mac Intire, but this subject is so appropriate to the present work, that we have dwelt longer upon his compositions than they would otherwise be thought to merit.

In his " Orain na Briogas," or song on the breeches, he said the Highlanders, with such a dress, blushed " when in presence of the fair." " Now," he exultingly exclaims, " our men appear in their beloved tartans: the coat that displays the strife of colours, but in which the carmine prevails. Gracefully flow our belted plaids, our hose reach not the knee nor obstruct the pace," &c. Duncan was appointed bard to the Highland Society, the proudest office he could hold, and he furnished it with many stirring addresses in his mother tongue at the annual meetings.

Many Mac an t-Saoirs were in the clan regiment of Stewart of Appin, in the campaign of 1745-6; but they were not out as an independent body.

The ARMORIAL BEARINGS are quarterly, first and fourth, or, an eagle displayed, gules, armed and langued sable. Second, argent, a galley, sails, furled, sable, flags, gules. Third, argent, a sinister hand couped at the wrist, fesswise, gules, holding a cross croslet fitchee, sable. Crest, a dexter hand holding a dagger in pale, proper.

The SUAICHEANTAS or badge, is that of the Mac Donalds, Fraoch gorm, common heath, *Erica Vulgaris.*

The figure which illustrates this clan, also shows how pertinaciously the Highlanders retained the form of the dress, if they were prohibited from wearing it in the manufacture of tartan. The expedients resorted to in order to evade the operation of the Prohibition Act, were ingenious, such as sewing the feilebeag between the limbs, to enable them to maintain the plea that such form was not the Highland dress. When Doctor Johnson visited the Isle of Skye, he was conveyed to Rasa in the boat of Malcom Mac Leod, a gentleman who had been Captain in the army of Prince Charles, and he is described as wearing a kilt of the colour here shown, the dye of which is procured from a native vegetable substance.

CLANN AN TOSAICH—THE MAC INTOSHES.

IT being " the unvaried tradition of the Mac Intoshes, that their ancestor was a son of the Thane of Fife," it may only here be observed, that Tosach is a chief or leader, and, as Dr. John Mac Pherson observes, that Malcolm Ceann-mòr gave a right to those

MAC INTOSH

powerful Thanes to lead the van, the name is in this manner accounted for. Shah, the younger son, accompanying Malcom IV. who reigned 1153—65, in an expedition against the rebels of Moray, was rewarded by the lands of Petty, Breachley, &c., in the county of Inverness, was appointed constable of the castle of that name, and is therefore held to be progenitor of the Mac Intoshes. Recent investigations have, however, led to a different conclusion respecting the derivation of this race, but that they are a branch of the great Clann 'a Chattan, there can be no doubt.

In 1291, Angus, married Eva, only daughter and heiress of Dugal Phaol mac Gilli Chattan, chief of the Mac Phersons, with whom he obtained a great accession of lands in Lochaber, and a numerous addition to his own hereditary followers. It was, therefore, " natural for the clan to follow their masters, whereby the family of the Mac Intoshes were ever afterwards called Captains of Clan Chattan." The family soon became very powerful, and wisely strengthened their patriarchal influence by obtaining crown charters and other feudal documents, an advantage which many of their neighbours, to their great loss, did not possess, but the enforcement of claims founded thereon led the Mac Intoshes into frequent and sanguinary collisions with others.

The important transactions, both civil and warlike, in which the Mac Intoshes were engaged, many of them full of romantic and chivalrous interest, are too numerous to be even incidentally referred to in this place.

In 1396 occurred that very extraordinary judicial combat, on the North inch of Perth, so graphically described by Sir Walter Scott, between the Clan Chattan and Clan Dhai, and the Mac Intoshes claim the honour of their ancestors having been the Chattans here mentioned, which the Mac Phersons as stoutly maintain belongs to them. The elucidation of this point, involved as it is in considerable obscurity, would occupy more space than can be here afforded.

The Mac Intoshes joined the army of Donald of the Isles, and fought with their wonted bravery at the sanguinary battle of Harlaw, 1411, in which his mighty army was repulsed.

Between the Earls of Huntly and Moray, the Mac Intoshes were often hard bestead, and they were forced, in 1624, as we find by an old chronicler, to take the field against the latter "upon foot, with swords, bows, arrows, targets, hagbuts, pistols, and other Highland arms;" this they did for their own protection, but they were frequently obliged to act offensively against the Camerons and the Mac Donalds of Keppach, who disputed their right to lands in Lochaber, and many desperate skirmishes took place between them.

The latter clan, who really had no feudal right to the property, refused to pay rent for it, and, to compel them, Mac Intosh took up arms, and, obtaining the assistance of a company of regular troops, the battle of Maol Rua', described under the sketch of the Mac Donalds of Keppach, took place, 1688, in which the lawless tenants were victorious! The contentions with their neighbours and kinsmen, the Mac Phersons, were scarcely less unsatisfactory to Clann an Tosaich; but the most disastrous quarrel in which they were engaged was with the Gordons. Their chief the Earl of Huntly, received a commission to subdue Lachlan Mac Intosh, a service which he executed with great vigour and relentless severity, for he put 300 of

the clan to death at one time! In the absence of Huntly, Lachlan presented himself at the castle of Strathbogie, and humbly supplicated the countess to intercede in his behalf; but the lady, not less stern than her lord, ordered the unfortunate chief to be forthwith beheaded! Tradition, which so often throws a mystery and horror over remote events, represents the countess as desiring Lachlan to lay his head on a table, as a token of his entire submission, when, seizing a knife, with her own hand, she cut off his head!

In Lachlan, who died 1731, without issue, the male line of William, the fifteenth chief, became extinct, and no male issue existing of his second son, William, the grandson of Angus the third, received the honours and estate. In 1741, he died, and was succeeded by Angus his brother, who married Anne, daughter of Farquharson of Invercauld. This lady acted the heroine in 1745. Angus was appointed to one of the three new companies in Lord Loudon's Highlanders, raised in the beginning of that year, and Lady Mac Intosh traversed the country in male attire, and enlisted, in a very short time, by her single exertions, every one of the hundred men required for a captaincy, except three! When the Prince landed, she was more active, if possible, in his favour, and although Mac Intosh was absent, and in the service of Government, she raised two battalions of the clan, and put them under the able command of Mac Gillivray of Dunmaglas, chief of that subdivision of Clan Chattan. It is well known with what bravery these men behaved at Culloden. It was their division which made that irresistible onset with sword and target, by which two companies of Burrel's regiment were at once annihilated, and those of several others broken up. Mortal men, however resolute, could not force their way through a barrier of three lines of well appointed troops, exposed to a murderous fire in front and both flanks, and the Mac Intoshes were compelled to retire from the hopeless contest, after the loss of a great number of men. On this bloody field they left their gallant colonel, Major Gillies Mac Bean, and several other officers, of whom some interesting particulars will be found in Numbers I. and XVII.

The clan had been out in 1715, and the division of King James's army, which so gallantly pushed into England, was under the command of Brigadier Mac Intosh, of Borlum. When they were obliged to surrender at Preston, the chief gave up his sword to an officer of the name of Graham, on condition that, if he escaped with his life, it should be returned to him, having been a present from Viscount Dundee, in the war of 1689. Mac Intosh was pardoned, but this officer forgot his promise. His regiment being sent, several years afterwards, to Fort Augustus, when Mac Intosh was dead, his successor required the holder of this heir-loom either to give up the sword, or fight him for its possession, when it was at once restored. It is a goodly weapon, the blade well-tempered, with a silver-hilt, on which is engraved the coat armour of Dundee. This is not the only sword preserved by this family. Another finely finished Clai' mòr was presented to Sir Lachlan, then chief, by King Charles I. before he came to the throne. These two were always laid across the coffins of deceased chiefs, whose funerals were conducted with a pomp suitable to their rank and popularity.

When Lachlan, the nineteenth chief, died, his body was laid in state from the 9th of December to the 18th of January, 1704, and

2,000 foot of his own clan attended his remains to the family vault at Petty. The number of the Farquharsons and Mac Phersons, who are branches of the Clan na Chattan, who followed, is not given in the document we have consulted, but Keppach was present with 220 foot, and there were 200 horsemen, the whole cavalcade being marshalled according to a fixed rule of precedency. The coffin was carried on "the spokes," a frame-work, or bier, which allows six or more to bear it up—the pipers preceded, with black flags to their pipes, and women followed, singing loud and wildly the saddening Coronach. Lachlan, this chief's successor, lay six weeks in state at the castle of Dalcross, where he died, and a much larger assemblage attended his funeral, the expense attending which amounted to £700 sterling. When Sir Eneas Mac Intosh, another worthy chief, died in 1823, six pipers preceded the corpse, playing the heart-touching Lament.

The chief seat of The Mac Intosh, is Moyhall, near Inverness. The original castle stood in an island in Lochmoy; but it has long been abandoned for a more commodious mansion. The barony was first obtained about 1340, by William, seventh chief.

The ARMORIAL BEARINGS of the Mac Intosh are—Quarterly: first, or, a lion rampant gules, as descended from Mac Duff; second, argent, a dexter hand couped, fesswise grasping a man's heart, pale-wise, gules; third, azure, a boar's head couped, or, for Gordon of Lochinvar; fourth, a lymphad, oars erect in saltire, sable, for Clan Chattan. Crest, a cat salient, proper. Supporters, two cats, proper. Motto, "Touch not the cat bot a glove."

The SUAICHEANTAS of this clan is Lus nam braoileag, Red whortle berry, *Vaccinium vitis idœa.*

It is to be observed that many are of opinion the box tree is the proper badge, but the mistake arose from the circumstance of those employed in recruiting in the French and American wars mounting sprigs of that shrub in their bonnets; its leaf is much like the whortle, and it could be more easily procured in town.

The CATH-GHAIRM, or rallying cry, is Loch Moidh, pronounced Moy—the lake of meeting.

The PIOBAIREACHD—Cu'a' Mhic an Tosaich, or Mac Intoshes' Lament, is one of the most touching of that species of music, and is a great favourite of the pipers.

In 1715 this clan had 1,500 men in arms, but in 1745 scarcely one half that number took the field.

The Mac Intosh, who is one of the most active and public-spirited proprietors of the north, has a variety of relics of the Rebellions, among which are the plaid, and several other articles, which belonged to the unfortunate Prince Charles Stewart; and his charter chest is full of important deeds and documents, interesting in the history of his own clan and of the North Highlands. In this work it is not possible to give any list of the gentlemen of this name, who have distinguished themselves in the civil and military history of their country, or contributed to science and literature. The late Sir James Mac Intosh alone is an honour to any clan.

The figure illustrative of the Clann an Tosaich is that of a gentleman in the Highland court dress of the beginning of last century, as represented in old prints, when the wig gave an air of gravity even to the young. The velvet coat and sword belt are richly ornamented with gold lace and embroidery. The Breacan is belted, plaid and kilt forming one large piece of tartan, the loose ends of which cover the sporan, or purse, and most part of the bidag, or dirk. The hose are of the same pattern as the plaid, and made of the same material, as we have seen in a pair belonging to old Sir Eneas, above mentioned.

There is a beautiful pattern, displaying a variety of colours, which is called the chief's full dress tartan—these illustrations represent that worn by the clan as their appropriate recognisance.

CLANN IMHOIR—THE MAC IVORS.

THIS clan trace their lineage as far back as the time of Malcolm IV., who reigned from 1153 to 1165.

Ivor, the progenitor, is represented in a manuscript of the family, as son of Duncan, Lord of Lochow, who flourished in the above period, so that the clan was a branch of the great Siol Diarmid or race of Campbell; and they appear to have acknowledged their dependance upon that powerful clan until the year 1564, when Gille

Easpuig, fifth Earl, made a formal resignation of all claim which he might have as chief paramount. By this deed, the Earl relinquishes for ever, to his cousin, Ivor Mac Ivor, and his successors, of "his awin frie motife, uncompellit, and for special cause and favors," all "ryght, title, and kyndnes quhatsumever, we, or our predecessoris had, has, or in any manner of way may claim, of the calpis aucht and wont to come to our house of the surname of Mac Ever, with power to use, uplift, intromit, and uptak the said calpis to thair awn utilitie and profite, and to dispone thairupon as thay sall think expedient, as anie uther freehalder, and as we wes wont to do of before, providing yat we haif the said Ever's calpe;" and by the title deeds of their estates they were bound to use the name of Mac Ivor. The calp here alluded to, was a horse, cow, or ox, which had belonged to a deceased clansman, and was given to the chief on his death. The reservation seems to have been made as an acknowledgment of Argyle's Earldom.

The original lands of this clan were Lergachonzie, Asnish, and others in Cowal; but they subsequently made great accesssions to their original property, and they spread out into many families of respectability, not only in Argyleshire, but in Caithness, Invernessshire, the Lewes, &c. Those who settled in Lochaber, went under the name of Mac Glasrichs, and were in the following of Mac Donald of Keppach, with whom they went out in the cause of Prince Charles, 1745-6. This small but brave clan received their designation from their progenitors in Argyle, who were often distinguished as Clann Imhoir Glasrich, from a district in Argyle. In the strong spirit of clanship they insisted, at the battle of Culloden, on being drawn up as a separate body, not being of the lineage of Clan Donald, and having officers of their own tribe. When the army was drawn up on that field of carnage, not forgetful of their origin, they refused to be placed in such position as that they should have to engage the Argyle militia, with whom they carried the same colours and wore their appropriate tartan.

The Mac Ivors were great favourites of the house of Argyle, from whom they held several posts of trust and honour, as the Keeping of the castle of Inverary, &c. When the ninth Earl was involved in some civil commotions, Ivor Mac Ivor promptly joined his standard with one hundred men of his clan, and when forfeited, on his return from Holland, Ivor, who had again joined him, shared his fate. After the revolution, when the Earl's forfeiture was rescinded, Mac Ivor recovered his estates from Earl Archibald; but the condition which his patron imposed upon him for this favour, was, that his son Duncan, and his heirs, should adopt the surname of Campbell, and quarter the arms of that name with his own, whereas they had previously borne that of Mac Ivor only.

Gille Easpuig bàn Mac Ivor, who lived in the middle of the seventeeth century, had only one daughter, who married Campbell of Barchbeyan, ancestor of Campbell of Craignish, and to her he gave the lands of Lergachonzie, and others, as her dowrie; after which the chief gave up that title, and the Mac Ivors were ever after distinguished as of Ashnish, another part of their property. Having no male issue, he resigned the estates in favour of his cousin, " a man of remarkable courage and intrepidity." He was heir-male to Duncan Mac Ivor of Sronshiarai', and by his succession the above family, those of Lergachonzie and of Pennymòr, were united. Duncan, the eighth chief, who lived in the beginning of the eighteenth century, distinguished himself by well-directed exertions to " civilize" the Highlanders. He married a daughter of Mac Alasdair of Loup; and the second son, who became his successor, married Catherine, daughter of Campbell, the captain of Dunstafnage castle. Angus, his son and heir, a man who is still spoken of with great respect, had by

Elizabeth, daughter of Mac Lachlan of Craigentarv, six sons, who all attained honourable positions in life, and four daughters, who were respectably married, and left issue. Robert Campbell, Esq. of Ashnish, eldest son and heir, who became an advocate of repute in the Court of Session, married a daughter of Mail of Maghide, in the county of Lancaster, in 1769, and, having but one daughter, the family became extinct in that line.

The Mac Ivors were hereditary crowners within a certain district; and latterly the chief seats were at Lochgair, on the side of Lochfine, and at Ashnish, on Loch Mealfort, in the county of Argyle.

The ARMORIAL BEARINGS are—Quarterly, first grand quarter, counterquartered first and fourth, gyrony of eight, or and sable, for Campbell; second argent, a dexter hand couped in fesse, grasping a dagger in pale, gules; third argent, a galley, sails furled and oars in action, sable. Second grand quarter, quarterly or and gules, over all a bend sable. Supporters, two leopards proper, collared azure, with chains passing betwixt their fore legs and reflected over their backs, or. Crest, a boar's head couped, or. " Motto, " Nunquam obliviscar."

The SUAICHEANTAS, was no doubt always that of the Campbells. All branches of a clan carried the same badge as a general mode of recognition and token of common descent; whereas the tartan might be different, and was usually dissimilar, for the very purpose of preventing mistakes as to who parties might be, when not engaged in any joint enterprise. It was common, likewise, for families to have hereditary patterns, in which they dressed when engaged in their own domestic and social employments; but these must not be confounded or allowed to rank with the regular clan tartans.

The figure is dressed in the long tunic, or coat, which was often thickly quilted, and is so frequently seen on the monumental effigies of Highland chiefs in the burial grounds throughout the country. In a baldrick, carried twice round the body, is suspended the clai'mor, of an old fashion, and he is also armed with the sleag, a short spear, or javelin, provided with the brazen ball, or cnapstarra, which, it has been before observed, was described by Dio, as being in use among the Caledonians in the second century. By means of a pebble, or pieces of metal, it made a rattling noise. It is to be observed that two were usually carried, which at times they used as missiles, being recovered by means of a thong, as shown in the figure of Mac Innes. The sgiath, or shield, is one according to primitive formation, but it was used at later periods, this having been painted from a genuine specimen. It was held by a grasp only, a method which admitted of a greater range, and was consequently of more utility than if confined to the elbow. The hood was a usual head-dress of the warriors of old, and was composed as the fancy of the wearer might suggest.

MAC IVOR

SIOL MHORGAN NO CLANN AODH—
THE MACKAYS.

THE origin of this clan cannot be satisfactorily discovered, but traditionary notices have been collected which carries its descent to the aboriginal Gaëlic inhabitants. The Norwegian Sagas mention their reputed ancestor as an Iarl, a norse term which would be used instead of the Celtic Maormòr, applied to a person of great power and dignity, who had the government of a district. Several Scottish writers account this clan a branch of the Forbeses, with whom there is certainly a similarity of badge and armorial bearings.

Morgan, son of Magnus, or Ma'nus, the undoubted ancestor of the Mackays, flourished from 1315 to 1325, and from him the clan has been called Siol Mhorgan, i. e. the race or offspring of Morgan. Donald, his son, married a daughter of Mac Nial of Gigha, and left a son named Aodh, a word so peculiarly Celtic as to have greatly puzzled orthographers, who anciently, were accustomed to use the letter Y as best indicating the sound; but Aodh, when occurring as a christian name, is, from some fancied resemblance, transformed into Hugh. It is from his son, Donald Mac Aoidh, that the clan has acquired the patronymic Mackay according to the present mode of spelling. Angus dubh, or dark complexioned, is the first chief mentioned in written record; he opposed Donald of the Isles when marching towards the South of Scotland in prosecution of his claim to the Earldom of Ross, and in the vain endeavour to arrest his progress at Dingwall, Mackay was defeated and taken prisoner, but, after a short confinement, he was released and the Lord of the Isles sought his alliance by giving him his daughter Elizabeth in marriage, with various lands, by charter 1415. In this document he is called "Angusis Eyg de Strathnaver," which was then the chief seat, but subsequently the whole property got the general appellation of the Rea country.

The Mackays were at this time very powerful, and Angus du', who had a following of 4,000 men, kept that part of the kingdom in agitation with frequent military expeditions. King James I., coming to Inverness resolved to curb so powerful a subject, and contrived to arrest the refractory chief and his four sons, one of whom was accepted as a hostage for the peaceable conduct of his father who was then liberated; but next year, 1427, he was treacherously killed when searching for the bodies of some relations who had fallen in a desperate clan battle near his castle of Tong.

The Mackays were involved in almost continual disputes with their neighbours, and the most afflicting harriships and bloodshed occurred on both sides. They were too powerful and jealous to brook aggression or insult from the Earls of Sutherland and Caithness, who were very ambitious to elivate themselves, and depress this indomitable clan. The inhabitants of Caithness under one or another leader, were prone to make inroads upon the Rea country; and it may give an idea of the state of vigilance in which the people must have been kept by their enemies, to mention that, besides petty slaughters, they fought ten pitched battles from the field of Tuttum-tarmhich, in 1406, to that of Gar-uarrai', in 1555.

The Mackays were early and zealous promoters of the reformation; and Donald who was chief in the beginning of the 17th century, raised a body of 3,000 men of his own clan, the Gunns, Munros, Sinclairs, and others, to battle for the Protestant cause; fifteen hundred of these he selected, and sent under the command of Col. Robert Munro, to the assistance of the king of Bohemia; but on his death, which soon after took place, they entered the service of Gustavus, king of Sweden, and performed such deeds of valour as drew forth the frequent and warm applause of that heroic monarch and his general officers.[*] Donald subsequently went over himself with a reinforcement, and on his return, after the death of Gustavus, he became of great service to Charles I., and, as a reward for his loyalty, he was raised to the peerage by the title of "Lord Reay."

Although thus ennobled by the Stewarts, the Mackays strenuously contended for the protestant succession, and it was Hugh Mackay of Scourie who commanded the troops of William of Orange against the Highlanders under Dundee at Killiecrankie, in 1689. In 1715 they were also in arms for King George I., and were of great service in keeping the adverse clans in check, and preserving the castle and town of Inverness from the adherents of King James. In 1745 they were equally active on the same side, having 800 men under arms, and gave much annoyance to those around them who were favourable to the cause of Prince Charles.

In 1795 the Reay Fencible regiment, or Mackay Highlanders, were embodied, and their services being extended to Ireland, they were hotly engaged with the rebels, whose signal defeat at the hill of Tara was accomplished by this regiment in gallant style.

Mackay was the last Highland chief who held his lands, as allodial territory, for it was not until the year 1499 that a feudal charter was thought necessary to secure its possession.

The present Right Hon. Eric, Lord Reay, leaving no male issue, the chiefship will devolve on the elder of his two brothers, the Hon. Major Alexander Mackay, or his surviving son; failing these, the title would go to a family in Holland. Mackay, of Auchness, is accounted chief presumptive, on failure of the direct line.

The COAT ARMOUR is az. a chevron arg. charged with a *rea* buck's head in point, and two hands grasping dirks, inclined towards it, all proper. Crest, a right hand holding a dagger in pale, proper.

* An interesting account of "Munroe's Expedition with the Scots regiment, Mac Keyes," was published in folio, 1637,—now a very scarce work.

MACKAY

Supporters, two soldiers as sentinels, in the dress worn by the clan regiment in the great civil war. Motto, "Manu forte."

The SUAICHEANTAS, or Badge, is Bealuidh, Broom, *Spartium Scorparium*.

The PIOBARIEACHDAN are Brattach bhan Chlann Aoidh, or the Mackay's white banner, which is the salute. Donald Duaghal Mhic Aoidh, Iseabel Nic Aoidh, Ban-tighearn Mhic Aoidh and Cumhadh Strath h-Alladail, are laments for the chief, his lady, his daughter, and Mackay of Strath Alladail.

The figure wears a flat bonnet, on which the clan badge is displayed, and an eagle's feather. The doublet, or jacket, is of a strong cloth formerly much worn, to which a dull red colour was imparted by a native dye. This is the first instance in which the Feilebeag is given without a plaid, a manner of dressing by no means uncommon; indeed, a simple covering for the lower portion of the body, by wrapping around the lions a piece of some material, was evidently the primitive garb of all nations, and the kilt is, therefore, the oldest, as it is the most characteristic relic of the Highland costume. The tartan is that recognized as peculiar to the Clan Aodh; the hose and garters do not differ from many already introduced; the brogs are similar in form to those painted in the figure, illustrative of the Chisholms, but are molach or of hide, from which the hair is not removed; the sword and target are of the forms in common use among the Highlanders.

CLANN CHOINNICH,—THE MACKENZIES.

THE MACKENZIES have been accustomed to believe themselves of Irish extraction, according to a tradition formed in the age of corrupted bardism, which makes the predecessor of this numerous and most respectable clan to be Cailean, or Colin, son of Fitzgerald, Earl of Desmond. This nobleman assisting king Alexander III. at the battle of Largs against the Norwegians in 1263, was rewarded, according to this account, by the lands of Kintail in Wester Ross, where he married a daughter of Coinneach Maonach, or Kenneth Matheson, and settled in the stronghold of Ellandonan; in proof of which origin, a charter of the above monarch is adduced, granted "Colino Hiberno." This document is, however, pronounced a forgery by our best antiquaries, but, were it genuine, it would not be any authority for an Irish origin, as the native Gaël received at that time equally the appellations Hiberni and Hibernienses. Clarke, in his observations upon the touching "Elegy on Du'choil," says, that this generous chief is accounted ancestor of the Mackenzies; it is more satisfactory to turn to Cailean òg mhic Chailean na h-airde, progenitor of the Earls of Ross, from whom it would appear they are descended.[*] We find Murdach du' Mac Choinneach, Chinntail, who was certainly ancestor of all the branches of this distinguished clan, receiving in 1362 a charter from David II.

In 1427 James I. made a progress to Inverness with the view to secure a more peaceful rule among his Highland subjects, and he there held a Parliament, and took vigorous steps to bring the most turbulent chiefs and others to punishment. On this occasion Mac Coinneach was arrested, and he is then said to have commanded a force of 2000 men.

The powerful Lord of the Isles resigned the Earldom of Ross in 1477, when the Clan Donald commenced a system of continued marauding on the mainland, and, under the command of Alastair Mac Gillieaspuig, having marched down on the territories of Clann Choinnich, were met by a body of them on the banks of the Conan, where the bloody encounter celebrated as Blàr na Pairc, took place, and the Mac Donalds were defeated with great carnage. This battle secured the independence of the Mackenzies, who rose very rapidly in importance from that time. An unavoidable consequence of their extensive acquisitions was involvement in desperate feuds with several clans, but, their termination being favourable, they only served to increase the power of the Mackenzies. The most stubborn of those who withstood this progress of aggrandizement, were the Mac Donalds, but, armed with letters of fire and sword, "the clan Chenzie did invade Glengarrie, anno 1602," took and blew up his castle of Sron Carron, assaulted and slew his eldest son, but were finally content to terminate hostilities with so troublesome an enemy, in an agreement whereby they obtained another accession of territory.

The lands of Strath Braan, and other parts of Easter Ross, where the seat of the chief was latterly established, appear to have been acquired in the time of king James IV. Kenneth, the twelfth chief in the genealogical history, was created Lord Kintail in 1609, and his son Colin was raised by patent, December 3, 1623, to the dignity of Earl of Seaforth.

The Mackenzies were firm supporters of Charles I. Earl William having ardently engaged in the rebellion of 1715, was attainted but made his escape to the continent. Although exiled, and his

[*] Skene, "On the Origin, &c. of the Highlanders."

MACKENZIE

property forfeited, his followers gave a striking example of the strength of clannish attachment by remitting to France the amount of rental, as if their chief were still in possession of the lands, conveying it to Edinburgh under a guard of 400 armed men. Sanguine in the power and feeling of the Highlanders, he landed with a body of Spaniards at Glensheal in 1719, to battle for the same cause, but the expedition was frustrated by a speedy defeat.

In 1725 Marshal Wade being commissioned to disarm the Highlanders, commenced by summoning the Mackenzies in eighteen parishes as having been the chief promoters of the different "risings," and he reports the manner in which he accomplished his object. They professed their willingness to submit, but considered that it would be incompatible with their honour, as having been the chief leaders in the war, to surrender in presence of any other clan. Their wish was acceded to, and having selected Braan Castle as the most suitable place for the transaction, the Marshal proceeded thither with 200 soldiers, when the Mackenzies "marched in good order through the great avenue, and one after another laid down their arms in the court yard, in great quiet and decency, amounting to 784 of the several pieces mentioned in the Act."

George I. was pleased to modify the sentence of forfeiture, and permit Seaforth to take and inherit real and personal estates, when he attached himself to the Hanoverian interest, and his son, Lord Fortrose, engaged with great zeal in favour of government during the troublous years 1745-6. His son Kenneth, eighteenth chief, was created Earl of Seaforth in the peerage of Ireland in 1771, but dying without male issue the titles became extinct, and the estates were purchased by his cousin Colonel Thomas Mackenzie Humberstone, a distinguished officer, who fell in India at an early age, when his only brother, Francis, succeeded to the estates in 1783, and died in 1811.

His son, the late Hon. Stewart Mackenzie, died in 1841, leaving the Hon. Keith Stewart Mackenzie, who has distinguished himself as an officer in India, and is author of an interesting narrative of the second campaign in China.

In 1831, Mackenzie, of Allangrange, was returned as male representative of the chiefs, but we have been given to understand that the birth of a son has been discovered, in the leabhar Comerach, an old MS. which, if properly authenticated, will give Captain William Mackenzie, of Gruinard, a claim to this honour.

In the year 1704, when an invasion on behalf of the Stewarts was intended to be made, the force which the Mackenzies offered to bring out was 1200; in 1715, they had 3000 under arms; and in 1745 they had 2500. Lord Seaforth, in 1777, made government an offer to raise a body of Highlanders, and receiving letters of service for that purpose, 1300 men were speedily enrolled, and the regiment was numbered 78, but they are now the 72nd. In the years 1793 and 1804, two other battalions were raised, which were fixed as the 78th, and are well known as the Ross-shire Buffs, from the colour of their facings. In the above year Lord Mac Leod, son of the attainted Earl of Cromarty, also raised two battalions amounting to 2,200 men, and thus, "without money or credit, except that of a long remembered and respected name, he attained command over a body of hardy and devoted followers." These regiments have distinguished themselves for their exemplary conduct and bravery in various parts of the world,

and their services have been ably recorded by the late general Stewart, who, for sometime, bore a commission in the 78th.

The ARMORIAL BEARINGS are azure, a stag's head cabossed, or. Crest, on a wreath, a mountain inflamed, proper. Supporters, two savage men, wreathed about the loins and head with laurel, each holding in his exterior hand a bâton, or club, erect and inflamed, all proper. Motto, "Luceo non uro."

The SUAICHEANTAS, or Badge, is Cuilf hion, Holly.

The SLOIDH-GHAIRM, or war shout, "Tullach Ard," a mountain on which the beacon fire was lighted.

Several PIOBAIREACHDS are appropriate to this clan. There are the Salutes to Seaforth, and Fear Comerach, or Applecross, and Laments for the chief and Sir Eachuin of Gairloch, &c.

Every clan had particular pieces of music, some of very high antiquity, the style of composition being quite peculiar to the Gaël, and they served to direct their warlike proceedings. In the "Scottish Gaël" will be found a list of the military pieces or music of the Mackenzies, and being curious, as shewing the use of the bagpipes in regulating the evolutions of a Highland army, it is deemed an appropriate addition to this sketch of the clan.

Daybreak . . .	Surachan.
Cruinneacha', gathering or turn out .	Tullach Ard.
Salute when the Chief appears on the field	Failte mhic Choinneach.
Slow march . . .	An Cuilf hionn.
Quick step . . .	Caisteal Donan.
Charge	Caber feidh.
Stimulus during the engagement .	Blàr Sron.
Coronach played at funerals . .	Cumha' mhic Choinneach.
Sunset	Suibhal Clann Choinnich.
Tattoo	Ceann drochait Aluinn.
Warning half an hour before dinner .	Blar Ghlinn Seill.
During Dinner . . .	Cath Sleibh an t' Shiora.

The 73rd regiment, now the 71st, having been raised by Lord Mac Leod, son of Mackenzie, Earl of Cromarty, they were dressed in the Mackenzie tartan, and this circumstance has led many to believe that the Mac Leod Highlanders wore the Mac Leod tartan.

There are seven Baronets of this clan, and, with the exception of one, their possessions are all in Ross:—Gairloch, who is the nearest Cadet; Tarbat; Kilcoy; Coul; Scatwell; Fairburn, and Delvine in Perthshire. Besides these are many families of ancient descent and respectability, such as Applecross, Suddie, Hilton, &c., &c. Easter Ross is studded with the old baronial castles and modern seats of gentlemen of this name.

The sketch represents a jacobite fugitive, who has escaped from the field of Cullòden, and still retains in his bonnet the white cockade of the Stewarts, and the badge of his clan, for mounting which many of his countrymen were then transported as felons. The green jacket and red cuffs were a favourite style at that time. Hose and kilt are of the clan tartan. The waist-belt was often worn around the skirts of the jacket, as it is shewn here, passing over the long waistcoat.

The dirk represents one in Mr. Mᶜ Ian's possession, the hilt of which is rather remarkable in shape. Shoes and buckles, a late innovation on the original costume, were generally worn at the time.

This Cearnach is evidently keeping at bay some of the " Hanoverian party," indicated by the weapons which are seen bristling before him.

SLIOCHD FHIONNON, NO MAC 'IONNON—
THE MACKINNONS,

ARE of royal descent, being a branch of the great Clan Alpin; and the family historians derive them from Fingon, or Findon, grandson of Gregor, whose father was the celebrated Kenneth Mac Alpin, King of Scotland. This ancestor lived about the year 900, but the name as we understand it, is one of the most ancient among the Gaël. The old chroniclers have made Findanus of it; and the poetical imaginations of the disciples of bardism have rendered the modern appellation, Mac Ionmhuinn, the son of love!

Finan, or Finon, occurs repeatedly in the national annals: several of the name were Cludee saints, and Loceni Mac Finin was king of the Cruthens, or Picts, anno 645. The prefix, Mac, renders the initial consonant quiescent, hence Mac Fhinnon— Mac'innon.

In 1639, a court was held at Iona for the enaction of regulations which were thought necessary to repress the power of the barons of the Isles, and they not only referred to their military arms and retainers, but their style of living. Mackinnon, with others of the same rank, were ordered to "sustain and entertain three gentlemen only in their retinue," who where not to carry hagbuts, or pistols, and none, except the chief and his immediate household, were permitted to wear swords, or other armour. No chief was to keep more than one Biorlin, or galley, of sixteen or eighteen oars; and those of Mackinnon's degree were prohibited from using more than one tun of wine a year, the tenants not being allowed to buy or drink any spirits or wine whatever; and no Bards, or Seanachies, were to be entertained in the houses of gentlemen! The sturdy chiefs of the isles, as may be supposed, did not long submit to such rigid laws.

In troublous times it was customary for clansmen and friends to enter into "Bonds of Manrent" for the sake of mutual assistance, and with this view the following were executed:

"Forsæmeikle as we, Lauchlan Mackinnon of Strathardil, and Finlay Mac Nabb of Bowaine, happening to foregether togedder, with certain of the said Finlay's friends, in their rooms, in the laird of Glenurchy's country, and the said Lauchlan and Finlay, being come of ane house, and being of ane surname and lineage, notwithstanding the said Lauchlan and Finlay this long time bygane oversaw their awn dueties till udders, in respect of the long distance betwixt their dwelling places, quhairfore baith the saids now and in all time coming, are content to be bound and obleisit, with consent of their kyn and friends, to do all sted pleasure, assistance, and service, that lies in them ilk ane to uthers; the said Finlay acknowledging the said Lauchlan as ane kynd chieff and of ane house, and siklike the said Lauchlan to acknowledge the said Finlay Mac Nabb his friend, as his special kynsman and friend. And baith the said parties grants them faithfullie that ane surer, firm band and contract be made betwixt them, by advice of men of law; and that quhasoon, God willing, the said Lauchlan shall come, either to Sterling, Perth, or Glasgow, or any part of the lowland, quhair they may easiest meet together. And for sure keeping and performing of this present minute, baith the said Lauchlan and Finlay are content to subscribe to the same, with their hands led to the pen, at Uir, the 12th July, anno 1606, before these witnesses, James Mac Nabb, Robert Mac Nabb, Duncan dow Mac Nabb, Archibald Mac Nabb, Gibbie Mac Nabb, John Mac Dhonnell rewich, and Ewan Mackinnons, with uthers.

(Signed) LAUGHLAND, mise (i.e. myself) MAC FINGON."

In 1671, a deed was executed at Kilmorie " betwixt the honourable persons underwritten, to wit, James Mac Gregor of that ilk on the ane part, and Lauchlan Mac Fingon of Strathardill on the other part, for the special love and amitie between these persons, and condescending that they are descended lawfullie frae twa brether of auld descent, quhairfor, and for certain onerous causes moving, we faithfullie bind and obleise us and our successors, our kin, friends and followers, to serve ane anuther in all causes with our men and servants against all wha live and die, the king's highness only excepted."[*]

About the year 1400, the Mackinnons fell into misunderstanding with other clans, who were jealous of their rising influence, and on occasion of the Lord of the Isles returning to his castle of Ardtornis from hunting in Mull, while Mackinnon was unsuspiciously stepping into his galley to follow, Lachlan Mac Lean of Duart, and Eachuinn of Lochbui', basely slew him, and, disarming his followers, they hastened after the Lord of the Isles. Apprehensive of his vengeance when they had overtaken his galley, they, in desperation, took him into custody, and forced him to grant them an indemnity before he was set at liberty.

On the death of John Lord of the Isles, Mackinnon being joined by the Mac Leods and Mac Leans raised a formidable rebellion in

*Baronage, apud, Mac Gregors and Mac Nabs.

favour of Ion mòr, a younger son; but Donald, the elder, succeeded in expelling his rival, who was obliged to take refuge in Ireland. He was afterwards pardoned, but Mackinnon, as leader of the insurrection, was put to death.†

Lachlan mòr Mackinnon, who lived in the middle of the seventeenth century, was brought up at Inverarai' by the Earl of Argyle; and, having married a daughter of Mac Lean of Duart, he was induced to join that chief in a descent on the lands of his former protector, with a body of 200 men. On their approach, being recognised by the badge of pine, the Campbells were so incensed that they would give no quarter, and a sanguinary rout took place, in which the Mackinnons were fairly cut up *

These notices will serve to show the military character of this clan, who were active partizans of the gallant Montrose, and were present at the fiercely fought battle of Inverlochai,' 1645.

In 1650, the chief of the Mackinnons received letters of service to raise a regiment of his clan, of which he was, of course, appointed colonel, and, having joined the army of King Charles I., they fought with distinguished bravery at the battle of Worcester, 1651.

In 1715, 150 Mackinnons joined the Earl of Seaforth, and fought valiantly along with the Mac Donalds of Slait, at the battle of Sherramuir. for which the chief was attainted, but received a pardon 4th of January, 1727. Feeling like most others that their loyal intentions had been underrated, and their interests overlooked, Mackinnon joined the army of Prince Charles on the 13th of October, 1745, with a battalion of his clan. Their force in 1745 was estimated at 240.††

The unfortunate prince and attendants were entertained in Mackinnon's castle when travelling in disguise through Skye; and he gave the use of his own boat to carry the fugitives off the island, conducting them himself to the country of Mac Donald of Boisdale, to whom he resigned his royal charge.

The military history of this clan would have been extended had government accepted the liberal offer of the present chief, who some years ago, undertook to raise a battalion of 1,000 Highlanders, who were to serve a certain number of years in Canada, where they would have been highly useful in quelling the unfortunate disturbances in that country, and where it was intended they should settle upon allotments of land, thus adding to the strength of the colony.

Lachlan mòr, who fought at the battle of Worcester, had two sons, John, whose great grandson died in London unmarried, 1808, and Donald, who, being taken prisoner by Cromwell, went, on his release, to Antigua, where he was called Daniel by a common corruption, and married Miss Thomas, a lady of that island, by whom he left a son William, who married a daughter of Lieutenant-Governor Yeamans, also of Antigua, and died at Bath, 1767, aged seventy, leaving a son, also called William, who married a daughter of Henry Vernon, Esq., of Hilton Castle, Staffordshire. His eldest son, William, married Harriet, daughter of John Frye, Esq., of Antigua, and he left several children, the eldest of whom, William Alexander Mackinnon, M.P., &c., since the death of the above John, is the chief of the name and race of Mackinnon as great great grandson of Donald, second son of Lachlan mòr.

The possessions of the Mackinnons were extensive. They had anciently lands in Arran; and Griban in Mull was, at one time, the

chief property, in fact, great part of the Leth-iocrach, or lower half of that island, was theirs, but it was reduced to the estate of Misnish, north-west of Tobarmorie. They had, likewise, lands in the Isle of Tiree, but Strath or Strathardel in Skye was latterly the principal residence, to which were attached the Islets of Pabay and Scalpa, properties acquired partly by excambion and otherwise from the following circumstance The heir of the chief of the Mackinnons was sent from Mull to be fostered by Gillies, who then possessed Strath; this person had an only son and a nephew, who, being on a hunting expedition to Pabay, unfortunately quarrelled, and in the contest both were slain, when old Gillies, being without heirs, became attached to young Mackinnon, and left him his patrimonial estates.

The chief seats were at Earey on the property in Mull, at Kilmorie, the fine situation of which is described by Pennant the tourist, and Mackinnon Castle, in the south-eastern coast of Skye.*

The "ENSIGNS ARMORIAL," as matriculated in the Lord Lyon Court, are quarterly; 1st vert, a boar's head erased arg, holding in its mouth the shank-bone of a deer, proper, for the name of Mackinnon; 2nd azure, a castle triple-towered and embattled arg., masoned sab., windows and portcullis gules, for Mac Leod; 3rd or, a lymphad or biorlin, the oars saltirewise, sab.; 4th arg., a dexter hand couped, fesswise, holding a cross croslet, fitchee, sab., the two last for Mac Donald. Crest, a boar's head erased, holding in its mouth the shank-bone of a deer, proper. They were also accustomed to carry a man's head crowned, coupèe, proper, and guttee de sang, in commemoration of the death of King Alpin, slain in 834. Motto, "Audentes fortuna juvat."

The supporters are, on the dexter side, a lion, and on the sinister, a leopard, both proper.

The SUAICHEANTAS, or Badge, is Guithas, *pinus sylvestris*, a slip of pine tree.

The CATH-GHAIRM, or Battle-shout, "Cuimhnich bas Alpin!" Remember the death of Alpin!

The burial-place was in the far-famed Isle of Iona, where, in the chancel, is seen, on an altar tomb, the monumental effigy of Abbat Mac Fingon, who died anno 1500. In conjunction with his father, Lachlan, he erected one of those elaborately sculptured crosses still remaining in the Reilig Ouran, in the same island.

The jacket is the first specimen given of the form prevalent in the beginning of last century; a form much more consistent with the other parts of the costume than the modern style. The pattern of the hose is that worn by the military in the ca'da' or cloth.

† Donald Gregory.   *Leabhar nan Cnoc.   †† MS. in King's Library, Brit. Mus.   * Collections penes W. A. Mackinnon, Esq., M.P.

130

MACKINNON

By a traditional account of the Mac Lachlans they are descended from the Milesians who settled in Ireland, as the chronicles of that country tell us, long before the commencement of credible history, and their Scottish progenitor is said to have been one of the invaders of Kintire, under the renowned Fergus. The appellation seems to point to a Scandinavian origin, Lochlin being the name under which that country was known to the Gaël. Whichever may be the origin, no clan has a better claim to antiquity, whether their first possessions were in Lochaber, as some are of opinion, or in Argyle, where they acquired lands in Cowal by marriage with an heiress of the Clan Laomainn or Lamond.

A curious genealogical MS., written in Gaëlic, about 1450, was accidentally discovered a few years ago, in the Library of the Advocates, Edinburgh, which gives the descent of many of the Scottish clans. It derives more interest in this place, from having been written, as is supposed, by one of this clan, chiefly, I believe, from the circumstance of the Mac Lachlan pedigree being more copious and particular than the others, as well as from the family of Kilbride, cadets of the chief, having possessed an unique collection of ancient manuscripts, to which much attention was drawn, when the controversy on Ossian's poems arose, and which were eventually purchased by the Highland Society of Scotland. This manuscript derives the Mac Lachlans from the Lords of the Isles, and as a specimen of the work, of which there are extracts in the Transactions of "The Iona Club." we shall here give a translation of the Genelach' ic Lachlan oig;" a good example of a Highland pedigree. It must, at the same time, be observed, that in several cases where we have compared these genealogies with authentic charters, there is a great, if not irreconcilable discrepancy, between the names of individuals.

" Keneth, son of John, son of Lachlan, son of Gille Patrick, son of Lachlan mòr, son of Patrick, son of Gille Christ, son of Dedalan, son of Anradan, from whom are descended also the children of Niel. Caitrina, the daughter of Duncan Mac Lamain was the mother of Keneth, Patrick and Gille Easpuig, and Agais daughter of Mac Donald was mother of John, and Culusaid daughter of the Maormor of Cowal, was the mother of Lachlan oig, and the mother of Gille Patrick was daughter of Donald, son of Eiri, son of Keneth, lord of Cairge, and the daughter of Lachlan, son of Rorie, was mother of Gille Patrick." There are also several other pedigrees annexed, which appear to be those of collateral branches.

The oldest Cadets of this clan were the Mac Lachlans of Coire-uanan, in Lochaber, who dwelt in the country of the Camerons, and held for many ages, the hereditary office of Standard bearers to the lairds of Lochiel.

A story is told of one of this branch which we do not recollect having met with in any publication. A quarrel having arisen between a young man and the Camerons of Glen Nevis, he took his revenge by the slaughter of his enemy, which was accomplished in a somewhat singular manner. Glen Nevis, passing the fold where the young women were milking the cattle, he was presented, according to custom, with a draught. Mac Lachlan, who had been lying in wait for him and was celebrated for his skilful archery let fly an arrow which simultaneously split Cameron's head and the vessel which contained the milk ! Mac Lachlan instantly fled, and was obliged to wander through the highlands and isles, for many years, in constant dred of being captured or slain by his enemies. During this time it was his practice to sleep in caves, or the least accessible mountains, and even when in the shelter of a house, he always rested his head on his naked dirk, a weapon peculiarly convenient in case of sudden or close attack. He is represented as having been the last of his family, and perhaps was therefore more reckless of his life ; however, in process of time, he ventured to revisit his native hills, and as he passed by the house of Glen Nevis he observed, by looking through an open window, a very fine gun, which he resolved to appropriate to himself. A broad ditch intervened between him and the building, but being remarkably athletic, he cleared it at a bound, and silently entering, he seized the gun—at the moment, when he was retreating by the window, Glen Nevis entered the room, and pouncing on the depredator, seized him by the arm with an iron grasp, exclaiming, "You are now in the talons of the mountain eagle, and a death struggle alone could disengage them !" A minute's portentous pause ensued, when Mac Lachlan, with unsuspected dexterity, stabbed Cameron with his dirk, and then, relieved from his hold, leaped across the ditch, and escaped ! The gun, a very curious piece, is still preserved by Glen Nevis.

The residence of the chief of this clan is Castle Lachlan, in Straith Lachlan, Argyleshire, an elegant building situated near the old tower, in the centre of the estate, which is about eleven miles in length by about one and a half in breadth, stretching along the eastern side of Loch Fyne.

The number of men which the chief of this clan brought to the field in 1745, amounted to 300.

The ARMORIAL BEARINGS are quarterly. First, or, a lion rampant, gules. Second, arg. a dexter hand couped in fess, hold-

MAC LACHLAN

ing a croslet pattee, in pale gules. Third, or, a galley, oars in saltire, sable, in a sea, proper. Fourth, arg. in base, in sea vert a salmon naiant proper. Supporters, two roebucks proper. Motto, " Fortis et fidus."

The SUAICHEANTAS, or badge, is, Faochag, no Gillefruinbrinn, Lesser Periwinkle, *Pervinca major.*

The PIOBAIREACHD or Mac Lachlan's Salute, a very musical and animated composition, is better known as " Moladh Mhairi," or, the praise of Mary.

The late Ewen Mac Lachlan, master of the grammar school of old Aberdeen, deserves to be mentioned as a poet of great excellence. He translated several of the books of Homer and other pieces, as well as composed original poems in his native language, and it is observable that his English and classic writings, although much admired, are deemed inferior to his Gaëlic compositions, thus, perhaps, proving the superior adaption of that language for poetry.

The figure is that of a young man in the act of parrying an attack by his sword and target. He wears a deer skin jacket or rather waistcoat, being in his shirt sleeves. The hose are of a different tartan from the clan pattern as was often the case. The brogs are similar to old examples given in former figures—the purse, dirk, target, and broadsword, are also from old specimens of armour. The badge is fixed in the bonnet by the appropriate dealg or pin, which was formed of the shank bone of a deer's leg.

CLANN LABHRAINN—THE MAC LAURINS.

THE Mac Laurins afford an instance of a clan of very ancient descent, having become of inconsiderable importance, compared with other more fortunate tribes. There is a traditional origin given of the Mac Laurins, with reference to a mermaid, which is among the most puerile of the many similar legends; but it was sufficient to induce the heralds to assign armorial bearings, allusive to the fancied occurrence, when the eminent Lord Dreghorn, who claimed the chiefship, applied, in 1781, for matriculation of these family honours in the Lyon College of Arms.

Loarn or Laurin, one of the sons of Erc, who settled in Argyle, 503, acquired that district, which from him is said to have obtained its name. This appellation, however spelt, is invariably pronounced Lawrin, by the Gaël; and there can be no reasonable doubt that it is a modification of Lawrence, the name of the saint who suffered martyrdom under Valerian, 261; its Gaëlic orthography is Labhrainn, the bh being quiescent.

In 843, Kenneth Mac Alpin, chief of the posterity of the above brothers and their followers, overthrew the southern Picts, took possession of their territories, and transferred the seat of Government to their capital, Abernethie, in Strathearn, county of Perth, where he was crowned King of all Scotland.

It was the well-known practice for conquerors to apportion the lands they acquired among their victorious followers; and it is somewhat stronger than assumption to say, that the chief of the tribe of Laurin, of Argyle, received a due share. Balquhidder and Strathearn has ever been known as "the country" of the Clan Laurin, and the identity of the appellation as demonstrative of a common origin, is corroborated by the tradition that three brothers from Argyle had this territory assigned to them; the eldest occupying Auchleskine, in the centre, the second the Bruach, at the west, and the third the Stank, at the extreme east of the district.

This tradition is borne out by an observance, jealously regarded to the present day; the burial places of the three branches being marked out in the kirkyard, from west to east, according to the above location! In the descent submitted to the Lyon court of arms, by Lord Dreghorn, he traces his ancestry through Donald Mac Laurin, to the ancient proprietors of the island of Tiree, in the county of Argyle; and it is certain that a friendship, grounded on a conviction of common descent, always subsisted between those of the name in the west, and the Clan Laurin of Perthshire.

The early history of the Seneschals and Earls of Strathearn, stretches too far back to be known; but there can be no doubt that they were the descendants of those settled in that district by Mac Alpin. In the reign of King David I. Malise, then Earl, led the " Lavernani " to the battle of the Standard, in 1138. Lord Hailes, so accurate and learned, in his annals of Scotland says, that these could have been no other than the clan Laurin, which must have comprehended both divisions, Argyle not being then a separate county; and hence they would form a body sufficient to deserve a special notice from the historian Aldred.

In the Roll of submission to Edward I, of England, which so many of the nobles of Scotland were compelled to sign, 1296, we find Maurice of Tiree, Conan of Balquhidder, and Laurin of Ardveche, in Strathearn, who are presumed by competent authority, to have been cadets of the Earl of Strathearn.

This Earldom underwent many changes, until it vested in the crown, 1370, when the Mac Laurins were reduced from the condition of proprietors to that of " kyndly " or perpetual tenants. In 1508, it was thought expedient that this celtic holding should be changed, and the lands set in feu " for increase of policie, and augmentation of the King's rental; " but it was justly considered that as they had punctually discharged what was exacted, and from " aye

MAC LAURIN

to aye payed compositions to the exchequer at the entry of heirs, built houses, planted yairds, parks, woods, and other policie, serving thair prince at all tymes, as at Bannockburn with King James III., Flodden with King James IV., and after at Pinky, whither it is agreeable to justice that so many honest gentlemen should be ruined altogether in thair estates, if that Earldome be again separated and evicted from the crown!" The farms of Invernentie and Craigruie were, however, at no distant period, the absolute property of persons of the name of Mac Laurin.

In the Roll of the Clans, who had captains, chiefs, and chieftains, " quhome on thai depend," drawn up in 1587, the " Clanlawren" appear, thus proving their independence. In another list, dated 1594, they again appear in a similar position.

Besides their services in the national wars, the Mac Laurins were engaged in many feuds and encounters which the former state of Celtic society rendered inevitable, and some notice of a few of these will farther show the former status of the clan.

One of the Mac Laurins who was an " innocent," or of weak intellect, having gone to a fair, held at Kilmahog, a place westward of Callendar, one of the Lenie Buchanans, a neighbouring clan passing along, struck Mac Laurin on the cheek with a salmon he was carrying, and knocked off his bonnet. The reply to this insult was, that it dare not be repeated " latha fheill aon'ais," or on the fair day of Angus, in Balquhidder, which is held near Auchleskine, an observation which met a contemptuous rejoinder. The fair day arrived, when the Mac Laurins, as usual, attended in considerable numbers. Early in the morning, the people of Auchleskine observed a great body of men, who had come in sight at Ruskachan, in Strathire, and expressing wonder as to whom they might be, the idiot for the first time, related his treatment at the fair of Kilmahog, and said these were the Buchanans come to clear the field of the Mac Laurins. They were thus taken by surprise; but the crois tara,' or warning cross, was immediately sent through the country, and every man ran to the muster. The Buchanans drew near, and were met at Beannachd Ao'nais, east of Auchleskine, by the Mac Laurins, who commenced the battle, although all their force had not arrived. They fought with great resolution, and their friends were coming to their aid from all quarters, but the Lenies pressed on, and drove the clan Laurin off the field, at least a mile. On the place where the manse now stands, they rallied, for a man, having observed his son cut down, shouting the war cry, he turned on the advancing foe with such fury, spreading death around with his Clai'mòr, that his clansmen, fired with the miri-cath, or madness of battle, rushed desperately after him. So furious an assault was irresistible, and the Buchanans were almost cut off; those who survived sought for escape by plunging into the river Balvie, at a deep pool, which has since been called the Linn nan seicachan. Of these, two only got over, but were pursued by the Mac Laurins, when one was slain at Gartnafuaran, and the other fell at the point, which from him, has since been known as Sron Lainie. These circumstances are detailed in Balquhidder with the particularity of oral tradition, and the period when they occurred is said to be the reign of the Alexanders, from 1106 to 1285.

John Stewart, third Lord Lorn, had an illegitimate son, Dugal,

by a lady of the Mac Laurins of Perthshire. According to feudal law, this son was incapable of succeeding to his paternal estates, which accordingly went by the entail to his uncle Walter. Dugal is the ancestor of the Stewarts of Appin, and on the death of his father, in 1469, he had to enforce his claims by strength of arms. Whether the contention was for the lands of Appin only, or for his supposed hereditary rights, does not appear; but a desperate conflict was the result, and tradition informs us that he was very strenuously supported by his mother's friends, the Mac Laurins, 130 of whom fell in the battle which took place at the foot of Beandouran, in Glenurchie.

About 1497, this clan again got into trouble, occasioned by their having carried off a creach from the braes of Lochaber. The Mac Donalds followed the spoilers, and, having overtaken them in Glenurchie, after a sharp skirmish, recovered the prey. The Mac Laurins went straight to their kinsman, Dugal Stewart of Appin, who, joining them with his followers, they marched hastily in pursuit, and intercepted the Mac Donalds somewhere about the Black Mount in Glenco, where a desperate conflict forthwith took place. There was dreadful slaughter on both sides; Dougal and Donull Mac Aonghais mhic Dhonuill, of Keppach, the chiefs of their respective clans, were slain! It may be remarked that the friendship of consanguinity always existed between these Stewarts and the Mac Laurins, who followed the Appin banner in considerable numbers, 1745-6. In the return of that regiment we find there were thirteen Mac Laurins killed and fourteen wounded.

The Mac Gregors were accused of a most shocking deed, committed in 1558, which seems to have consummated the decadence of Clan Laurin. It is thus described in their trial for the slaughter of the Colquhouns, 1604:—" And siclyk, John Mc Coull cheire, ffor airt and pairt of the crewall murthour and burning of auchtene houshalders of the Clan Lawren, thair wyves and bairns; committit fourtie-sax yeir syne, or thairby!" Nearly half a century had thus elapsed, when the verdict was, that he was " clene, innocent, and acquit of the said crymes." The Mac Gregors, however, occupied the farms which had belonged to the slaughtered householders, and it is singular that these very lands are now the property of the chief of Clan Gregor, having been purchased about 1798 from the Commissioners of Forfeited estates. Whatever was the original ground of quarrel; or how far provocation had been given, the most friendly feeling afterwards prevailed and now exists between the two clans, which is strengthened by frequent intermarriage.

Balquhidder, " the country of the Mac Laurins," is eighteen miles in length and seven in breadth; by the last census the number of inhabitants was reduced to 1,049 souls, of whom, perhaps, not more than twenty bear their appropriate patronymic. It was formerly very different; so numerous were those of the name that no others durst go into church until the Mac Laurins had entered and taken their seats, and the first question usually asked on their return was, " what fight or quarrel has happened to-day?" As all parties were armed it is easily seen that deeds of blood would frequently arise from these unseemly brawls, and a curious entry in the Lord High Treasurer's account under the year 1532, appears to refer to the practice. In this record we find that a Sir John Mac Laurin, Vicar or Balquhidder, was killed, and that several of his kinsmen were implicated in the slaughter and were outlawed. There is no other reference to this transaction than the above; and it is very probable that the Vicar lost his life in a humane endeavour to prevent the shedding of blood on one of these unhallowed occasions.

Mac Laurin, of wester Invernentie, was taken prisoner after Culloden, and marched for Carlisle to take his trial. When the party reached a height near Moffat the prisoner desired to step aside, when, seizing the moment, he tumbled himself to the bottom of the declivity, and ran off with the utmost speed; gaining a morass he plunged into the water, immersed himself to the neck, and covering his head with a turf he remained until night, when he made his way to his own country, where, in the disguise of a woman, he lived undiscovered until the act of indemnity relieved him from all fear. This is the foundation of the story of " Pate in Peril," given in the Waverley novel of " Redgauntlet."

Among the most distinguished members of this clan is Colin Mac Laurin, son of a clergyman in Argyle,—successively professor of mathematics in the colleges of Aberdeen and Edinburgh. His various philosophical works, which do him lasting honour, procured him the friendship of a large circle of the most eminent men of his day, but he fell a victim to his loyalty at the age of forty-eight. Having taken an active part in providing for the defence of Edinburgh in 1745, when that city fell into the hands of Prince Charles, he was forced to make a precipitate retreat, on which he was exposed to cold and hardship that led to the complaint which carried him off in June 1746. His son John, who became a senator of the College of Justice, Edinburgh, under the title of Lord Dreghorn, in 1787, was highly eminent as a lawyer, and was author of some professional and other pieces.

Ewen Mac Laurin, a native of Argyle, raised, at his own charge, the " South Carolina loyalists " in the first American war.

James Chichester Mac Laurin, M.D., was physician to the Forces. In 1794 he accompanied the British army to Holland, but his health becoming impaired, he died, with the brightest prospects, at the early age of thirty-eight.

Colonel James Mac Laren, C.B., has distinguished himself very highly in the Indian army. His bravery in leading on the 16th Bengal native Infantry at the victory of Sabraon, where he was severely wounded, elicited the pointed commendation of the Governor-General. His father was well known as the " Baron Mac Labhrain," and we cannot but regret to find that this gallant officer like so many others, has adopted the modern corrupt spelling of his name.

The ARMORIAL BEARINGS of the Clan Laurin of old are, or, two chevronels gules, in base a lymphad, sail furled, oars in action sable, all within a bordure, ingrailed gules. Crest, on a casque and wreath of the colours, a lion's head erased, between two laurel branches orlewise proper, meeting in an eastern crown of three points or. Motto, over the achievement " Dalriada," underneath " Ab origine fidus."

SUAICHEANTAS, or badge, Labhrail, otherwise Buaidh craobh, wild Laurel, *Laureola*. CATH-GHAIRM, or war cry, Craig Tuirc, the rock of the Boar.

The figure illustrative of this clan represents a chief of former days; on his head is the clogaid or conical helmet, and he wears a short lurich, or shirt of mail, under a leathern doublet, for which there is old authority. The Breacan fheile, or Belted plaid, is of the clan tartan, and the feet are protected by short Cuarans of deer hide. The bow which he holds is from one found in a moss and now preserved at Inch, in Lochaber. With such a weapon a young chief of the Mac Laurins, by a singular act of coolness and dexterity slew Caillain uaine, the leader of a predatory band of Campbells, and recovered the cattle they were driving away. His cairn is still pointed out, and the traditional " sgeulachd," or legend, is interesting. The quiver is of badger's skin, with which old Gaëlic poetry tells us they were usually formed.

CLANN GHILLEAN, OR THE MAC LEANS.

THE MAC LEANS consider themselves derived from a hero, said to have been contemporary with Fergus II., who flourished in 404, whose name was Gilleän or Gilleòin, which would either signify simply the young man, or the servant or follower of John.* This personage was farther distinguished as an tuagh or " of the axe," from the dexterous manner in which he could use that formidable weapon in the battle field.

* Leathan is broad, so Gill'e'an might imply a broad-shouldered man.

The first, however, who appears in national record is Gilleän, who lived in the time of Alexander III., 1249—86, and his son being Mac Ghilleän, that designation became the patronymic of the clan. Eoin, surnamed Dubh, from his dark complexion, is the first who is described in charters as being settled in the Isle of Mull, in the reign of David Bruce, anno 1330.

Eachuin, an appellation which has most strangely been translated Hector, is a favourite name among the Mac Leans. One of the chiefs so called, was celebrated for deeds of arms, and hence was distinguished as " rua'nan cath," or red Eachuin of the battles. He was second in command under the Lord of the Isles, in the great contest for the Earldom of Ross, 1411, and at the sanguinary cath Gariach, or Battle of Harlaw, which checked the advance of 10,000 Highlanders, he met in a hand to hand encounter with Irvine of Druim, a powerful baron of Aberdeenshire. So well matched in prowess were these chiefs, that, after a long and strenuous contention, they fell by mutual wounds; from which circumstance the Duart and Druim families were long accustomed, in accordance with a Scottish usuage, to exchange swords.

Eachuin, the chief who led the clan to the field of Flodden, in 1513, fell in the attempt to save the life of James IV., by generously throwing himself between the king and the English bowmen!

Besides the national wars, in which the Mac Leans always bore a distinguished part, they had to maintain long, protracted and desperately supported feuds with adjoining clans. " The troubles in the west isles between the clan 'Lean and the Clan Donald," which raged from 1585 to 1598, " to the destruction well near of all their country," were quenched by the death of Sir Lachlan Mac Lean, of Duart, who fell with eighty gentlemen, and 200 common men at Loch Gruinart in Isla, which he had vainly endeavoured to wrest from his victorious opponents, the Mac Donalds.

Sir Lachlan, who was chief in the reign of Charles I, led his clan to Inverlochie, where he was of great assistance to Montrose in gaining his celebrated victory there; he had a share in the succeeding battles of that extraordinary leader, and his son, Sir Hector, was at the battle of Inverkeithing, 1651, with 800 resolute followers, standing with the Buchanans the brunt of that sharp action with the Protector's forces. It was a maxim of the high-spirited Mac Leans, that they should never turn their backs on a foe, and the effect of its practice on this occasion was, that the chief fell, and his followers were cut up almost to a man ! They went out, notwithstanding, with Viscount Dundee, 1689, and rose with the Earl of Mar, in 1715. Under the command of Mac Lean of Druimnin, for the chief had been imprisoned, they fought bravely at Culloden with 500 men, and their leader sealed his devotion to the cause with his life.

The military history of Great Britain exhibits the members of this clan bearing a prominent share in all its glories; numbers have received the distinctive honours which their bravery deserved, and General Sir Fitzroy Mac Lean, Bart., is the Ceannard of his race.

The chiefs of Clan Gilleän resided in the strong and spacious castle of Duart, built by Lachlan Cattanach, about 1518, which is still entire, and occasionally occupied by troops.

The ARMORIAL BEARINGS are quarterly, 1st argent, a rock gules ; 2nd arg. a dexter hand couped fesswise, gules, holding a

crosslet fitchee in pale az.; 3rd or, a lymphad, oars in action, sable; 4th arg. a salmon naiant, proper, and in chief two eagles' heads erased, affrontee, gu. Crest a tower embattled, arg. Supporters, two selches or seals proper, on a compartment, vert. Motto, " Virtue mine honour." This is borne by Sir Fitzroy, whose baronetcy is of the creation of Charles I., 1632; but the old crest still borne by Coll, Ardgour, and other families, is a lochaber axe within a laurel branch on the dexter and cypress on the sinister, proper.

The SUAICHEANTAS, or Badge, is a sprig of Cuilfhionn, Holly bush, *Ilex aquifolium*.

The PIOBAIREACHD, is called Caismeachd Eachuin mhic Aluin an sop ; the alarm or march of the son of Allan of the wisp, an appellation which this warrior, who lived about 1595, received from his propensity to set fire to the places he reduced. It was composed by his prisoner, Mac Lean of Coll, whose liberty was the reward of this fine specimen of his musical skill.

In this illustration the belted plaid is again given with the doublet of the time of Charles I., when we know that " a slasht out coat beneath her plaides," was the general fashion among gentlemen. From the arrangement of the breacan, the Highlander's sword-belt was necessarily long, as here represented, a style in which the French still wear it. The sporan, or purse, was painted from one now in possession of Robert Stewart, Esq., of Ardvoirlich, and originally belonged to his unfortunate progenitor, James Stewart, of Ardvoirlich, the prototype of Allan Mac Aulay, who figures in Sir Walter Scott's " Legend of Montrose." It is furnished with short thongs ornamented with tassels, to keep it close, much in the manner of a lady's reticule. The handle of the dirk is concealed by the plaid. In the hose and brogs there is nothing peculiar. Three eagles' feathers, indicative of a chief, are fixed in the bonnet.

The figure is designed to illustrate a singular incident in the history of the Mac Leans of Coll. When the Reformation was advancing through the Highlands and had reached this island, the laird found his people very reluctant to abandon the religion of their fathers, but for some time he did not interfere with their belief. At last he thought it necessary to bring them, by some means, into the reformed communion, and for this purpose he posted himself one Sunday in the path which led to the Roman Catholic place of worship, and as his followers approached, he drove them successively back with his cane. Like obedient clansmen, they at once retreated, making their way to the Protestant Church, and from this persuasive mode of conversion, the people ever after called presbyterianism the religion of the gold-headed stick.

MAC LEAN

IT has been observed in former Numbers, that many of the Highland patronymics are derived from the circumstance of the founder of the clan or family having acquired his name in consequence of becoming a devotee to some particular ecclesiastic, or receiving his name from the parents, as indicative of dedication to his service. Finan was a very celebrated saint in the Highlands, to whom many religious buildings were consecrated, and it is from his cognomen that the clan now illustrated, derive the appellation by which they are distinguished. The traditional account of the Mac Lennans gives them the following origin.

There was a noted chief of the Logans of Druimdeurfait, in Ross-shire, called Gilliegorm, who, having fallen in a sanguinary battle with the Frasers, his widow was carried off, and a son, to whom she soon after gave birth, was either naturally deformed or was intentionally injured, as is alleged, that he might have no wish or ability to promote a feud for the slaughter of his father, for the Highlanders had a strong aversion to follow a deformed leader. He was therefore placed with the monks of Beaulieu, as best able to impart to him the religious instruction suited for the profession he was destined to follow. On coming to age he took holy orders, and travelled to the west coast, the Isle of Skye, &c., and built the churches of Kilmòr in Sleit and Kilchrinan in Glenelg. He was known from his personal appearance as crotach Mac Ghilliegorm, and although he lived in the time of Pope Innocent III., who held the pontificate in the beginning of the thirteenth century, he did not observe the decree which was then made, strictly enjoining the celibacy of the clergy, but married and had several children. One of his sons he called Gillie Fhinan, in honour of the renowned Saint Finan, and the son of that man was, of course, called patronymically Mac Gill'inan. His successors were the Siol'inan, the race of Gillie Fhinan, otherwise Clann or Mac Ghillie Inain, now, for euphony's sake, corrupted to Mac Lennan.

Another etymology of this name has certainly been given, but it appears to be merely founded on similarity of sound, and is not so agreeable to Highland usage as the former, which has, besides, the authority of a well known tradition. Mac Lennan according to some, is simply the son of a sweetheart or young woman, an appellation, it may be supposed not very usually adopted.

The Mac Lennans were generally enrolled among the Frasers and Mac Kenzies in the different rebellions, and as they were thus lost in the ranks of those predominant clans, their numbers do not appear, nor, for the same reason, do they agree as to who is the present chief; but it is certain that they were at one time of considerable note among the tribes of Ross-shire.

The district of Kintail has still scarcely any inhabitants but those of the names Mac Rae and Mac Lennan, the boundary between them being a river, which runs into Loch Duich; but slight as the line of demarcation is, the two clans keep up a marked distinction. It is remarkable that frequent intermarriage seems not yet to have amalga-

mated them. The Mac Lennans were entrusted with the standard of Lord Seaforth at the battle of Aultdearn, in 1645, and they proved the estimation in which they held this honour, by the great numbers who were cut down in the strenuous defence which they made of the renowned "caber feidh," as the banner of that clan was called, from the armorial bearing of the deer's head—eighteen of their widows married their neighbours the Mac Raes.

We have heard many laughable stories told of a Mac Lennan, who was exceedingly dexterous in carrying off the cattle and other effects of his neighbours, as well as those inimical to himself or his clan; such as cutting the rope by which a Highlander was leading some horses in a dark night, getting off with the prize, while the owner believed they were following, and afterwards selling them to him, having contrived to alter the animals so as not to be recognised—joining a party of smugglers, and by passing in the dark as one of themselves, obtaining an anker of whisky, as if to assist in carrying it, with which he dropped behind and unperceived slipped away. It was a practice among Highland gentlemen to have the bards at their bedsides when going to rest, that they might be lulled to sleep by the recitation of ancient poems. Mac Lennan officiating on one occasion in this capacity put the laird into a profound slumber, when he slipped out, stole some horses, with which he crossed a loch, and returned so speedily that the gentleman was still asleep, when sitting down by the bedside he commenced the recitation, which he continued until morning, when the laird awoke. Believing that the dexterous robber had never left the house, he was not suspected, but an innocent person being taken up on suspicion, Mac Lennan generously confessed his guilt, and by making some restitution escaped punishment.

The battle of Dunblain, as the highlanders call it, or Sheriffmuir, as it is otherwise named, was fought 13th November, 1715, between the Duke of Argyle for the Government, and the Earl of Mar for King James. Although the left wing of each army was routed, and both claimed the victory, the battle terminated this formidable rising; Mar, who alleged the treachery of one Drummond as the cause of his victory being indecisive, retired from the field, and his forces soon after disbanded. A very humorous song on this battle was composed by the late Rev. Murdoch Mac Lennan, minister of Crathie, in Braemar. It consists of twenty-one verses, in a peculiar measure, and describes the operations very graphically, at the same time giving the names of all the chiefs and principal parties engaged on either side, with allusion to their conduct during the fight.

The ARMORIAL BEARINGS are argent, three piles, sable, in

MAC LENNAN

chief, and in base, a cross croslet, fitchee, gules. Crest, an arm and broadsword, proper, Motto, " Dum spiro spero."

The figure introduced for Mac Lennan is simply enveloped in his ample garments of tartan. In this style elderly persons usually dress, particularly when engaged in pastoral occupations; and many a time has the highland drover to sleep on the heath beside his cattle, with no other protection from the weather. It was a practice to wet the plaid before lying down, by which it was rendered less pervious to the cutting winds, and Captain Burt, who wrote his

Letters from the Highlands, in 1725, was surprised when the places where the hardy Celts had spent the night were pointed out to him, cleared as they were of the surrounding snow, which the heat of their bodies had melted away! What advantage had such men over more effeminate troops in time of war? During the campaign in Holland, when the cold was so intense that brandy was frozen in the bottle, the 42nd Regiment, with their limbs exposed to the severity of the winter, scarcely lost a man, whilst other better clad troops were knocked up in course of the march!

CLANN LEOID—THE MAC LEODS.

"It is universally acknowledged," says the writer in Douglas's Baronage, " that the Mac Leods are descended of the Norwegian Kings of Man;" but "the Chronicle" of that island does not afford satisfactory authority for this supposition. We much more readily believe that they are the descendants of the ancient inhabitants of the Western Highlands, an origin which is surely as honourable as a derivation from these insular invaders. Their principal and allodial possession was Glenelg, bestowed on Malcolm, son of Tormod, by a charter from David II., in consideration for which, the reddendum was to provide a galley of thirty-six oars for the King's use whenever required. The lands in Skye, where the chiefs of this Clan have so long resided, were obtained by marriage with a daughter of Mac Arailt, a Norwegian settler.

The Mac Leods, at an early period, became divided into two Clans, or rather divisions. Torcul, son of Mac Leod of Harris and Glenelg, obtained a charter from David II., of the barony of Assynt, and the island of Lewes appears to have been previously in his possession. From this ancestor, the Lewes' branch were designated Siol Thorcuil,—"the Race of Torquil,"—while, from his elder brother, the succeeding chiefs and their followers were distinguished as the Siol Thormod. The former were situated so far from the locality of the others, that they became independent, and even disputed the right of chiefship with characteristic pertinacity They acquired great power and extensive possessions, which were forfeited in the time of James VI. and Roderick, then chief, dying without male issue, the representation devolved upon the Laird of Rasa, descended from Malcolm, second son of Malcolm, eighth Baron of Lewes, from whom that branch were designated Clann mhic Ghillichallum.

The Mac Leods of "that ilk," as the chiefs in Scottish parlance were called, acted prominently in the dissensions of their own country, and in the national wars. They were among the clans who fought with Bruce, and although they had sanguinary feuds with the Macdonalds, William, who flourished in the time of Robert III., having undertaken the most daring expeditions, and given that Clan a signal defeat, they became reconciled, and his son accompanied Donald of the Isles in the extraordinary raid of 1411.

It is impossible, in this condensed memorial of the Mac Leods, to give anything like a satisfactory account of so important a Clan, replete as its annals are with all those stirring and romantic incidents which marked the history of a numerous and independent tribe. They generously assisted the Mac Leans in their feuds with the Clan Donald of Isla, in the 16th century, and enabled their allies to gain a complete triumph over that people. Their long animosity with Clan Ranald, which led to the barbarous suffocation of the people of Eig, about 200 in number, who had for some days concealed themselves in a cave, is a lamentable instance of the horrors produced in the excitement of war. "The troubles" in which the Mac Leods were involved with various Clans are amusingly detailed by Sir Robert Gordon in his history of the Earldom of Sutherland.

Sir Roderick, still spoken of with veneration as Sir Ruarie mòr, or the great knight, from his eminent qualities, added much to the family estates; and, instead of keeping alive any old, or giving cause for fresh dissensions, he endeavoured to live on friendly terms with his neighbours. Like his contemporary, Roderick of Lewes, he had disobeyed the order of King James VI., that all land owners in the highlands should produce their charters, and, consequently, his property was declared to be forfeited, on which it was granted to Spens of Wormiston, and the other "undertakers," as a body of lowland gentlemen were called, who had, to civilize the islanders, and benefit themselves, associated to establish a fishing town in the Lewes, a project to which the natives unanimously offered unceasing opposition; and the design, after many attempts, was finally abandoned. Ruarie prevented this company from getting possession of his lands; and he had the address to procure a free remission of all offences in 1610. He built that portion of Dunvegan Castle which is called Ruarie mòr's Tower, on which were placed curious effigies of himself and lady, a daughter of Mac Donald of Glengarry, the last of which still exists, but is thrown from its original position.

The chief was a minor when Cromwell usurped the Sovereignty, but the whole clan went to the service of King Charles, under the leading of Sir Roderick of Talisker and Sir Norman of Bernera; and, at the unfortunate battle of Worcester, in 1651, the Mac Leods

MAC LEOD

suffered so severely, that it was agreed amongst the other clans they should not come out on any warlike expedition until their strength had been recruited. This was not the only loss they sustained. In 1655, Mac Leod was obliged to purchase absolution from his treason against the "Common wealth," at the price of £2500, and give security for his future obedience to the amount of £6000 sterling!

In 1715, General Wade reported this clan as 1000 strong; in 1745, Mac Leod could bring out 900; but he was induced to remain quiet, to the great mortification of his clansmen, many of whom foreswore their chief, and joined the highland army.

There are several castles which were raised by the Mac Leods throughout their territories; Dunvegan, the seat of the chief is a fine old castellated building, situated on a rock overhanging the sea, and isolated by a deep and wide ditch on the land side; and there are still displayed from its battlements several old iron cannon.

The ARMORIAL BEARINGS of Mac Leod are azure, a castle, triple towered and embattled argent, masoned sable, port and windows, gules. Crest, a bull's head, cabossed sable, between two flags, gules, staves of the first. Motto, "Hold fast."

The SUAICHEANTAS, fixed in the right side of the bonnet, is craobh Aiteann, Juniper bush, *Juniperis communis*.

Many PIOBAIREACHDS were composed in commemoration of the battles, and other transactions, in which this clan were engaged, events which offered favourable opportunities for the exercise of the musical abilities of the Mac Cruimins, hereditary pipers to Mac Leod. These pieces of music are a species of historical record; and some of them refer to circumstances which took place many centuries ago. In a list before us, besides the Salute to the Chief, and Lament played at his funeral, which were transferrable from generation to generation, there are eight other pieces, most of which, with historic notes, are given in the publication of Her Majesty's Piper.

Nor was this clan deficient in members of poetical ability. Mairi Nighean Alasdair ruaidh, or Mary, daughter of Alexander the red, a relation of the chief, is the most celebrated composer of poetry in the Isles; and as it is believed she could neither read nor write, she affords a striking instance of the natural gift of poesy. Her style is quite original; and some of her modes of versification have neither been attempted by any one previous, nor since her time. She was born in 1569, and died at the age of 105; and she is described as wearing the tonnag, a sort of shawl, which is given in the female representative of the Mac Nicols, fastened with a large ornamental silver brooch; and she, latterly, used a silver-headed cane. There was another daughter of a red Alexander, who likewise wooed the muses, but her name was Fionaghal, or the Fair Stranger—

a name translated Flora, with as much propriety as if it had been made Fortuna!

Among the relics, which most highland families possessed, and which the clan reverenced as charms, the Brattach sith, or fairy flag of Mac Leod, was highly celebrated. Pennant saw this banner, which has long disappeared, with the antique iron chest which contained it; but none of those disastrous consequences, which were predicted to follow its loss, appears to have occured. It was given to a certain chief of the clan, by an ecclesiastic, and its production was to avert any great calamity. It seems to have been one of the trophies gained in the holy war, of which there are yet several preserved in old families, but the mode of their acquisition is forgotten.

Norman, the present chief, distinguished among the Gael as an Leodach, emphatically, "Mac Leod," is the 22nd in lineal succession, according to the family genealogy.

The figure which illustrates this clan is clad in the dress usually worn when not fully armed for war. This plaid was a most useful vestment in so watery a climate as Skye; nor was it less necessary for the highlanders, who, in a thinly-peopled country, might, on occassion of sudden tempests, be storm-staid on desolate isles: in such cases it would enable them to bivouac in sufficient comfort.

It has previousely been observed that, after the repeal of the act which proscribed the highland dress, considerable difficulty occurred in many instances, to determine the almost forgotten patterns of clan-tartan, so long an illegal manufacture and material for dress. To this day, there are, consequently, contentions respecting the breacan appropriate to respective clans; and this is the case with the Mac Leods, who claim that of the Mac Kenzies. No motive can animate us but a desire to make statement of facts, as far as our information may enable us. It is possible that one clan may choose to wear the tartan of another, just as different regiments appear with the same facings; but we believe the misunderstanding in the present instance thus arose:—When Lord Mac Leod, son of the Earl of Cromarty, raised the Mac Leod highlanders in 1778, who amounted to 1800 men, from the property which had been forfeited since 1746; being himself a Mac Kenzie, he very naturally ordered the tartan to be of his own clan pattern, In this way, the misapprehension has arisen. This body, formed into a regiment of the line, is now the 71st, or Glasgow light Infantry; but, after having long disused the feilebeag, the trows and scarf plaid of the same tartan has been adopted.

There is a fine full-length portrait of the Mac Leod of 1745, at Dunvegan, which appears in the trows and an ample plaid, like the figure which the artist has here given; but that was manufactured by a lady of the name of Fraser, and presented to the Laird, as a token of gratitude for some favour. To the best of our recollection, it is the exact Breacan Friosailich, as given in the sixth number of this work.

CLANN GHILLE MHAOIL—THE MAC MILLANS.

THE traditions respecting the origin of this clan are rather conflicting, one representing Argyle as being the original seat, another Braidalban, and a third Lochaber, in the county of Inverness.

We are assured by an old historian, it was the "uncontroverted" belief that the ancestor of the Mac Millans was brother to the chief of the Buchanans, who flourished in the time of King Alexander II. whose reign extended from 1214 to 1249. The name of this person was Methlan, from which, by the same authority, we are told the patronymic is derived; but the Gaëlic appellation, pronounced Gille-Vaolain, although much resembling the aspirated sound of the other, indicates the religious character of the individual, who was bald-headed, i.e. was distinguished by the clerical tonsure.

This was the most considerable of the cadets of the clan Buchanan. They lived around Loch Tay, Lawers on the north side being their principal residence, from whence they were driven in the reign of David II. annis 1329 to 1369, by the Chalmers's, or Camerarii, who held a feudal grant of the lands; but it was a work of no slight difficulty. Mac Millan had ten sons, and on their expulsion, some of them went to Braidalban, and were ancestors of the families of Ardournag and others. Those who went to Argyle settled in the southern part, where the chief was distinguished from his residence, as Mac Millan of Cnap, the name of the property which had been obtained from the Lord of the Isles; and, it is said, that he had the charter engraven on the top of a rock, at the boundary of the land, in the Gaëlic language and letter. Here they rose to considerable importance; and in the burial-ground of the chapel of Kilmorie, which was built by them, is a stone cross, at least twelve feet in height, covered with beautifully-executed foliage, and other ornaments, amid which is represented a spirited deer hunt. On one side is inscribed, in rude Saxon characters, "Hæc est crux Alexandri Mac Millan."

One, named Marallach mòr, who is called a stranger, had established himself in Cnapdale, where he became very obnoxious by his harshness and pride; particularly to a son of "the great Mac Millan," who resided at Kilchamag, and having slain this man, either in a general fight or personal duel, he was obliged to leave the country, and, with six associates, he retired to Lochaber, where Locheil took them under his protection, and granted them some lands beside Locharcaig. Such is the traditional story, which does not support the opinion of some, that Lochaber was the first seat of the Mac Millans; but this locality may account for their alleged connection with the Clan Chattan. One of the Clann Ghille Mhaoil subsequently returned to Argyle, and taking up his residence at Badokennan, by the head of Loch Fine, was progenitor of the Mac Millans of Glen Shera, Glen Shira, and others.

On the extinction of the family of Cnap, Mac Millan of Dunmòr, a property on the south side of Loch Tarbert, assumed the chiefship, with apparent right; but this house also became extinct, when the Campbells immediately laid claim to the lands, but were opposed in a counterclaim by the Mac Niels. The contention was finally settled in favour of the Campbells, by some mutual concessions, and in 1775, the estates became the property, by purchase, of Sir Archibald Campbell, of Inver Niel.

The Mac Millans in Lochaber, or the Clann Ghille Mhaoil Aberaich, latterly dwelt in Muir Lagan, Glen Spean, and Caillie, and they were among the trustiest of the followers of Locheil, "being generally employed," says Buchanan of Auchmar, "in any desperate enterprise," and the following is related concerning them. In the latter part of the seventeenth century, there arose a quarrel between them and the Mac Ghille'onies, a branch of the Camerons, when a collision with a body of twelve of them, one of the Gille Mhaoils was killed, on which the whole of their adversaries made off to the hills, to avoid the consequences, and determined there to maintain themselves, until the wrath of their enemies had become subdued, and the impending feud suppressed, a proceeding which leads to the presumption that they must have been the aggressors. The Mac Millans loudly demanded permission from Locheil to march against the fugitives, declaring, that if prevented from bringing the guilty to justice, they would wreak their vengeance on the whole tribe! Locheil acceded to their request, on which they went to work so vigorously, that in a very short time, the whole twelve were either slain or made prisoners, without any loss of life to the Mac Millans, although many of them were sorely wounded.

There is another traditional account of a rather curious circumstance, in the life of a Mac Millan. One of the family of Cnap, called Gille Easpuig bàn, happened, unfortunately, to kill some person of consequence, in chaud melee at a fair, upon which he fled, and a hot pursuit immediately followed. Breathless, Mac Millan reached the Earl of Argyle's castle, when in desperation he rushed in to obtain refuge from his infuriated pursuers, and he made his way to the kitchen, where he found the cook engaged in baking. Without delay he effected an exchange of clothes, and began very busily to knead the barley bannocks. By this ruse he eluded his pursuers, and some "assythment" having been made for the slaughter, he lived in peace thereafter, his posterity, from this event, being called Mac-Bhacstear, or the son of the baker, of whom the ceann tigh, or patriarch, lived in Glendaruel, in the district of Cowal.

The military force of the Mac Millans in Lochaber, was reckoned one hundred good men; respecting that of the others, we have met with no data.

The ARMORIAL BEARINGS are, or, a lion rampant sable, as descended of Buchanan, and on a chief, party, per bar, gules and azure, three mullets, argent.

As Buchanans, the Badge would be that of the original stem, but in Lochaber they would assume that of the Camerons.

The figure represents a Mac Millan defending himself with fierce resolution against a person, who may be taken to represent one of Cromwell's soldiers, such actions having frequently taken place. He wears moggans, or stockings without feet, and he is otherwise undressed, with the exception of his kilt. This part of the dress has been called a late improvement, and introduced by an Englishman! We are prepared to maintain its antiquity. The Highlanders retained the practice of stripping off their plaids when hotly engaged, so late as Killiecrankie and Prestonpans, and, had the belted plaid been the garment then worn, they must have stood " pugnare in nudo corpore," at least with the exception of the shirt, which we know was also cast off, on some occasions, by those who were provided with that comfortable portion of dress. The tartan is that of Buchanan, a pattern of a rather singular but effective design.

CLANN AN ABBA—THE MAC NABS.

It has been supposed that this clan are Mac Donalds. That powerful race was accustomed to claim all who could not clearly established another connexion, but a different origin must be asserted for the Mac Nabs: they were of the Siol Alpin, the chief division of whom was the Mac Gregors. A son of the chief who flourished in the time of David the first, became Abbat or Prior of Glendochart, and from him arose the patronymic, which is, literally, the Abbat's son, and " An Abba uaine Mac mhic Griagar o Sron uaine," is a saying descriptive of him.

The Mackinnon of Strath, was an undoubted branch of the greas Clan Alpin, and a curious document proves the Clann an Abba to have been so also.

In the year 1606, Lachlan Mackinnon, then chief, and Fiunla' Mac Nab, of Bowain, having met in Glenurchai', in Braidàlban, and taken into consideration that they were both " come of ane house, and being of ane surname and lineage, notwithstanding this lang tyme bygane" they had " overseen, their ain dueties till udders, in respect of the lang distance betwixt their dwelling places, quhairfore baith the saids now and in all tyme coming, are content to be bound and obleisit, with consent of their kyn and friends, to do all sted, pleasure, assistance and service that lies in them, ilk ane to uthers, &c. and baith the said parties grants them faithfullie, that ane surer firm band and contract be made betwixt them by advyce of men of aw, and that quhasoon the said Lachland shall come either to Stirling, 'erth or Glasgow or any part of the lowland quhair they may easiest eet." These worthy patriarchs, " for sure keiping and performing this present minute," agreed to subscribe the document " with ir hands led to the pen." Writing was an unnecessary quali- tion for such personages in the opening of the 17th century.

The original possessions of the Mac Nabs were extensive tracts westward of Loch Tay, on which they were located from the earliest period, but having joined the Lord of Lorn in his rebellion against King Robert Bruce, and particularly distinguished them- selves at the battle of Dal Rhi, that monarch visited them with a severe retribution, and a section of Glendochart seems to have been the only portion of their lands which were then left in the chief's possession. Of this, the principal messuage of which was Bowain, he received a Crown charter from David Bruce, in 1336, which was renewed with additions in 1486, 1502, &c.

Mac Nab joined the Royal party under Montrose, and fought bravely at Kilsyth, after which he was appointed to garrison the castle of Kincardine, where he was so closely besieged by General Leslie, that he found it impossible to stand out. He therefore sallied forth with his 300 clansmen, sword in hand, during the night, and all got clear off but the Chief and a private, who were taken prisoners and sent to Edinburgh, where Mac Nab was condemned to die ; but the night before his execution, he contrived to make his escape and joined King Charles in England, where he fell at the battle of Worcester, 1651. His house, during this time, had been burnt, and his charters and other documents destroyed, the property being given to Campbell of Glenurchai', who alleged that he had sustained heavy losses by the Mac Nabs. So reduced was the family by these reverses, that during the minority of her son, the Widow of Mac Nab made supplication to General Monk for relief, who directed the Governor of Finlarig castle to "preserve the rights that to them (those who were peaceable) belong, and to enter and receive them into their lands as if the said order (for depriving them of their estates) had never been made." This attempt to repair the injuries inflicted on the Mac Nabs had, un-

MAC MILLAN

fortunately, little effect; but on the restoration, the Scottish parliament awarded them a portion of their estates which they had so long enjoyed, amid surrounding clans of great power and no friendly disposition. The property is now merged in the domain of Braidàlban, and the line of the chief has become extinct, except the claim which a gentleman in America prefers, is to be held good.

The late chief, a most eccentric but good-hearted man, was the last specimen, in Perthshire at least, of the old Highland Laird. He was of a remarkably tall and robust frame, and spurned all suggestions to keep on the march of improvement, which he only viewed as innovation on the good old mode of living and acting with plainness and blunt sincerity. The anecdotes which are related of this remarkable picture of the primitive school, would form a very amusing volume. He had the highest opinion of the dignity of a chief and could not well be persuaded that his will should not be law. Having raised a body of Fencibles, he proudly marched at their head to Edinburgh, but was met by some excisemen who unceremoniously ordered a halt that they might make a search as they had received information that a great quantity of Whisky was concealed among the baggage. Mac Nab indignantly refused to stop, and the gaugers resolutely maintained their right as being on his Majesty's service. "I also," exclaims the offended chief, "am on his Majesty's service, halt! this, my lads, is a serious affair, load with ball!" The officers of excise knowing the character of the leader, and disposition of the clan, prudently allowed them to proceed.

Close to the old mansion is seen Inisbhui', an island in the river, the romantic burial place of this ancient family. It is a spot of singular beauty, where the solemn and deep silence is only broken by the gentle murmur of the surrounding stream or the sound of the passing breeze in the aged pines. Here rest many generations of these Alpine chiefs, under the grey stones which mark the narrow dwelling of the heroes of old.

The ARMORIAL BEARINGS are, sab. on a chevron arg. three crescents vert; in base an open boat with oars of the second, sailing in a sea proper. Crest, the head of a savage, affrontee proper.

MOTTO, "Timor omnis abesto."

The SUAICHEANTAS, or Badge, as a branch of Clan Alpin, is Giuthaš. Pine, *Pinus Sylvestris*.

The PIOBAIREACHD is "Failte mhic an Abba" or the Salute to the Chief.

The figure wears the usual broad bonnet, with the feather, which marks the rank of gentleman, the badge of distinction is likewise displayed. The coat and waistcoat are in the style worn about 1715, the latter being usually lower than the coat. The ample plaid is belted, as the Highlanders wore it when going on a compaign, or in droving. The sporan is of a plain old pattern, but is almost hid by the folds of the breacan. There is a small belt introduced, in which pistols were slung, as is seen in the rare prints of the soldiers of the Black Watch, engraved from portraits taken when they were quartered in the Tower, in 1743. The Tartan is according to that given in the "Scottish Gaël, and the hose are Cath da', thick home-made stuff, of an old pattern, reckoned appropriate to this clan. He wears shoe buckles, and his hair is tyed in the manner represented in the above curious prints. He is armed with the broadsword and target, the trusty companions of the old Highlanders.

SIOL NEACHDANN, OR MAC NACHTANS.

THIS tribe may yield to few others in the antiquity of its name. Tradition derives this clan from Nachtan, a hero in the reign of Malcolm IV., who succeeded to the crown in 1153, but it is believed that they were long previously a powerful tribe in the province of Moray.* The name is identic with the Pictish Nectan, celebrated in the regal chronicle of that nation, one of the great Celtic divisions in Scotland, and the appellation is among the most ancient in the north of Ireland, the former seat of the Cruthen Picts.

* Skene on Authority of the Gaëlic Genealogy, MS. 1450.

The chiefs were for ages Thanes of Loch Tay, possessing all the country between Loch Fin and Loch Awe. In 1267, "Gillichriosd Mac Nachdan" was appointed heritable keeper of the fortress and island of Fraoch Ellan in Lochaw, by charter of Alexander III., on condition that he should be properly entertained when he should pass that way, whence the castle was assumed as an heraldic insignia.

Donald, who was chief in the beginning of the fourteenth century, being nearly related to the Mac Dughals of Lorn, he joined them

MAC NAB

against Robert the Bruce, but, observing the heroism of the king at the battle of Dalree, particularly his cutting down three men who had set on him in a narrow pass, he changed sides, and Duncan, his son, was a steady royalist in the reign of David Bruce.†

David II., as a reward for the loyalty of the Mac Nachtans, conferred on Alastair, their chief, all the lands of John, son of Duncan Mac Alastair of the Isles, and of John Dornagil (white fist), which had been forfeited, by which he obtained extensive insular possessions.

Alastair, who lived in the beginning of the sixteenth century, received the honour of knighthood; and, accompanying James IV. in his fatal expedition into England, he fell with his sovereign in the field of Flodden, 1513, leaving a son John, who was succeeded by Maolcolum of Glenshira, his second son.

John, second son of Maolcolum, became rich, and purchased lands in Kintire, being indebted for his good fortune to his handsome person, which induced King James to appoint him one of the pages of honour on his accession to the crown of England.

Alexander, the next laird, was a firm adherent of King Charles I., and received a commission in 1627, "with ane sufficient warrant to levie and transport twa hundrethe bowmen," to serve in the war against France. This is a very curious fact respecting a weapon then almost forgotten, save in the Highlands. The men were, however, speedily embodied, the Laird of Mac Kinnon furnishing a small quota, and set sail with the suitable accompaniment of pipers and a harper, but were twice driven into Falmouth, and were " hetlie followit by ane man of warr," who seems to have been deterred from pursuit by the strange effect of their " baggpypperis and marlit plaidis."*

He was a great favourite with Charles II., who retained him at court, where he was known as Colonel Mac Nachtan; and dying in London, he was interred, at the expense of his Majesty, in the Chapel Royal. John, his successor, joined Viscount Dundee with a goodly number of his clan; and it is said that their efforts materially contributed to the victory at Killicrankie in 1689. After that indecisive action, he retired with those who held out for King James, and, with his son Alexander, signed the spirited address, or defiance, of those resolute leaders, to General Mackay, commanding the troops of King William; shortly afterwards he joined in a bond of association with other chiefs, engaging to meet his confederates with fifty men for the royal service, wherever it might be agreed on. Forfeiture, in 1691, was the unfortunate result of his activity in the Stewart cause.*²

He married a daughter of Sir John Campbell of Glenurchai', and was succeeded by his son Alexander, who was a captian in Queen Anne's guards, and was killed in the expedition to Vigo, 1702; and having no issue, the chiefship devolved upon his brother John, who also leaving no successors, it is now held to be extinct.

When Lord President Forbes made his report, 1747, on the forces which could be raised by the respective chiefs, he does not give the strength of the Nac Nachtans individually, but classes them with several others inhabiting the same district.

Their possessions, it has been observed, were formerly very extensive: by the " risings" in which they were so frequently engaged, the patrimonial territories were much reduced. Charles II. meant to bestow on the Mac Nachtans the hereditary sheriffship of Argyle; but, in consequence of some court intrigue, the patent never passed

the seals: and James VII. intended to reward the devotion of the clan to his interest, by giving the chief a commission of stewartry and heritable bailliary over all the lands which belonged to him, or his ancestors had ever possessed, and the deed was signed by the king, and subsigned by the Duke of Perth; but the revolution, which upset all his Majesty's designs, disappointed the hopes of Mac Nachtan. With a reduced estate and increasing troubles in the country, the family got involved, and the estates which remained in their possession were finally wrested from them by process of law.

It has been remarked of the Mac Nachtans, that, unlike most other clans, who have either from fortunate circumstances been brought into prominence, or by reverses been overborne by others, they have appeared throughout their history independent, and preserved a uniformity of state, neither much elevated nor depressed, a situation not easily maintained, surrounded as they were by the powerful Campbells, Mac Dughals, and others.

Their ancient residences, situated far apart, some of which have been works of magnitude, attest their former power. Fraoch Ellan was the ancient seat of the chiefs in Argyle. The Castle of Dunderaw exhibits the ruins of a building of great strength; besides which were Mac Nachtan Castle in the Lewis, and several others; and if we are to consider the race "ab origine" in that district, Dun Nachtan, in Strathspey, was a still more ancient stronghold.

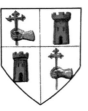

The ARMORIAL BEARINGS are quarterly, 1st and 4th arg.; a hand fesswise proper, holding a cross crosslet fitchee, az.; 2nd and 3rd arg.; a castle embattled gules. Crest, a castle embattled gules. Supporters, two roebucks proper. Motto, " I hope in God."

The SUAICHEANTAS, or Badge, is Lusan Albanach, *Azalea procumbens*, or Trailing Azalea.

The CATH-GHAIRM, or Battle-shout, we have heard, is Fraoch Ellan, and this is also a cry of the Mac Donalds, but there were many islets which were equally " heathy" as that in Lochaw. The Castle was frequently given as the rallying cry, or gathering, and probably those in different localities might be used for rendezvousing the neighbouring clansmen.

The figure represents a gamekeeper or shepherd dressed in the modern fashion, and resolutely facing a storm, in which the utility of the ample plaid, and the original flat bonnet, as protective from the effect of " the cauld blast and the drift," is so apparent. The pattern of the breacan, or clan tartan, is well shown by the breadth of drapery. The hose are of a pattern, dubh a's dearg, or black and red, at present very commonly worn.

---

† Abercrombie's Martial Achievements of the Scots. Douglas's Baronage, 418.

*¹ Donald Gregory in Archæologia Scotica, III. 248.

*² Acts of Scottish Parliament, IX.

MAC NACHTAN

CLANN NICAIL—THE MAC NICOLS.

THE Mac Nicols, although they have been for some time, what in olden phraseology would be called, a broken clan, are of ancient gaëlic origin, and were formerly a tribe of considerable importance.

Their first known possessions were in Coigach, a district of Ross. On one occasion, they were so fortunate as to intercept a band of marauders, who were driving along a large herd of cattle, which had been carried off from Sutherland, and having recovered the booty, in requital for such a service, the Thane of that county, it is said, gave them the adjacent lands of Assynt, on which they afterwards got a crown charter.

The individual then at the head of this clan is called Mac Rycul, or Grigul; but it is to be observed that the letters r and n are commutable; and it is not a little singular, that the highlanders are accustomed to pronounce invariably the latter as it were the former: thus, cnoc is sounded croc, &c.

About the beginning of the 14th century, the family of the chief terminated in a female, who married Torcuil Mac Leod of the Lewes, who obtained a crown charter of the district of Assynt, and other lands in the west of Ross, apparently those which had become vested in his wife. The clan, on this event, came by the patriarchal rule, or law of clanship, under the leading of the nearest male heir; and the Mac Nicails subsequently removed to the Isle of Skye, where their chief residence was at Scoirebreac, a beautiful situation, on the margin of the loch, close to Port Rhi.

They seem to have been considerable benefactors to the religous establishment at the head of Loch Snisort, of which the ruins are still to be seen, on an island formed by the river, to which access is obtained by means of stepping stones. There is a small chapel on the south side of the chief building, which is still known as aite-adhlaic Mhic Nicail, or Nicholson's Aisle; and here lies an effigy of a warrior, dressed in the long quilted coat, or habergion; and the clogaid or conical helmet, represented in the figure of the Lord of the Isles, No. XI. It is to be regretted, that, with few exceptions, the inscriptions on those stones, numerous in the islands, are now illegible.

There were many Mac Nicails in Argyle, and several traditions are current respecting them, especially of one accounted a seer, or prophet, who went under the designation of "Gualan Crostadh," because he never looked behind him, from which habit he was also named an Teallsanach, or the philosopher; and of him, curious stories are told. One Gillieaspuig Mac Nicail was a notable cearnach. A widow's son having fallen into the hands of the Saigh-dearan dearg, or government troops, they were carrying him away when Gillieaspuig attacked them with such resolution, that he rescued the captive, slew one or two, and put the rest to flight, escaping himself with a stroke on the face which carried away his nose.

The following singular occurrence is related by some old people in Skye. One of the chiefs of this clan, called Mac Nicail mòr, from his great size, being engaged in a warm discussion with Mac Leod of Rasa, which was carried on in the English language, his servant coming into the room, imagined they were quarrelling, and drawing his sword, he gave Mac Nicail a deadly blow! A council of chiefs and comhairlich, or elders, was forthwith called to determine in what manner so unhappy a deed could be satisfactorily avenged, and the unnecessary shedding of blood avoided; when it was agreed, upon some old precedent, that the meanest person in the clan Nicail should behead the Laird of Rasa. It speaks highly for the respectability of the Mac Nicails at that time, that the individual of least note, who could be found among them, was one Lomach, a maker of keisans, which are a sort of woven baskets that are slung on each side of a horse's back, and are used for the conveyance of grain and like commodities. Rasa was accordingly executed near Snisort, and by this judicial decree, a feud was prevented. The sgeulachd, or oral tradition, informs us that, so cleanly did Lomach sever the head from the body of the unfortunate chief, who was at the moment in the act of speaking, that as it rolled from the hill, the half articulate sounds, "ip ip," were said to have been distinctly heard, and hence the little eminence on which the execution took place has since been distinguished as "Cnoc an h-ip."

About sixty years ago there was a banquet given in the highlands on some joyful occasion, and during the evening there was a call for the bards to be brought to the upper end of the room, on which Mac Nicail of Scoirebreac exclaimed, "the bards are extinct." "No," quickly replied Alasdair bui' Mac I'vor, "they are not extinct; but those who delighted to patronise them are gone!" This genuine highlander felt keenly the decadence of those ancient, social manners, which characterised his ancestors.

The ARMORIAL BEARINGS of the Mac Nicails are party per fesse, indented, gules and argent, in chief two mullets, and in base a crescent, counterchanged. Crest, a battle axe, proper. Motto, "With heart and hand." There are respectable families of the name in Ireland, whose crest is a demi lion, and, motto "Generositate."

"The children of Nical" are now reduced in numbers, and thinly scattered abroad: several individuals have distinguished themselves in different professions, but, little of any importance can now be gleaned of their history as an independent tribe.

Nicholson of Nicholson, or that ilk—of Carnock, and others of this name resident in the low country, appear to have received the appellation as descendants of Nicholas, of which the English Nicholls

MAC NICOL

is a plain corruption; but the Nicols and Nicolsons of Scotland, are acknowledged Mac Nicails.

From intermarriage, this clan came under the following of Mac Leod, and as we have never met with a tartan peculiar to them, it is probable they adopted that of their superiors.

The figure illustrative of the Mac Nicols, represents a Banarach or Dairy-maid, who bears in her hand the vessel called cuman, which receives the milky tribute of the fold. The dress is such as usually seen among young persons; the chief peculiarity is the Tonag or Guail-leachan, as it is otherwise called, from being worn over the shoulders.

It is, as represented, a square piece of tartan resembling a shawl, but smaller, and is a useful article of female attire both for warmth and protection from the rain. The pattern is from a web, home made, by Mrs. Cameron, wife of the schoolmaster, of Kil, in Morven. The silver brooch fastens it in front, an ornament prized by both sexes in the highlands, often valuable, and transmitted as an heirloom through many successive generations. The striped pattern in her dress is much esteemed by the smarter Cailleagan, and the colours are often rich and very tastefully blended.

CLANN NIAL—THE MAC NIELS.

NIAL or NIEL, as it is now spelt, is one of the oldest Celtic personal appellations, and is, in this respect, distinguished from those names which are of local derivation. It is unsafe ground when we venture beyond the period of written record, and it is not always very satisfactory to substitute oral tradition for more legitimate history. It may be sufficient here to say, that Nial, the ancestor of the Mac Nials of Barra, is the first who appears to occur in a charter, a document which is dated in the reign of King Robert the Bruce. This chief is distinguished by the adjunct òg, or younger, from which it would appear that his father bore the same name. At this time the clan was located in Knapdale, a district in Argyle, where they were hereditary constables of Suen Castle.

Nial was succeeded by Murchard, or rather Murchadh, pronounced Murachie, and now translated Murdoch, whose son was Roderic, which is the Gaëlic Ruarai' anglicised. His son, Gillieonan, was settled in the Isle of Barra, in the time of King James I., as seen by a charter, dated 1427; it conveys to him the land of Boisdail also; but this possession led to a dispute with Ian Garbh Mac 'Lean of Coll, who asserted his right to the property, and in his effort to maintain it, Gilleonan was slain; but his son, who bore the same name, received a charter confirming de novo all his possessions, dated 12th August, 1495. His successor, likewise called Gilleonan, was deeply engaged in the cause of his superior, the Lord of the Isles,

These princes, whose dependence on the crown of Scotland was little more than nominal, were involved in frequent disputes, which brought them into collision with government, and their efforts to maintain their independence brought on them, and all the chiefs of the west Highlands, severe retribution, but no measures could repress the dissensions which were continually distracting the country. The insular and remote situation of these clans, served to protect them from the rigorous punishment which their inflexible resistance to extraneous coercion would have brought on them. By issuing commissions of fire and sword to the Campbells and others, against the contumacious clans, some of them were reduced to obedience, and paid the penalty of loss of land, and frequently of life; but the isles which the Mac Niels inhabited, were so very distant and difficult of access, that it was found impossible to serve the personal

summons requisite to compel attendance before a court of law; and parliamentary record often informs us that " Mac Nele sæpe vocatus, sed non comparet."

The frequent processes of treason, and rising in arms against such sturdy island chiefs as held out, were ultimately dropped; from those who were forced to submission, hostages were taken for their peaceable behaviour; and, when captured, the principal leaders were often fined or subjected to long and severe imprisonment.

Roderic 7th chief, by the family history, was celebrated for his bravery and enterprise. When the Earl of Argyle received his commission to proceed on that notable expedition against the catholic lords, the Earls of Angus, Errol, and Huntley, Mac Niel of Barra joined the array with his clan, snd after contending with their wonted energy and valour to avert the signal discomfiture which befel the army of Mac Cailain mòr, in Glenlivat, he fell with honour at that battle, which was fought 1594.

Barra's castle of Kismul was reckoned impregnable. A warder, called Gocman, paced along the battlements night and day, and so jealous of intrusion were the watchful keepers, that a gentleman of considerable note, about 150 years ago, who held an official situation in the Isles, was peremptorily denied admission.*

The Mac Niels of Barra, have intermarried with the families of Clan Ranald, Cameron, Mac Leod, Duart and other west Highland chiefs, The present Lieutenant Colonel Mac Niel, who is deputy Lieutenant of Inverness-shire, has distinguished himself by the introduction of manufactures, the promotion of agriculture, and improvement of the native breed of cattle.

There are several highly respectable cadets of this clan, and those of Gigha, an island so remote from Barra, as to render anything like regular intercourse impossible, were obliged to do for themselves, and came to assert a claim to the chiefship. Tradition invariably gives that honour to Barra, but in latter times they acted independently. Malcolm Mac Niel of Gigha, a person of consideration, was chief in the year 1493. Both branches have produced numerous individuals celebrated in various walks of life; and there are now living of the family of Colonsay, several highly distinguished personages.

* Martin in his History of the Western Isles, 1705.

MAC NIEL

The ARMORIAL INSIGNIA of the chief, are quarterly; 1st vert, a lion rampant, or; 2d arg., in base the sea, with a castle issuant therefrom, proper; 3d or, a long-fada or lymphad, sails furled, sable; 4th or, a dexter hand palewise, couped gules, within an orle of nine fetterlocks. Crest, a rock gules. Supporters, two lions proper. Motto, "Vincere vel mori."

The SUAICHEANTAS, or Badge, is the plant Luibheann, Dryas, *Octopetala.*

In this figure, is represented the costume of a Highland equestrian, on which occasion the trews were the fitting garment. He is mounted on a genuine specimen of a Highland garron, the qualities of which are truly valuable, particularly their hardiness and sureness of foot in crossing bogs and dangerous passages.

The trews are made in the same manner as the cath-dath hose, being cut from the cloth with great ingenuity, and adapted to the form of the limb and foot. The jacket is short, with round skirts, and is kept close to the body by a waist-belt; the waistcoat is much longer, and is provided with large pockets in each flap. The ample shoulder plaid is seen in all portraits, clad in trews as here represented. The 'sporan, or purse, is small, and of plain leather; it is worn high, and attached to the waist-belt by a swivel-ring. The long fowling-piece is a manufacture of Spain, from which the Highlanders imported them in large quantities, and the one here introduced was painted from a specimen seen by Mr. Mc Ian in London, on the stock of which is cut the name of "Grant." There is nothing peculiar in the brogs; the flat bonnet is cocked up by means of a dealg, or pin, which was usually formed of the small bone of a deer's shank, and it very conveniently served the purpose of fixing the badge, and giving smart effect to the bonnet.

The simple caparison of the horse betokens its antiquity, but the same rude style is yet to be seen in many secluded districts; and this design was suggested by a Celtic charger in possession of Mac Donald of Agais, Strathglas; the harness is composed of withies, or twisted rods of hazel; a "rung" is used for a crupper, and the rein is a rope of hair; the covering, instead of a saddle, is a fine goat skin! We have heard that a Highland gentleman of some eccentricity astonished the Auld reekie Athenians, when George IV. visited Scotland, by appearing in a similar costume!

CLANN PHARLAIN—THE MAC PHARLANS.

MOST of the great Highland families trace their descent from some individual of warlike celebrity. By the usual account of this clan, a hero who arrived in Ireland with the first colonists from Spain, and subsequently settled in Scotland, is given as its founder, an origin which must be classed among the Milesian fables. The original name is Partholan, or Par'lan, which by the addition of Mac, is aspirated or softened into the sound of F, thus—Par'lan Macpharlain.

The chief seat of this clan was Arrochar, a district in Dunbartonshire, where the chiefs maintained themselves in respectable independence, amid the tumults and distractions which raged around them, and luckily escaped the designs of ambitious and grasping neighbours, by whom other tribes were involved in ruin.

The Highland chiefs long held their lands as allodial possession, and they accepted feudal charters with great reluctance, esteeming it a mark of dependance quite unworthy of their rank and descent. When Robert the Bruce had established himself on the throne, he issued a proclamation in which he desired all his barons, or freeholders, to produce their charters, and prove the right by which they held their lands. He found, however, that a spirit of indignant hostility was excited, which he was glad to allay by recalling the obnoxious order. James VI. tried the same experiment with like success. The Mackays were, perhaps, the last who retained their extensive estates by the ancient right of prescriptive occupation, a charter having been given no earlier than the middle of the fifteenth century. At a much later period, Mac Donald of Keppach spurned the offer of a crown-charter of his lands, observing with scorn, that he would never hold his paternal inheritance by the writing on a sheep's skin! The property was lost to that family, in consequence of this stubborn refusal. "By our swords," said those haughty chiefs, "we first acquired these lands, and by our swords shall we retain them!"

In the "Baronage," the Mac Pharlans are derived from the old Earls of Lennox, and it is not until the time of David Bruce, who commenced his reign in 1329, that there appears in this work a chief of the name of Par'lan, of which the old scribes made Bartholomew! but in the name of this king's father, Robert I., a charter was given to "Dowgal Mac Farlane, of the lands of Kindavie, Arynschauche, &c." Subsequently several others were obtained, either adding to the former possessions, or securing those which the clan already held.

The laird of Mac Farlane appears in the rolls of chiefs made out in 1587—94, with the view to enforce a law which prevailed in

MAC PHARLAN

Scotland, by which they were held accountable to government for the peaceable behaviour of all their followers. This was a Celtic practice, and was well adapted to the state of society, for if the natural head or governor of a clan was responsible for the members individually and collectively, it was evidently his interest to prevent them from becoming turbulent. It likewise tended to secure and increase his heritable power and influence. Should any property be stolen, as cattle frequently were, those through whose lands the robbers passed were bound to pursue and apprehend them if they could, and if the trace should be lost, the chief in whose lands they were last discovered was obliged to produce the offenders, with whom he was otherwise held to be guilty, "art and part."

In 1544, when Lennox took arms to oppose the regent Arran, and Donald Dubh of the Isles, had entered into a treaty with the king of England for an invasion of Scotland, in prosecution of which a landing was made at Dunbarton, Walter Mac Pharlan, of Tarbet, joined "the English party" with a body of his clansmen, amounting to 140 men. It is noted by the historian that these troops were able to speak both "English and Erse." They were what the Highlanders call Cearnaich, or light-armed troops, being provided with coats of mail, two-handed swords, bows and arrows, and they did good service then and in the subsequent operations. John, who lived in the reign of James VI., was a hospitable and generous chief, and endowed a house for the free lodging and entertainment of passengers.

Among the distinguished members of this clan, the late chief, Walter, who was a noted lawer, must be mentioned for his celebrity as an antiquary. He copied with great labour, the chartularies of the bishopricks and monasteries preserved in the Advocate's library, and left many other monuments of his industry and deep research into national history. In the army, the members of this clan have nobly shewn their national spirit, and many have risen to deserved distinction and rank.

The Mac Pharlans were among the few clans who opposed Queen Mary, and at Langside, "the valliancie of ane Highland gentleman, named Mac Farlan, stood the Regent's part in great stead, for in the hottest brunte of the fight he came in with 300 of his friends, and so manfullie gave in upon the flanke of the queen's people, that he was a great cause of disordering of them." On this occasion they carried off in triumph three of the enemy's standards.

Their force was estimated, in 1745, at 250, but by the proposal for a rising in 1704 it was calculated that they would muster 300.

The ARMORIAL BEARINGS of the Mac Pharlans are arg., a saltire ingrailed between four roses, gules. Supporters, the courtesy of Scotland allowing these marks of nobility to all chiefs of clans, are two Highlanders dressed in belted plaids of appropriate tartan, with drawn swords, bows, and arrows, proper. Crest, a demi-savage grasping in his dexter hand a sheaf of arrows, and pointing with the sinister to a crown, or. Mottos, on a compartment wavy, " Loch Sloidh," and above the shield, " This I'll defend."

The SUAICHEANTAS, or Badge, is Muillieag, Cranberry bush, *Oxycoccus palustris.*

The CATH-GHAIRM, war cry, or battle shout, is " Loch Sloidh," pronounced Sloy, the lake of the host, the plain along its bank being the place of rendezvous for the clan previous to an expedition.

The castle of Arrochar is situated in a very pleasant locality. Part of it was very old, but recently this venerable building has been pulled down for the purpose of being re-built in a beautiful style. The castles of Ellanbhui and Inveruglas, on islands in Loch Lomond, were also ancient seats.

The Mac Pharlans, as we have observed, were fortunate in avoiding the feuds which weakened and destroyed so many others. They had, however, occasional contentions with their neighbours, particularly the Colquhons, and it is affirmed that the unfortunate chief of that clan, who was slain in his castle, 1604, fell a victim to the Mac Pharlans, although, from the recent defeat at Glenfruin by the Mac Gregors, that unfortunate tribe was accused of the crime.

The figure represents an aged man, who having caught a fish, has lit a turf fire, and is broiling it for a plain repast. Since the abolition of clanship, the poor Highlanders do not receive that patriarchal protection which was neither given nor accepted as an almsgift. On the rugged shores of a stormy sea many an old and forlorn Gaël, like this figure, has now to seek for fish, where his ancestors were wont to subsist by hunting and the less precarious supply of corn and cattle.

CLANN DHUBHI—THE MAC PHEES.

THE Gaël have a predilection for softening the pronunciation of words, whence a language, which to a stranger would appear, from its numerous consonants, to be harsh and unpleasing, is rendered very euphonious. The Clann, or Mac, in this case, aspirates the d,

the indication of which effect is the h which follows; but the name has been farther softened, in common parlance, by elision of the first syllable, into Mac Phee.

This clan is a branch of the great Siol Alpinich, or race of Alpin,

MAC PHEE

the name implying a dark-coloured tribe, and their ancient possession was the island Colonsay, county of Argyle, of which Oransay, only isolated at high water, forms a part.

Munro, dean of the Isles, in his description of those parts, tells us that this "was the property of ane gentle Captain, called Mac Phie, but perteined of auld to clan Donald of Kintire." This island was held by the Mac Phees as late as the middle of the seventeenth century, and there are still several freeholders and many respectable families in the county. A branch of the clan who followed Locheil has been also settled in Lochaber from time immemorial.

In the burial ground of Iona, that venerated and ancient seat of piety and learning, there was, when Pennant visited the isle, 1772, a monument commemorating a chief of this clan. He described it as presenting the effigy of a warrior in high relief, armed with the claidheamh mòr, great or two handed sword, and among the ornaments was a Long-fada, or galley, the lymphad of the heralds, that invariable ensign of an insular or west highland chief, with the inscription "Hic jacet Malcolumbus Mac Duffie de Collonsay." Oransay contained a priory of canons regular, the ruins of which are little inferior in extent or architectural interest to those in Iona, but the cell of Columba and cemetery of so many kings was preferred by the Gaëlic nobles as the most hallowed resting-place.

Coll Mac Donald, better known by the appellation Ciotach, or left-handed, the faithful companion of the great Marquis of Montrose in the civil war of 1645, was accused with his followers, of having been "art and guilty of the felonie and cruell slaughter of umquhill Malcolm Mac Phie of Collonsay."

This clan, having been dispossessed of its original inheritance, became what has usually been termed "broken," i. e. lost their independence, and were obliged to rank in the following of others more powerful. It has been observed that a branch of them settled in the country of the Camerons, where they were much respected, and were useful auxiliaries to the laird of Locheil, distinguishing themselves by their bravery. In the battle of Culloden, the Camerons were one of the few clans who made that furious onset, which nearly annihilated the left wing of the Duke of Cumberland's army, and almost led to a brilliant victory. They suffered fearfully for their temerity, and, with the Camerons proper, fell slain and wounded a proportionate number of the name of Mac Phee. One of them was engaged in the vain attempt which was made to prevent the dragoons from getting through the wall which protected the flank of the Highland army, and he brought down both horse and rider with his broadsword; but ere Duncan could get clear of them the horse gave him a kick which broke his back; next day he was carried off the field, and although he lived long after, he walked on his stick, bent entirely to the ground. He used to say " she was a sore morning for him, but he made ae southern tak a sleep it would be lang ere he wakened fae."

There is at present living in an island in Loch Quoich, Invernessshire, "an outlaw" of this name—a sort of Rob Roy in his way, as he holds himself free of the laird or the law, paying no rent, or making acknowledgment of a superior. Ewen Mac Phee is a deserter from the army, but although his retreat is well known, he receives no molestation. He, however, does not consider himself entirely secure,

for his constant companion is a loaded rifle, which, it is said, his wife is as dextrous in the use of as himself. He leads in other respects a harmless life, maintaining his family chiefly on his goats and the fish and game he may procure. Some curiosity has lately been excited respecting this man from the unusual circumstances in which he is placed, and a clansman, a worthy baille of Glasgow, in lately passing along the Caledonian canal, and hearing Ewen's history, left a sovereign for his use.

The ARMORIAL BEARINGS for Mac Phee are or, a lion rampant, gules, surmounted by a fess, azure. Crest, a demi lion rampant, gule. Motto, "Pro Rege."

The SUAICHEANTAS, or Badge, is Guithas Pine, *pinus sylvestris*, as being a branch of the Clan Alpin. If in the ranks of the Cameron, the badge of the superior would be adopted.

The figure which illustrates this clan is dressed in the shirt of mail, of which the highlanders so long retained the use. It is called lurich in Gaëlic, a word, which it has been observed in a previous number, bears a close resemblance to the Latin lorica, applied to a similar piece of defensive armour by the Romans, and which Varro tells us is a word derived by them from the Gauls, who would hence appear to have been its inventors. The form in this instance is rather remarkable, but there is old authority for it. The openings in the skirt gave freedom to the wearer, and the sword was thrust through a hole, as the most convenient method of carrying it. The head is protected by the clogaid, skull-piece, or helmet, of the conical form, worn by both the Gaël and the nations of Scandinavia, but longest retained by the highlanders. He wears in it the eagle's wing, which we find from Ossianic poetry was the peculiar distinction of the chiefs. He is armed with the da Sleag, two missile spears or darts, which are often alluded to as having been carried by the heroes of old. The ball at the lower end, called the cnapstarra, is mentioned by Dion Cassius as having been used by the ancient Caledonians to disturb the enemy and their cavalry by a rattling noise which it made. This weapon is seen on sepulchral monuments, and is mentioned in Gaëlic poetry of late ages.

CLANN MHURICH—THE MAC PHERSONS.

THIS is the oldest branch of the great Clan Chattan, who are believed to be descended of the German Catti, and whose original possessions were the northern part of Scotland, now forming the counties of Sutherland and Caithness, the latter of which being the original name of both, was derived from this people.

The generic appellation of this clan was Cattanich, which denotes shaggy-haired, rough-looking men; and it is remarkable that the Catti are described by Tacitus as presenting a more stern aspect than the other Gauls, from the practice of fashioning their hair and beard in a certain rough and grizly manner, so that, by the fierceness of their visage, they might be the more terrible to their enemies. The name certainly does not arise from their ancestors putting a herd of ferocious cats to the route when they first landed from Germany, as some historians are pleased to tell us! It came to be changed in this manner:—Muraich, or Murdach, who was second son of Diarmid, the chief, betook himself to the Church, and became parson of Kingùsie, a religious establishment in the lower part of Badenach. The elder brother dying without issue, in 1153, the succession devolved on Muraich the younger, and this cognomen being aspirated in the genitive, thus: Mhuraich, pronounced Vurech, his descendants were designated indifferently from his own name, Clann Mhurich, or were called Mac Phersain, from his office. Procuring a papal dispensation, he married a daughter of the Thane of Calder, and left two sons, Gille Chattan and Eoghan bân. Dugal-dàl, the grandson, had only a daughter, called Eva, who, about the year 1292, married Aongas, ancestor of the chief of the Mac Intoshes, who thereby acquired a great accession of lands, and many of the Cattanich remained with the heiress, and assumed the name of Mac Intosh; but as the rule of clanship, like the salique law in France, excluded females from succession, Eoghan, i. e. Ewen, second son of Muraich, was accordingly acknowledged by the great majority of the clan as their legitimate chief. It is from Kenneth, the eldest of his three sons, that the distinguished family of Mac Pherson of Clunie, chief of the Clan Chattan, known in the Highlands as "Mac Mhurich Chluanaidh," is descended, in the direct male line.

It was at this time that the clan left Lochaber, which they had possessed for several generations; and for the great service they had rendered King Robert Bruce, by expelling the Cummins from that country, and killing their turbulent chief, they obtained a grateful reward from that heroic monarch, who bestowed on this clan the possessions in Badenach, which had so long sheltered his inveterate foes. Those who adhered to Eva remained in Lochaber, and hence appears the origin of a right to that district, which the Mac Intoshes always so strenuously, but often so unsuccessfully, maintained, for the weakened strength of Eva's clansmen did not enable them to maintain their rule, and repress repeated insurrections.

In the beginning of the reign of Robert III. a desperate war was carried on between the Camerons and the Clan Chattan. The former, on one occasion, came down to Inver-na-h-avan, a plain at the juncture of the river Truim with the Spey, where they were met by the united forces of the Mac Phersons, Mac Intoshes, and Clann Dhai', or Davidsons. An engagement at once took place, but unfortunately, the Mac Phersons, indignant at finding the post of honour assigned to the Mac Dhai's, withdrew from the fight, and their friends were defeated; but next day Clunie retrieved the disgrace. He fell on the enemy with his own clan, unassisted by the others, and routed them, with great slaughter—a running fight being kept up from Badenach to Lochaber. A violent feud between the Davidsons and Mac Phersons was the consequence of the preference so inconsiderately given to the former by Mac Intosh, who, as captain of Clan Chattan, marshalled the troops, and who, no doubt, had the command of the united forces, as the quarrel was about the lands in Lochaber to which he laid claim

The commotion thus excited in the North Highlands must have been great, when it was deemed necessary to send the Earls of Moray and Crauford on a special mission to try whether they could compose those differences which so much distracted the country. Their mediation was unfortunately ineffectual, and the sword alone could stanch the mortal strife. A proposition was therefore made, which was at once embraced by both parties, that the quarrel should be decided by thirty men selected on each side, who were to fight on a plain called the North Inch of Perth before King Robert III., the officers of state, and nobility, armed with two-handed swords only, that the right should be decided "by the just judgement of God; and in the year 1396 this extraordinary conflict took place. When these stern warriors were drawn up on each side it was found that the Clan Chattan were one short of the prescribed number, but both parties were determined for the onslaught, and no man would leave the rank on the opposite side to equalise the combat. The Mac Phersons equally resolute, offered a reward, no greater, it is said, than half a mark, to any one present, who would join their clan in this mortal contention. The reward for this imminent peril of life seems to us small; but there were chivalrous spirits in those days, to whom it was sufficient temptation; and one Henry, a blacksmith, living in the "wynd," or lane of Perth, from which he was familiarly designated "Harry of the wynd," promptly stepped forward, when the battle forthwith commenced, and our readers will recollect the graphic narrative of the sanguinary combat, which is given in "The Fair Maid of Perth," one of Sir Walter Scott's interesting novels.

With such unflinching bravery did the indomitable heroes maintain the fight, that it did not cease until twenty-nine of the Clan Dhai' had fallen on the spot, when the unhappy man who alone remained, although unhurt, seeing all his comrades stretched in death, plunged with desperation into the river Tay and swam across. Eleven of the

Clan Chattan survived the conflict, but they were all so severely wounded that they were unable to pursue the fugitive, who, it is believed, was killed by his own clan, infuriated by their defeat, for his cowardice in not preferring death in the bed of honour to retreat. As to the valiant blacksmith, the general belief is that he accompanied the Mac Phersons to Badenach, and was incorporated in the clan, his progeny being distinguished as " Sliochd," a ghobha chruim, or the race of the stooping smith ; but a tradition exists, that in his way north he stopped in Strathdoun, Aberdeenshire, where his descendants are still known by a similar appellation.

Ewen of Clunie was a staunch friend of the unfortunate Queen Mary, and John was with his clan at the battle of Glenlivat, in 1594, where the royal forces under the Earl of Argyle were entirely defeated. The Mac Phersons were active in the service of King Charles I., and suffered much for their loyalty. An anecdote is related of a gentleman of this clan, who, when preparing to engage a party of the enemy's horse, was observed to be crouching down, some way in the rear, on which, believing it was from cowardice, Mac Pherson of Nuid ran up to him, indignant that he should set so improper an example. " I have only," observed he, " been fastening a spur to the heel of my brog, for I mean to be mounted on one of these horses in five minutes," and he soon accomplished his object.

The Mac Intoshes were more numerous than the Mac Phersons, and their chiefs were most anxious to be acknowledged as supreme head of the whole race of the Cattanich. The latter were, however, extremely jealous of any attempt to assume this honour, and much bad blood was engendered by these adverse claims. In 1665, when Mac Intosh went on an expedition against the Camerons for recovery of the lands of Glenluy and Locharkaig, he solicited the assistance of the Mac Phersons, who were to receive some part of the lands to be recovered, when, so fearful were they lest their attendance might be construed into a duty, that a regular notarial deed was executed, wherein Mac Intosh declares that it was of their mere goodwill and pleasure that they did so ; and, on his part, it is added—" I bind and oblige myself and friends and followers, to assist, fortify, and join with the said Andrew, Lachlan, and John Mac Pherson, all their lawful and necessary adoes, being thereunto required." Notwithstanding this, Mac Intosh continued to assert his right to the chiefship of the Mac Mhurichs, the consequence of which was prolonged and violent dissensions between the clans. The Marquis of Huntly being Lord of Badenach, took the part of the Mac Phersons, and letters are preserved in the charter chest at Clunie castle, from his tutor and relative, Lord Aboyne, declaring that they would " espouse the quarrel against the Mackintosh." At last a protest was raised by Mac Intosh before the Privy Council, in order to have it determined by a judicial decree, as to the right of either party to the proper ensigns armorial. It was rather a delicate matter to be decided, and from the example given on the North Inch of Perth it might be matter of doubt whether the award would not produce a serious clan war; but the Council steered a middle and just course, and, after protracted litigation, an order was issued for both chiefs to give surety for the peaceable behaviour of their respective clansmen, thus deciding, in terms as inoffensive as could well be used,

that they were each independent. This process excited great interest in the north, and Clunie received the hearty congratulations of many friends on his return from Edinburgh—Keith, Earl Marischal, and others, entertaining him by the way, and acknowledging that they were of the Catti, and freely accepted him as their chief.

Among other grievances which the Mac Phersons had to complain of against their neighbours, was the erection of a mill, about 1660, by Mac Intosh, which, although on his own property, it was alleged would be injurious to one belonging to Clunie, lower down the stream. Remonstrance having no effect it was determined to appeal to arms; the crois tara' was sent through the country to raise the clann Mhurich, who were stimulated by the assertion of some seanachai's, that it had been prophesied of old, that at this time a great battle should be fought between the rival clans. They accordingly met each other at the sight of the intended mill; but Mac Intosh finding himself inferior in numbers, sent down to the laird of Grant for a reinforcement. This chief was a young man, and, entering keenly into the design, he promised to dispatch a large body to assist his friend early next morning. This transaction affords us a fine instance of the effect or " working" of clanship, a system so different from what it is generally represented. The elders, comhairlich, or councillors, on learning their chief's determination, immediately went to him, and remonstrated against his involving the clan in a dispute with which they had nothing to do. " The Mac Phersons," they observed, " are our near neighbours, and in memory of man there has not been so much as a quarrel or slaughter between us. It therefore becomes us to preserve that peace and goodwill for our children, which has been handed down from our fathers to us, and not stir up a war of which no one can foresee the consequences." The resolute manner in which those men delivered their advice could not be resisted, and The Grant, arbitrary as a chief is supposed to have been, immediately countermanded the proposed levy. Mac Intosh then made a similar application to his relation, the chief of the Farquharsons, but with no better success, for, though many of his people were inclined to take arms, he bluntly desired the messenger to say, that his master was greatly mistaken, if he thought that, because he had married his sister, the Clann Fiunla', were to be embroiled in a war with the Mac Phersons. Under these circumstances, the two clans having faced each other for some days in the month of October, Mac Intosh drew off his men, the Clann Mhurich threw down what of the walls had been built, and the erection of the mill was abandoned.

Ewen Mac Pherson of Clunie, who was captain in Lord Loudon's highlanders, threw up his commission on the arrival of Prince Charles Edward, in 1745, and raised the clan in his favour, joining the army soon after the victory at Prestonpans. The bravery of this battalion was evinced on various occasions during the short campaign, particularly on the admirable retreat from England; and had not Clunie been too late for the battle of Culloden, his 600 men, it is believed, would have been sufficient to retrieve the misfortunes of that day, but in vain did he urge the Prince, whom he met in the retreat, to return to the charge. The Mac Phersons were stimulated to take a determined part in this unfortunate rising, chiefly from the fate of three of their clansmen, who suffered for the extraordinary mutiny of the Black-watch, now the 42nd two years

TOUGH ME CAT BOT A GLOVE.

MAC PHERSON

before. This regiment having been marched to the vicinity of London, were apprehensive that it was intended to send them abroad, contrary to their terms of enlistment, and almost the whole body decamped at night in the hope of being able to reach the highlands, but they were intercepted in Northamptonshire, and marched to the Tower. Being brought to trial, many were banished to different colonies, and three were shot. These three were Samuel and Andrew Mac Pherson of Druminourd, and Farquhar Shaw.

Sorely did their chief pay for his favour to Prince Charles, whom he not only so bravely fought for, but afterwards concealed for some time from the vigilant pursuit of his enemies. Clunie was himself for the long period of nine years a disconsolate refugee, moving from wood to wood and cave to cave, in avoidance of the parties sent to capture him, from whom he made many hair-breadth escapes, and although his retreats were well known to his clansmen, no one could be bribed to divulge the secret. His house had been burned, and his lands forfeited; his lady, a daughter of Lord Lovat, giving birth to a son, afterwards colonel in the third regiment of foot-guards, in a kiln for drying corn. The Prince's military chest, with a considerable sum of money, was left in Clunie's possession, which with high honour he preserved intact and carried with him when he made his escape to the Continent, where he soon afterwards died.

In 1689, when the Viscount Dundee took arms for King James, Clunie, received a commission from the Estates "to convocat and call together all his friends, kinsmen, vassels, followers, and tennants, and other fencible men, under his command or influence, and reduce them into troops, companies, or a regiment, with power to name his inferior officers, &c. &c." *Acta Parl.* app. 18.

In Clunie Castle, a handsome modern building, are preserved various relics of the Rebellion of 1745. Here is the Prince's target, which lay buried under ground until the death of Clunie. It is mounted richly and with much taste in silver trophies and other ornaments, and is lined with leopard-skin. There are also a pair of gold-inlaid pistols and his sporan, or purse, formed of seal-skin, with silver mounting and tassels. The colour which waved over the battalion on that occasion is still preserved, and in a good state, considering that it has been nine times perforated with musket balls. This is the Bratach uaine, or green banner, of which it is said an old woman foretold the Duke of Cumberland, that, should he await its arrival, he would assuredly meet his defeat. There are also the lace ruffles which ornamented Charles's wrists, and were given by him to Cameron of Fassifearn: an autograph letter from the Prince, promising an ample reward to his devoted friend Clunie, and a plate intended to strike off notes for the use of the army. A leathern belt of red morocco, called the Crios breac, is likewise shown, which has been so called from its numerous silver studs These represent the Agnus Dei and head of St. John alternately with other ornaments; and there can be little doubt but that it was brought from the Holy Land, by Murdach, or some other chief, who had made pilgrimage thither. The Feadan du', or black pipe chanter, must not be forgotten—the prosperity of the house of Clunie is popularly believed to be dependant on its preservation, and it is not doubted by all true clansmen that it is the veritable instrument which fell from heaven to supply the loss of that used by the piper at the battle of Perth !

The ARMORIAL BEARINGS of Clunie Mac Pherson, as he is generally designated, are party per fess or and azure, in dexter chief a hand, fesswise, grasping a dagger, palewise, gules, and in sinister a cross crosslet, gules; in base a lymphad, sails furled, oars in action of the first. Crest, a cat sejant proper. Supporters, two Highlanders in slashed-out blue doublets, their shirts, or leinn croich, fastened between their bare thighs, steel caps, swords by their sides, and targets on their arms. Motto, " Touch not the cat bot a glove."

The SUAICHEANTAS, or Badge, is—Lus nam braoileag, red whortle berry bush, *Vaccinium vitis idœa.*

The CATHGHAIRM, " Craig dhu !" the name of a high precipitous rock, over which falls a small stream, and at the base of which are two pretty little lakes called Lochan-uvie.

The PIOBAIREACHDAN.—The Mac Phersons claim " Ceann na drochait mòr " as their piobaireachd, alleging that it was composed on occasion of the battle of Perth, fought at " the end of the great bridge " over the Tay, but the Camerons belive that it is theirs. There seems to be a mistake in this for " the end of the *little* bridge," another piece of music. The claim to the composition of one of the pipers, who regretted in the field of battle that he had not three hands, so that he might both fight and play, is not disputed.

The figure is that of a Highland gentleman in full dress. The breacan fheile, or kilt and plaid, of one piece, is of " the grey plaid of Badenach," as worn by Captain Ewen Mac Pherson, present chief, and twenty-third from Gillichattan mòr. It is, however, somewhat different from the old pattern, which is plainer, and has the colours otherwise arranged. That worn by the clansmen in general as the appropriate tartan, is a pretty composition of the red class. In the hose a sett is shown, interesting as having been painted from a plaid woven about two hundred years ago, of remarkably fine texture, the colours still retaining their brilliancy, and it is one of the earliest specimens of hard tartan. The material was spun by one of the ladies of the house of Crubin, represented by Colonel Barkley Mac Pherson, and it is now in possession of Mrs. Mackintosh, of Stephen's Green, Dublin, to whom she was great great grandmother. It is not considered the common clan tartan, but it has been called the full dress pattern of the chief. The Eideadh ghaelich, or Highland dress, is usually worn by Mac Mhuraich Chluanadh, and he is one of those who always addresses his countrymen in their mother tongue, the revered language of their fathers.

James Mac Pherson the distinguished translator of the poems of Ossian was descended of William, second son of John of Nuid, who succeeded to the chiefship in 1722.

CLANN GHUAIRI'—THE MAC QUARIES.

THE race of Mac Quarie is of royal descent, and the generations of the chief are traced by the Seanachies, or Celtic genealogists to the second son of Gregor, son of Alpin, the famous king of Scots, who fell in battle, anno. 837.

The name of this personage has appeared under various forms; in the national annals it is Cor or Gor-bred, which was latinised by the norman appellation, Godfredus or Godfrey, and hence, by a euphonious mutation, it became in the hands of Culdee chroniclers, Mac Gotherie, Mac Gofra, Mac Gorrie, &c.

An indigenous Gaëlic appellation is not with propriety translatable. The proper orthography is Guarai' which is still preserved by some of the branches of the clan. The Mac Guarans, of Ireland, have generally called themselves Mac Guire, but they are an undoubted offspring from the Scottish tribe, and the lineage is attested by the identity of their coat armour with that of the lairds of Ulva, chiefs of the name.

Of these, Cormac surnamed mòr or the great, lived in the time of Alexander II. whom he joined with his followers and three biorlins or gallies of sixteen oars each, in the great expedition which that monarch undertook against the inhabitants of the Isles, which were then under the Norwegian rule. The king's death in the island of Kerera, rendered the design abortive, but Cormac by appearing in the armament brought on himself a severe retaliation; being attacked, his forces were overthrown, he himself was slain, and his sons Allan and Gregor were compelled to take refuge in Ireland, and the latter, surnamed garbh, or the rough, founded the branch distinguished by the above appellation, which, under the Earls of Inniskillin, became so powerful in that country, Eachuin, translated Hector! was chief when the illustrious Bruce contended for his crown and Scotland's independence, and he fought with his clan in the army of that hero at the ever memorable Bannockburn. Another of the same name, who flourished in the commencement of the sixteenth century, became deeply involved in the troubles which then agitated the highlands, and we find in judicial record, 1504, repeated summonses to "Mac Corry of Ullowaa" to make his appearance before Parliament on a charge of rebellion. In those times such decrees could not be very easily inforced; Mac Quarie neither gave himself up, nor was apprehended, but in 1517, Lachlan Mac Lean, of Duart, in obtaining his own remission, stipulated for a similar indemnity to his ally of Ulva. This chief married a daugther of Mac Niel, of Tainish, and the bride's tocher or dowry appears very singular in the present state of society: it consisted of a pie–bald horse, with two men and two women, the descendants of whom were long recognised.

Eachuin's son Donald was one of thirteen chiefs who were denounced in 1545 for traitorous correspondence with the king of England, but like his father, the sturdy chief set at defiance the power of his lawful sovereign and escaped the penalty. Allan, his successor, was slain with most of his followers at the battle of Inverkeithing, during the great civil war, 1651.

Lachlan the sixteenth and last chief in regular succession died in 1818, at the patriarchal age of 103 years; having disposed of his lands for behoof of his creditors, he entered the army when upwards of 63. Leaving no male issue, the late general Mac Quarie, long the respected governor of New South Wales, repurchased much of the ancient patrimonial property; and if not accepted as chief, was assuredly the first Ceanntigh or cadet. He married Miss Baillie of Jarviswood; and his only son, Lachlan, by his second wife, daughter of Sir John Campbell, of Airds, died without issue.

The ARMORIAL BEARINGS for Mac Quarie are quarterly, first and fourth vert, three towers in chief arg., second and third gules, three croslets fitchee, arg., in middle base, a ship and salmon, naiant-proper. Crest, from an antique crown, in token of the royal descent, an arm embowed, couped at the shoulder, in plate armour proper, grasping a dagger, arg. pommeled, or. Motto "Turris fortis mihi deus." Supporters, two greyhounds proper, leashed and collared, or.

The SUAICHEANTAS is Giuthas, Pine, *Pinus Sylvestris*.

The CATHGHAIRM or battle shout "An t-Airm breac dearg."

In the Chapel of St Ouran, the oldest of the ruins in the far-famed island of Iona, lies an effigy of one of the ancient chiefs of Ulva. It is executed in a superior style, and is still in good preservation. Had it been placed in a niche so that it might not have been trodden upon, an inscription, still almost legible, could no doubt have been easily deciphered. We have often in other cases observed, with great regret, the indifference which is displayed respecting these, and similar ancestral honours.

The illustrative figure appears in a jacket and feile-beag, without a plaid, and wears Cuarans or highland buskins. Those who have seen the curious woodcuts in Derricke's "Image of Ireland," reprinted in Lord Somers' Tracts, by Sir Walter Scott, will recognise the similarity of costume in that country and the highlands of Scotland, some centuries back.

The Clai' mòr, or genuine two-handed sword, is slung on the back, the only method in which it could be carried. A very fine specimen of an old target is given. It was grasped by a handle in the middle of the central boss, and not fastened to the arm, a method of wielding it, which much lessened its utility. It is steel-mounted and a ring around the umbo, is dextrously contrived, so that it might entangle the weapon of an adversary. It is provided with a hook, to enable the bearer to suspend it over his shoulder, in which way it was carried on a march, or when not in use. The figure shews the manner of highland archery; the Celt drawing the bow to the breast, the Saxon to the ear. Although apparently a disadvantageous method, as not giving sufficient power or precision, the Cearnaich, or those who carried bows and arrows, were good marksmen, and it has surprised us that the use of this weapon has been so entirely dropt in the highlands, especially by poachers, to whom it afforded the facility of bringing down the prey without giving the alarm of a report.

Mulroy i. e. Maol-ruadh, the bare, red point, in bræ Lochaber, fought 1688, was the last clan battle, in which bows and arrows were used. A body provided with this weapon, we think, might still be employed as a useful arm in the British forces.

Quivers were sometimes of wattle-work, but usually of skin, and that of the badger was preferred.

CLANN RATH—THE MAC RAES.

THIS is a Ross-shire clan of great antiquity, which was at one time both numerous and powerful; but through vicissitudes, such as those we have given instances of in the history of other tribes, the Mac Ra's fell into decadence. From being independent they were brought under the following of the Mac Kenzies, when that clan obtained the ascendancy in the north; and, although the name remained very extensively in the country, they possessed but little landed property and had not any great independent influence. As the ancient mode of holding lands was by immemorial possession, and not by feudal charter, the Mac Ra's were not in a singular position, for, like many others, they long continued in undisturbed occupancy, as "kyndly tenants," i. e. they were continued on the land in perpetuity, on payment of a stated rent, often nominal. This primitive system is found, in some instances, still to exist.

We have not heard any satisfactory account of the origin of this clan, which seems to have been indigenous. Mac Rath, pronounced Mac Ra', corruptly Rae, would signify the son of good fortune, and it is traditionally accounted for by the exclamation of a father, on learning that his son had achieved some wonderful exploit.

The practice of fostering, or having children brought up in the families of others, was a favourite Celtic usage, and it gave rise to bonds of friendship more strong and lasting than the ties of relationship. The powerful family of Bisset of Lovat, was forfeited in the time of King William the Lyon, who reigned from 1165 to 1214, at which period the Mac Raes were of considerable note. Mary, daughter of the last Lord Bisset, who carried the estates of Lovat to the Frasers, was fostered with Mac Rae, of Cluns, for whom she naturally entertained the highest respect, in which feeling her husband cordially participated, and a firm alliance continued long afterwards to subsist between their descendants. It is said, that a stone was erected at the door of Lord Lovat's castle, intimating that no Mac Rae should lodge without while a Fraser resided within.

There was one Donchadh, or Duncan Mac Ra', grandson to Duncan Mac gille Chriosd, a distinguished Cearnach, or warrior, among the Clann Choinich, in whose following we have remarked the Mac Raes were latterly ranked. This man, on one occasion, undertook with a choice, but small, company of associates, a hazardous expedition, in order to intercept the great Mac Donald of Glengarry, who had carried off a spraith of cattle from the Mac Kenzies' lands of Loch Carron. Having discovered the Biorlins, or galleys, of the enemy, Mac Rae boldly attacked them, and singling out the vessel in which Glengarry sailed, he furiously assaulted her, broke most of the oars, and otherwise greatly damaged the hull. Finally, after a severe contention, she was driven on a projecting rock at the point of Cailleach, when the chief and his whole crew were put to the sword. The victory was, however, dearly bought by the heroic Mac Rae, who lost his own life; but he left a son, who had subsequently ample opportunities, which, tradition says, he did not overlook, to revenge the death of his father.

The PIOBAIREACHD of this clan is very ancient, and was composed on occasion of a desperate battle, which took place in Strathconan. The Lord of the Isles having invaded Ross-shire with a numerous army, the Mac Kenzies took the field to protect their lands and property, and endeavour to recover a great booty which their enemies were driving away. They thought it necessary for this object, to obtain the assistance of the Mac Raes, who would not, from this circumstance, appear to have been at that time in any way dependent on the Clann Choinich. They accordingly joined with their force, and one of them, called Surachan, acquitted himself with admirable bravery; having slain a notable personage in the Mac Donald ranks, he is described, in the tradition, as coolly setting himself down on the body of the slain. Conduct so extraordinary attracted the attention of the chief of the Mac Kenzies, who went up to Surachan, and asked how he could sit with so much indifference

MAC QUARIE

while the battle raged around? "I have done my day's work," replied the stoical Celt, "and if every man do as much it will go well with us." "Kill more," exclaimed Mac Kenzie, "and I shall not reckon your labour by the day," on which Surachan started up, and dealt fearful destruction amongst the Mac Donalds, who were defeated with great slaughter! "Spaidseareach mhic Rha'," commemorates this battle, and, as its name imports, it is the "march" of the clan.

The ARMORIAL HONOURS of Mac Rae are argent, on a fess, gules, between two mullets in chief, and a lion rampant, in base, of the last, a mullet of the first. Crest, a hand holding a sword, proper. Motto, "Fortiter."

The military strength of this clan must have been at one time very considerable; but from their attachment to the house of Seaforth, they suffered much in the battles of Sherriffmuir, Glensheil, &c. When the late Sir John Sinclair published his great work, the Statistical Account of Scotland, 1793, all the inhabitants of Kintail were Mac Raes, except two or three families, and when the 78th regiment or Ross-shire Buffs, were raised in 1804, one gentleman brought eighteen of his own name in his complement for an ensigncy

John Mac Rae, better known among his countrymen as Mac Uirtsi, was the last of a race of bards, the gift of poesy having descended from father to son for some generations. He emigrated to America from sheer discontent with the invasion of ancient habits by the schemes for improving the Highlands and their population, for he was in comfortable circumstances, and feelingly regretted, in native verse, his folly in taking that step. A poem which he composed, on a heavy loss of cattle which he sustained, is reckoned, by many, to be equal to a ything in the Gaëlic language. One of this clan was an able governor of Madras, in commemoration of whom a monument is erected on a rising ground in the parish of Prestwick, county of Ayr.

The figure is dressed as a modern forester would appear, and carries without apparent difficulty, a large fat deer, which his unerring shot has brought down. The "Glengarry" bonnet has been taken into such general favour, that it seems useless to object to it as an innovation, or point out its inconvenience; neither defending the wearer from rain, nor the scorching rays of the summer sun. The sporan, or purse, is closed by a snap of the common old fashion.

CLANN MHATHAIN—THE MATHESONS.

THIS clan has experienced the fate of many others, which are now reduced from their former high standing among the independent tribes of Caledonia.

The etymon of the name Mac Mhathain, or Mathaineach, pronounced with the *th* quiescent, seems to be Maithean, heroes, or rather Maon, a hero, a term now obsolete. The form of the English translation is rather unaccountable, but the Mathesons of the Highlands are not to be confounded with those in other parts, whose name is a corruption of Matthew's-son.

Tradition represents the clan Mhathain as settled in Lochalsh, a district of wester Ross, in the time of Kenneth Mac Alpin, 834-53, whom they assisted in his wars with the Picts, and that in the twelfth century Coinneach, then chief, left two sons, Cailean, who carried on the line, and Coinneach, or Kenneth, from whom the Mac Kenzies derive their patronymic.

Alastair Mac Ruarai', who flourished in the beginning of the fifteenth century, was involved in a feud with the Earl of Sutherland, who marched to Lochalsh to chastise this haughty chief, but he was defeated and slain at a place since called Cnoc nan Cattich. In consequence of these proceedings, and the rebellion of Donald of the Isles, in which Alastair was engaged, King James I. seized him at Inverness, when he is said to have been commander of 2,000 men, and carried him to Edinburgh, where he was executed, 1427. He left two sons by a daughter of the chief of the Mac an Toshachs, who afterwards married a son of Mac Leod of the Lewes, between whom and the sons such dissensions arose as compelled them to leave the country: the younger retiring to Caithness, and John, the elder, to his grandfather. Here he lived for some time, but intent on obtaining possession of his inheritance, he obtained the assistance of a body of men from Mac Intosh, and commenced his march. Great caution

MAC RAE

was necessary to effect his purpose, for Mac Leod had adopted the most vigilant measures to prevent surprise; but, favoured by the trusty clansmen, he entered Lochalsh unobserved, and forthwith assaulted and set fire to the castle; yet anxious to save his mother, he stationed himself at the gate, that he might prevent her being slain in the *mêleé.* When forced to come out, she was, of course, permitted to pass through the body of the assailants without molestation, but in the darkness and tumult it was not perceived that she had concealed her husband under the ample folds of her Arisaid, the dress in which the illustrative figure is arrayed; when beyond observation, he quickly made off, and effected his escape to Lewes, while Matheson took possession of his property. Mac Leod was not slow to seek revenge: he landed with a strong force, and speedily encountered the Mathanaich, but he was repulsed with great loss, occasioned chiefly by being galled in retreat to the biorlins; or galleys, by Ian ciar mac Murdhai' mhic Thomais, who commanded the bowmen, from which the battle is called " Blar nan saigheadear." In a second attempt Mac Leod was slain, and the feud was thereby staunched.

John, a succeeding chief was appointed constable of Ellan-Donan castle by Mac Kenzie of Kintail, and had ample opportunity of proving his fitness for the responsible duty, sustaining successfully the attacks of the ferocious Donald gorm of Sleit, in one of which, 1537, he was slain by an arrow which entered a window where he stood. The possessions of the Mathesons were at this time greatly reduced, for his son Dugal had no more than the third of Lochalsh, and was engaged in frequent squabbles with his turbulent neighbour, Glengarry, who at last seized and put him in prison, where he soon died. His son, Murdach buidh, burning to revenge his father's wrongs, relinquished all his remaining possessions, except the farms of Balmacara and Fearnaig, to Mac Kenzie of Kintail, for a sufficient body of men to enable him to attack his enemy; the lands were accordingly made over, but the success of the enterprise was not so apparent. His elder son, Ruarai', was of great assistance to Seaforth, when he stormed Glengarry's castle of Sròn, in Lochcarron.

In process of time the " kindly " tenancy or occupation of land by prescription was converted into a stipulated rent, for Balmacara and other properties, and this once independent clan became dispersed, and in great measure lost among others, but many individuals of great worth and respectability are still to be found among its members. James Matheson, Esq., M.P., who has lately added the island of Lewis (thirty-six miles long by about ten broad) to his other property, rivals in extent of territorial possession, the ancient chiefs of Lochalsh. It is due to say of this gentleman that the exercise of patriotism and benevolence which do not always meet the public eye, render his important connexion with his native country a real blessing.

By the MS. history of this clan in our possession, which is the chief authority consulted, it appears that Alexander Mac Mhathain, who lived in Sallachie, 1822, was the representative, in lineal descent, of the eldest branch of the ancient house of Lochalsh.

THE ARMORIAL INSIGNIA borne by Matheson of Balmacara are, gyrony of eight, sable and gules, a lion rampant, arg. within a bordure of the last, charged with eight crosslets fitchee, of the second. Crest, a naked arm holding a drawn sabre, proper. Motto, " Fac et spera." Many others carry or for arg., and a cock for crest.

The worthy member for Ashburton carries in the bordure the addition of bears' heads, with two hands grasping daggers, to indicate his maternal descent from the Mac Kays, and the motto is " Heart and hand."

The CATH-GHAIRM, or rallying cry, was " Dail acha'n da thear nai'," the field between two descents, which was the place of assemblage before the clan went on any expedition, for it was reckoned a presage of misfortune if an enterprise was undertaken without this preliminary muster.

The principal figure in the illustration of this clan is a female, who wears that antique and now disused garment called an Arisaid, the same in which the lady of Lochalsh effected the escape of her husband. It is white striped with yellow, but the pattern varied according to the taste of the wearer. Martin describes the Hebridean ladies in this dress, which was " made of sufficient length to reach from the neck to the ankles, and being nicely plaited all round, was fastened about the waist with a belt, and secured on the breast by a large brooch. The belt was of leather and several pieces of silver intermixed, giving it the semblance of a chain, and at the lower end was a piece of plate about eight inches long and three broad, curiously engraven, and ingeniously adorned with fine stones, or piece of red coral." They wore sleeves of scarlet cloth like those of the men, laced with gold or silver, and adorned with buttons of plate set with precious stones.* The hair was plaited on each side, the ends being tastefully fastened with ribbons.

The boy wears a doublet and feilebag of the appropriate tartan, with deer-skin cuarans high up the leg.

*Scottish Gaël, i. 264.

MATHESON

MENZIES.

THE MENZIES' have been noticed, by Scottish historians, as bearing one of the surnames which first came into use about the time of Malcolm Ceanmor, A.D. 1090. The name having frequently been spelt Meyners, they have come to be considered a branch of the English family, Manners; but this opinion, although generally received by genealogists, does not appear well-founded: ancient orthography is very unsettled, and the name is as often spelt in one way as in the other. The Gaëlic appellation is Meinn, which is Meinnanich in the plural, and is often corruptly, Meinnarich

The clan has been settled in Athol from a very early period, and has held an important position among the Gaëlic tribes. The name occurs in charters of the reign of William the Lion, 1213; and in the time of Alexander II., about 1250, Robert de Meyners, Knt., was Lord High Chamberlain. His son, Alexander, we find in possession of the extensive territories of Fortingal, Weem, and Aberfeldy, in Athol, Glendochart in Breadalban, Durrisdeer in Nithsdale, and many others.* To Robert, the elder son of this potent chief, descended those great estates; while to Thomas, the younger, reverted the lands of Fortingal. It is from the elder that the present chief is descended. The Fortingal branch terminated in an heiress, who carried the property to the Stewarts, by marriage with James, natural son of the celebrated "Wolf of Badenach."*[1]

Sir Niel Menzies, Bart., creation 1665, as "principem claræ familie," who, with characteristic loyalty, performed his homage at Taymouth, is the respected representative (the twenty-sixth it is believed) of a long line of illustrious ancestry, who distinguished themselves in various important diplomatic services, and in the frequent fields of national war. The family of Pitfoddels, in the county of Aberdeen, who branched off early in the fourteenth century, is one of the most respectable in the north; and the present venerable laird, who was for forty years convener of the county, has distinguished himself by the endowment of a catholic college, for religious services and instruction, at the expense of most part of his large estate. Gilbert Menzies, of this family, carrying the royal standard at the last battle of Montrose, refused quarter, and fell rather than relinquish his charge.

This clan has long been famed for attention to the rearing of cattle, from which circumstance their lands were a favourite field for predatory inroads; " a fat mart from the herds of the Menzies" being proverbially offered as a tempting reward for a good piper, or a meritorious action. Under the active encouragement of the present chief, pastoral, agricultural, and other improvements are prosecuted with characteristic zeal and success.

"The Menyesses in Athoill and Apnadull," appear in " the Roll of Clans that have Captanes, Chiefs, and Chieftanes, on whom they depend, 1587."*[2] The clan has been otherwise distinguished by producing many celebrated individuals, and the Meinnanich were reckoned to be always peaceably disposed. They could not, how-

ever, avoid sharing in the usual troubles of the times. They were the first who suffered in Montrose's wars, their lands being ravaged in revenge for the death of a trumpeter, whom the Menzies unhappily had slain, the first blood drawn in that chivalrous campaign.† Several names are found of "gentlemen vassals," taken prisoners at the battle of Dunblane, 1715.* In 1745, Menzies of Shian took out the clan, and held the rank of colonel, although his chief remained at home.

The possessions of the clan were formerly very extensive, not only in Athol and Breadalban, but in the lower districts of Kippen, and Killearn, and even in Lanark and Fife. The FOLLOWING was consequently great: the numbers which they were able to bring into the field, in 1745, was 300 men, a much reduced force compared with their ancient vassalage.††

The ARMORIAL BEARINGS of Sir Niel Menzies, Bart., are arg., a chief gu. Crest, the head of a savage erased proper. Supporters, two savages wreathed about the head and loins proper. Mott, " Will God I shall."

The SUAICHEANTAS, or Badge, is the beautiful Fraoch na' Meinnanich, or Menzies' heath. A sprig of ash has, indeed, been mounted; but this tree is not an evergreen, and is, consequently, unfit for the designed purpose of being at all times a mark of distinction.

The BREACAN, or Tartan, is that simple but showy pattern which so particularly attracted attention, in contrast with the dark coloured Campbell, on occasion of Her Majesty's late visit, and has since become so popular: its appropriate name is Geal 'us Dearg.

The CATH-GHAIRM, or Battle-shout, in allusion to this peculiarly coloured plaid and the coat armour, is "Geal 'us Dearg a suas!" The red and white for ever !

The PIOBAIREACHD is Failte na' Meinnanich—the Menzies' Salute; played in compliment to the chief, or his visitors.

The chief seat is the picturesque Weem Castle, situated under the precipitous but well-wooded Craig Uamh, whence its name. It is one of the finest specimens of an old castellated mansion. In 1502 it was burned by Niel Stewart of Fortingal, in consequence of a dispute respecting the lands of Rannach. An action of damage and skaith was raised by Sir Robert Menzies for this raid, and a curious account is preserved of the losses sustained, which is interesting as

---

† Hist. of the King's Majesty's Affairs.   * Hist. of the Rebellion.   †† Forbes' Memorial.

*[1] Baronage, Index of Charters, &c.,   *[2] Acts of Scottish Parliament.

MENZIES

showing the warlike furniture of a baronial mansion in the Highlands at that time, with its provision stores.*

Menzies of Culdairs and two of his brothers were made prisoners in 1715, but they were all pardoned; and although he remained at home in 1745, his attachment to the Stewart family induced him to send a handsome charger for the use of Prince Charles. The Highlander who took the horse into England was made prisoner, and, being condemned, was offered his life if he would discover the person who had sent it, but the faithful clansman scorned the bribe, and was executed. This gentleman introduced the larch into

* Archæalogia Scotica.

Scotland, 1737, and from two plants which he gave to the Duke of Athol have arisen the stately and valuable woods of that tree in the district.†

The figure which illustrates the striking costume of this clan appears with the plaid arranged in imitation of the old Breacan an fheile, or belted plaid, a form adopted by the 42nd, and still retained by the Highland regiments, which, in succeeding Numbers, will be more fully illustrated. The coat is of the favourite colour, ruadh, or dark reddish. The basket hilt of the sword is very old and uncommon. The brogs are given from a pattern found in the Island of Isla.

† General Stewart.

CLANN ROTHICH—THE MUNROS.

THE genealogists of this clan, like those of so many others, have adopted the tradition of an Irish origin, and tell us, that, from their ancestor having lived on the bank of the river Ro, in the county of Derry, the name by which his descendants have been distinguished was thus derived.

The first recorded Scottish progenitor, was Donald O'Ceann, whose patronymic would indicate his descent from "the chief person." He lived in the time of Mac Beth, and is represented as residing on the lands which the clan has ever since possessed. They lie on the north side of the Cromarty firth, and from him they were designated, as Fearrann Donull, or Donald's country, the chiefs being distinguished as the Munros of Foulis, from the place of their residence. They were so closely connected with the Earls of Ross, that they accepted feudal charters from those powerful lords, but in one which was granted about 1350, the various lands therein enumerated, are expressly said to have belonged to them in free possession ever since the time of the above Donald. For better security, new grants were obtained from the Scottish Kings and others at various times; the reddendum in one charter, being a pair of white gloves, or three pennies, and in another, a ball of snow at Midsummer, if required, which although apparently a tenure which could not be long maintained, the hollows in his mountain property could at all times furnish!

Sir Robert Munro fought in the army of Bruce, at Bannockburn, where he lost his only son. The clan was noticed by Buchanan, as among the most considerable who attended Queen Mary, when she visited Inverness: "imprimis Fraserii et Munroi hominum fortissimorum in illis gentibus familiæ." The Munros distinguished themselves very highly in the German wars, and in the army of Charles I., the chief, who was himself a Colonel, had one son, a Major-General, two of the rank of Colonels, and one a Captain. In the latter rebellions they supported the revolution settlement, and, in 1715, were of great service in checking the advance of the Mackenzies and other jacobite clans. They took arms for King

George, on the landing of Prince Charles, and in the battle of Falkirk, which took place on the 17th of January, 1746, Sir Robert Munro was unfortunately slain, along with his brother, Doctor Duncan, who had from affection followed his chief to the field, and so much respected were these gentlemen that the victors gave them a funeral in the churchyard with military honours.

This clan was involved in feuds with various parties, and one of the most sanguinary contentions in which they bore a distinguished part, was in consequence of an insurrection against the Earls of Ross, by the Clans Ivor, Lea, and "Tallwighe," about 1300. Their leader having been made prisoner, they succeeded in capturing the Earl's son in retaliation, on which " the Munroes and the Dingwalls, with some others, gathered their forces, and pursued the Highlanders with all diligence, so overtaking them at Beallach na broig, betwixt Ferrindonnel and Loch Broun; there ensued a cruell fight, wel! foughten on either side. The clan Ivor, &c. were almost all utterlie extinguished, but the Munroes had a sorrowful victory, with great loss of their men, yet carried back again the Earl of Ross, his son. The Laird of Kildun wes ther slain, with seven score of the surname of Dingwall. Divers of the Munroes were slain in this conflict, and ther were killed eleven of the house of Foulis, that were to succeed one another, so that the succession fell unto a child then lying in his cradel."

About 1341, occurred another remarkable event in the clan history. John Munro, Tutor of Foulis, having met with some indignity from the inhabitants of Strathardail, in Perthshire, when passing homewards, his clansmen eargerly desired to have revenge. He accordingly marched with three hundred and fifty picked men on this expedition, and amply gratified their wishes; but when on his return, he was " driving the spreidh" by the castle of Moy, the Laird of Mac Intosh demanded a share of the prey, as due to him by custom. Munro, it seems offered him a less portion than he would accept, for he claimed one half " whereunto John Monroe wold not hearken nor yield, bot goeth on his intended journie homeward.

MUNRO

Mac Intosh conveens his forces with all diligence, and followes John Monroe, whom he overtook at Clagh ne Hayre, besyd Inverness, hard by the ferry of Kessack. John, perceaving Mac Intosh and his company following, then hard at hand, sent fiftie of his men home to Ferrindonald, with the spoile, and encouraged the rest to fight: so ther ensued a cruell conflict, wherein Mac Intosh wes slain, with the most part of his companie: divers of the Monroes wer also ther killed. John Monroe wes left as deid in the field, and wes taken up by the Lord Lovat, who carried him to his house, where he was cured of his wounds, and wes from thenceforth called, John Bacclawigh, becaus he was mutilat of one of his hands all the rest of his days."

The military strength of the Munros in 1715, was four hundred, and in 1745, five hundred.

The ARMORIAL BEARINGS are, on a shield or, an eagle's head erased, gules. Crest, an eagle on the perch, proper. Supporters, two eagles, proper. Motto, "Dread God."

The SUAICHEANTAS, or Badge, is the Garbhag an Ghlinn, otherwise called, Crutal a mada'-ruadh, Common club moss. *Lycopodium clavatum.*

The CATH-GHAIRM, or battle shout, is " Caisteal Foulis na theine," Foulis castle in flames, an exclamation which was enough to rouse up the ire of every clansman.

Failte Rothich, or the Munro's Salute, is the Cruinneachadh, or gathering; and it is a fine piece of music. There is also a Piobaireachd, composed on the battle of "Beallach na Broige," which would therefore be about five hundred years old!

There is nothing particular in the figure which illustrates this respectable clan. The dress is that of a modern Highlander. We have given the pattern of tartan which the best authorities assign to the Munros; but a claim is made for that of the forty-second Highlanders, which is supported by the allegation, that when Sir Robert Munro commanded that regiment, he introduced his own tartan as the uniform. This corps derived its original name, "the Black Watch," from the darkness of the Tartan, and it is not at all likely that when embodied, any clan pattern would be adopted, such a selection being calculated to give great offence to others.

CLANN MHORAIDH—THE MURRAYS.

FRESKIN, a chieftain in the army which suppressed the insurrection of the people inhabiting Moray, at that time so extensive a district, was rewarded for his heroism by the gift of a great tract of land then forfeited.

This occurred in 1130, and he immediately commenced building a castle of great strength for his safe residence at Duffus. Here his descendents flourished for many generations, and added by marriage the lordship of Bothwell, in Clydesdale, to their possessions, William, who was sherrif of Invernarn, and died about 1220, being the first who appears to have assumed the surname "de Moravia."

One of the hostages for the ransom of King David II. was Thomas Lord Bothwell, who died at London of the plague, in 1361, leaving a daughter only, who married Archibald the Grim, Lord of Galloway, and thus the male line became extinct. Among those of the house of Bothwell who distinguished themselves in the national wars, Sir Andrew, sixth chief, is most prominent. When Wallace raised the standard of Scottish independence, he was the first to join him, and when, from an unworthy jealousy, the other barons deserted that redoubted liberator, he was the only man of conse-quence who stood by the champion of his country's freedom, which they so triumphantly vindicated. His son, Sir Andrew, was not less distinguished for his steady adherence to the fortunes of the Bruce.

Sir John de Moravia, undoubtedly descended of the ancient Morays, was sherrif of Perth in the time of William the Lyon, 1165-1214. In a charter, dated 1284, his son is called " Dominus Malcolmus de Moravia, miles, Vicecomes de Perth," and his successor, William, obtained by marriage with Adda, daughter of Malise (Maol-Iosa) Seneschal of Strathearn, the lands of Tullibardin, whence his descendants were so designated.

The peerage was conferred on Sir John Murray in 1604, and Charles I. created John, third Lord Tullibardin, Earl of Athol, in right of his mother. John, who succeeded, was raised to the dignity of marquis in 1676, and his son to that of duke in 1703. His lady, by her mother, was related to the Prince of Orange, whose cause he consequently espoused, and raised his followers to oppose Viscount Dundee when he mustered the Highlanders for King James. He, however strenuously opposed the Union, and voted against every clause of that act. His son William, Marquis of Tullibardin, was one of the

MURRAY

first who joined the Earl of Mar, when he unfurled the royal banner in Strath Dee. He escaped to the continent on the defeat at Sherramuir, but returned with the body of Spaniards who joined the Mackenzies in another attempt, 1719, and again escaped after their repulse at Glensheil. His steady attachment to the Stewart family brought him once more to Scotland with Prince Charles, in 1745, when being made prisoner, he was committed to the Tower, where he died next year, in the 58th year of his age. His brother, Lord Charles, was also with the Earl of Mar, and commanded a regiment, at the head of which he always marched on foot in the Highland dress, Lord George, his next younger brother, who had been at the affair of Glensheil, joined the army of Prince Charles, and was, from his military knowledge and influence, appointed lieutenant-general, for which he was attainted, but escaped to the continent. The ability of Lord George Murray for the responsible situation assigned to him, cannot be questioned:—he brought up the rear in the retreat from England in a masterly manner, was present at all the battles, and it is only on occasion of the engagement at Culloden that he has fallen under reproach. There is scarcely a child in Scotland who has not heard of "the traitor Murray," the loss of that battle being imputed to his treachery. We believe the charge was first made by Colonel roy Stewart of Kincardine, a veteran officer who had served abroad, and who harboured a strong jealousy of his lordship's preferment. His attainder does not look like the reward which he should have received from the government, nor was his saying when 4,000 of the Highlanders rendezvoused at Ruthven, like that of one who meant to betray his party, that he regretted the order to disband by the prince exceedingly, for, with such a force, as long as there was meal in the Lowlands and cattle in the Highlands, he could well keep up the war. The Chevalier Johnstone, one of his Highness' aide de camps, expressly charges the Irish who were about Charles with obtruding those counsels which were the cause of his sudden abandonment of the daring but not hopeless attempt.

It is supposed to have been Lord John, his youngest brother, who, upon receiving the Colonelcy of the 42nd, or royal Highlanders, in 1745, introduced a red stripe in the plaid to render it of a similar pattern to the Murray tartan, but this distinction is now dropt.

The military strength of the Murrays was great, yet it is somewhat singular that there are fewer of the name in Athol than in many other parts, the various septs in his Grace's vassalage retaining their own patronymics. When the civil wars, in the time of Charles I., broke out, John, first marquis, raised 1,800 men for his majesty, and his son augmented the force of the Earl of Glencairn, who had raised the royal flag in 1653, with 2,000: President Forbes reported the number in 1745 at 3,000.

The ARMORIAL BEARINGS for the name of Murray are, on a field azure, three stars arg. within a double tressure flory, or. In the 2nd quarter of the Ducal Coat are three legs armed proper, conjoined at the upper part of the thighs, flexed in a triangle, garnished and spurred or, on a field gules, for Lord of Man, and in the 4th, paly of six, or and sable, for the insignia of Athol. The duke has, besides, his appropriate quarterings from different intermarriages. The Crest is a demi-savage, wreathed vert, holding a dagger proper in his right, and a key or, in his left. Supporters, on the dexter side a lion, gu. collared az. thereon three stars arg., on the sinister a savage wreathed about head and loins, his feet in irons, proper. Motto, " Furth fortune and fill the fetters."

The SUAICHEANTAS Clann Mhoraidh is Bealaidh Chatti, Butcher's Broom, *Ruscus occiliatus.*

By the marriage of the first marquis with Lady Amelia Stanley, daughter of the Earl of Derby, James, second duke, succeeded as heir of line to the sovereignty of the Isle of Man; and it is said that his right was accidentally discovered by President Forbes, when inspecting a pedigree at Blair Castle. In 1765 the lords of the treasury executed, under an act of parliament, a contract, by which government purchased, for £70,000, and annuities of £2,000 each, all the peculiar interests and privileges which the duke and duchess possessed, reserving to them their manorial rights, for an annual payment of £101 : 15s : 11d, and two falcons. In 1805 the reserved privileges were finally purchased by the crown.

THE LORDS DUNMORE.

Lord Charles Murray, second son of John, first Marquis of Athol, is the ancestor from which this branch is descended. He was created Earl of Dunmore, Viscount Fincastle, Lord Murray of Blair, Moulin, and Tullimet, in 1686. The second earl, when the Hon. William Murray of Taymouth, engaged in the rebellion of '45: after the battle of Culloden he surrendered himself, and pleaded guilty at his trial, on which he received pardon.

Lady Augusta, sister of the late earl, was married at Rome in 1793, and re-married at St. George's, Hanover-square, to his late Royal Highness the Duke of Sussex, but the marriage was dissolved, as having been made without consent of the crown, but with the express declaration that there was no reflection on her ladyship's honour, who left issue Colonel Sir Augustus Frederick, and Mademoiselle d'Este.

The Scottish title of his Royal Highness, who became an early subscriber to this work, was Earl of Inverness, which is the capital of the north Highlands, and he was distinguished for his attachment to the national manners and observances. It is believed that it was the circumstance of his retaining a piper in his establishment which induced her Majesty to pay a similar compliment to the Gaël. The Duke was colonel of the North British Volunteers, a patriotic body of Scotsmen in London, who wore the kilt, and he was for a long period chief of the Highland Society of London. His portrait in the full Highland costume of the appropriate Breacan, ornaments the hall of the Freemason's Tavern.

The Hon. Charles Augustus Murray, brother to the present Earl of Dunmore, and master of the royal household, is distinguished for his attachment to the customs and costumes of his native land.

The Dunmore branch had no following in the way of clanship but possessed, of course, great influence and authority as feudal superiors of extensive property.

The coat armour is quarterly, 1st and 4th for Murray, 2nd and 3rd quarterly, 1st and 4th or, a fesse cheque az. and arg. for Stewart, 2nd and 3rd paly of six or, and sable for Athol, and over all the arms of Man.

The figure illustrative of this clan wears a loose doublet of a dull red colour, produced from the crotal, or lichen, found on stones; in the old round shaped bonnet is the clan badge and the white cockade which marked the adherents of the Stewarts.

The waistcoat is of a brighter red, and, like the doublet, has the button-holes worked in gold, with some farther slight ornament. There is nothing peculiar in the hose:—on the toes of the brogs will be perceived the Friochan, a piece of additional leather, cut in Vandyke style, added to strengthen them, being exposed to considerable friction in walking over the heath. The sporan, or purse, from the position is scarcely seen, but the one used in the painting is an old one, small, and neatly formed. The target is from an old and fine specimen preserved in the armory of Colonel Mac Lean, chief of the Mac Leans of Coll.

The Murrays can justly boast of their nobility, and their wide dispersion throughout the kingdom. No fewer than thirteen baronets of the name, resident in different counties appear in the baronial genealogies of Sir Robert Douglas.

CLANN O' GHILLE BHUI'—THE OGILVIES.

THE original possessions of this great family lay in the counties of Angus and Mearns, and the noble ancestor who appears at the root of the genealogical tree, is Gillichriosd, who was created Iar'la', or Earl of Angus, by Malcolm Ceannmòr, about the year 1120. His successor was called Gilli' Breid, from which it would appear that he chose rather to be a devotee of the holy Saint Breid, or Bride, than, like his father, to be distinguished as the follower of Christ. Appellations from religious profession are the origin of many Scottish surnames.

The family historians inform us that the name Ogilvie was first assumed by a son of the second Earl, from his lands. There is, indeed, a part of the property called Glenogil, which seems to have been so named from *ochal* lamentation; but it is much more probable that this patronymic was derived from some noted ancestor who had been remarkable as a "fair complexioned young man;" bhuidh, pronounced vuie, being a usual epithet applied to those who have light-coloured or yellow hair. This derivation is more agreeable to Celtic usage, than that which is territorial; at the same time, there are some lands called Ogilvie, in Linlithgowshire; but we do not find that any family of the name ever lived there.

The Ogilvies act a distinguished part in Scottish history, and besides several barons of high consideration, they numbered the illustrious Earldoms of Findlater and Airly among the honours of the name.

It is not to be expected that more can be here given than a slight detail of some of the transactions in which the clan were more particularly engaged, which may serve to illustrate its character and the manners of the people, to whom these pages are devoted. The rough times in which the elder branches lived, when the whole population was obliged to hold itself in warlike preparation, led to the formation of habits which lingered long after the state of society had undergone a change. In the turmoils of other ages, property was continually changing hands. Sometimes it was acquired by force, and retained by the sword; sometimes intermarriage gave a title, to which, in many cases, it may be asserted that power alone could obtain acknowledgment, and possessions have been transferred to parties, in fuedal form, who being considered aliens by the original residents, were forthwith assailed as intruders, and compelled, perhaps, at last to relinquish their acquisition on the best terms they could obtain.

The Airly family held territorial possessions in Angus in the reign of William the Lyon, 1165—1214. They became heritable sheriffs of that extensive district, a situation which brought the Ogilvies into frequent collision with their enemies, and lawless freebooters from the Grampian hills. Sir Walter Ogilvie, of Achterhouse, who was sheriff in 1391, lost his life in one of these desperate raids, which is thus described. Duncan, natural son of Alexander Stewart, Earl of Buchan, made a southern expedition in the above year, plundering the country and committing great ravages, when Sir Walter, with a large force, marched in pursuit, and, having overtaken the marauders at a place called Glenbrereth, a furious combat immediately ensued, in which the sheriff and his brother, with about sixty of their followers, were slain!

The Earls of Airly were actively engaged in the wars of King Charles I., and again displayed their loyalty in gallantly taking the field in the risings of 1715 and 1745. On the last occasion, David

Lord Ogilvie joined Prince Charles, when the Highland army reached Edinburgh, with 600 men, and after the battle of Culloden he escaped, through Norway and Sweden, to France, where he served with great honour in command of a regiment called by his own name, until he obtained a pardon, 1778, and returned home. Bonaparte offered to pay up the arrears of the pension which had been allowed him by Louis XVI., but he disdained to receive from the revolutionary government an acknowledgment for the defence of a monarchy which had been destroyed. For participation in the above rebellions they were forfeited; but as Lord Ogilvie had been attainted before he succeeded to the Earldom, an Act of Parliament was passed in 1826 to remove all disabilities supposed to result from his attainder, in favour of David, present earl, and the thirteenth baron.

The branch of the Ogilvies settled in the North were not less distinguished for their loyalty, which frequently involved them in hostilities with their neighbours of an opposite feeling, and there were hot feuds of long standing between them and the Gordons, &c.

It must not be omitted to state here that it was to the brave George Ogilvie, governor of the castle of Dunottar, during the usurpation, that the preservation of the Scottish Regalia; crown, sceptre, and sword of justice, is owing. They had been deposited in this strong fortress for safety, and the reward he received for this important service was the title of baronet, and an honorary augmentation to his coat armour!

Another party had, however, a share in this transaction—the honest minister of the neighbouring kirk of Kinnèf having communicated with the governor, who was apprehensive that the castle might fall into the hands of the enemy, it was arranged that the clergyman's wife should carry off the regalia, which she did in a bundle of flax; and having carefully wrapped up the national treasures, the loyal couple buried them under the pulpit, where they remained until the Restoration; but no reward whatever was bestowed on these honest royalists!

The ARMORIAL BEARINGS are argent, a lion, passant, guardant, gules, crowned with an imperial crown, or. Crest, a lion rampant, gules, holding between the paws a plumb rule, proper. Supporters, two lions, guardant, gules. Motto, " Forward."

The SUAICHEANTAS, or badge of recognition, is Seorsa luibh, evergreen Alkanet, *Anchusa.*

The illustration represents a highland gentleman in the costume of 1745, and is painted with the exception of the Ogilvie tartan, from a portrait of James, sixth Earl of Perth, lieutenant-general of the highland army, preserved at Drummond Castle. The trews were the usual dress of gentlemen, as seen in old portraits; but in this, as in some other pictures, knee breeches and stockings are worn. The pistols slung in the sword-belt is unusual, and this is the only instance which has come under our notice.

CLAN DONNCHAIDH—THE ROBERTSONS.

THE common tradition has derived this clan from the Mac Donalds, but recent investigations have led to proofs of a different origin. They are shown by these authorities to be descended from the ancient Earls of Athol, carrying on the male line of inheritance after the death of Henry, last of these nobles. Donnchadh, or Duncan, who flourished about 1360, appears to have given the patronymic to the clan; while, from Raibeart ri'ach who died in the reign of James II., the more common designation, Robertson, was acquired.* From their principal residence the chiefs were distinguished as the Struan Robertsons, a style only used besides in the case of Clunie Mac Pherson. The Gaëlic Struthan—streamy, is prettily descriptive of the landscape surrounding the mansion.

In 1392 we find Clan Donachai' taking a prominent part in a fierce irruption made by the Highlanders into the county of Angus; and in subsequent periods they distinguished themselves by numerous warlike exploits. The chief being then a minor, the clan were, under the able command of his uncle, Donald the tutor, in the campaigns of Montrose, and fought with notable resolution at the battle of Inverlochai,' on which occasion one of them was particularly noticed for his personal valour. He had slain, according to the tradition, nineteen of the enemy with his own hand, and, after the conflict had ceased, he proceeded with others to cook some victuals. Montrose observing Duncan thus employed, and desirous himself to make use of the good pot he had provided, asked him for it; but the Celt bluffly refused to part with the utensil, saying, that, as he had well earned the meat which was in it, he though that to be permitted to refresh himself therewith was the least favour which could be allowed him. "I wish," says Montrose, good humouredly, "that more little tinkers had served his majesty so well to-day," alluding to the appellation Duncan was known by from his occupation—Caird beag.*

*Skene's History of the Highlanders. Donnachadh is pronounced Donachie.

* Collections penes me.

OGILVIE

Alasdair, or Alexander, the Struan chief, raised his followers in the Stewart cause, and fought bravely with Viscount Dundee in 1689, with the Earl of Mar, in 1715, where he was taken prisoner, but made his escape, and with Prince Charles Edward in 1745-6. He was celebrated for his poetic talents, and possessed a conviviality of feeling and humour bordering on eccentricity. A collection of his pieces was published, with a curious genealogical account of his family, very creditable to his literary acquirements.

The territories of the clan were formerly very extensive. Besides possessing Struthan, otherwise called Glenerochie, which was erected into a barony in 1451, the chief was Dominus de Ranach, and held the fifty-five merk land of Strath Tay; but a minority occuring on the death of William, who was unfortunately killed in a feud with the Earl of Athol, about 1510, that gentleman seized a great part of the lands of the Robertsons, which they could never again recover. They were forfeited in 1690, and were finally annexed to the crown in 1752, but part of the original property is again in possession of a descendant of this ancient family, it having been restored in 1784, and is now held by Major-General Duncan Robertson of Struan, who is descended from Donncha' mòr of Druimachinn, third son of Robert, the fifteenth chief.† Robertson of Lude is the oldest cadet.

This clan was connected by intermarriage with many noble and most respectable families, as the Earls of Athol, Braidalban, and Errol, Menzies of Weems, the Drummonds, &c.; and many considerable branches have settled in different parts, of whom are the Robertsons of Inches, in the county of Inverness, who trace their descent from Struan to a very early period; and from that house sprung, about 1540, the Robertsons of Ceanndace and Glencalvie in Rosshire. In the districts of Athol and Braidalban, as may be supposed, the families of this name are numerous.

The Skenes are believed also to be descended of the house of Struan. Donnchai' mòr an sgian— great Duncan of the dirk, having crossed from Athol to Braemar, and descending Strathdee with his followers, founded the family of Skene. The designation of John le Skene, who signs the Ragman's Roll in 1296, favours this account, le being personal, de territorial, but the words might be readily misapplied. The sgians in the coat armour, and Highland supporters in antique costume, are corroborative circumstances also; but is it probable that Skene of Skene would have given an inexpressive name to the Parish, rather than have been designated from it?

The military force of the clan in 1715 was reckoned 800, in 1745, 700, but only 200 of these resided on the estates, which the chief then retained. A regiment was raised in this clan about 1795,

† Family History.

which was distinguished by the appropriate name of the Clan Donnachai' Fencibles, and was commanded by Robertson of Auchleeks.

The COAT ARMOUR is gu., three wolves heads erased, arg., armed and langued, az.; Crest, a dexter arm, couped in pale, holding a regal crown, proper. Supporters on the dexter side, a serpent, and on the sinister a dove, the head of each encircled with rays. Motto, "Virtutis gloria merces." Robert ri'ach, the chief, having personally arrested Graeme and the Master of Athol, the murderers of King James I., 1436, received the honourable augmentation to the arms which his successors have been so proud to carry, viz., a savage man prostrate and in chains, placed beneath the escutcheon.*

The SUAICHEANTAS or Badge, is Dluth fraoch, erica cinerea, fine-leaved heath.

The PIOBAIREACHDAN, are "Failte Tighearn Shruthan"— Salute to the Lord of Struan and "an Riban gorm"—the blue ribbon, in allusion to a streamer of the national colour of Scotland.

There was a stone set in silver at Struan, which was preserved as a valuable relic, and from the name given to it—Clach na Bhratach, the stone of the flag, it must have been supposed to give assurance of victory. It seems from description to have been a Scot's pebble.

General Robertson does not now reside at Struan; his seat is Dun Alasdair, or Mount Alexander in Rannach.

The figure chosen to represent the clan is from the pen and ink sketch in the possession of Mr. Mc. Ian, of a Highland gentleman who resided some time at the court of Louis XIV., and adopted the gay style of dress, fashionable at that period, which well suits the gaudiness of his own many-coloured breacan; and it may be observed that the Gaël usually adopted the doublet or jacket worn in the country where they might sojourn. At that period the numerous Highlanders, who were compelled to expatriate themselves for attempting the restoration of their old line of kings, familiarized the inhabitants of the continent with the singular costume of "les braves Ecossias."

A white stripe has lately been introduced in the tartan, which is hence called the new Robertson—we, of course, reject it.

*Nesbit's Heraldry.

CLANN NA ROSAICH—THE ROSES.

THE Roses of Kilravock, although their residence lay in "the barbarous north," have enjoyed their property through a descent of nineteen generations.

It was a strange propensity of the old genealogists to derive most of the highland families from Ireland, and it is remarkable that they were prone also to bring them from England, or give

ROBERTSON

them a Saxon origin, even although the name be plainly Gaëlic. The person who furnished the account of this family for Sir Robert Douglas's "Baronage" is inclined to adopt this last opinion, because he found the same charges borne in the coat armour as are carried by the Roos's, or Roses, of that country—a very summary and rash, but frequent method of conclusion. With due respect for the noble science of heraldry, its professors indulged their fancies too much in tracing similarities of names, and adapting punning devices for them, to induce us to expect an identity where there was no connection.

Ros, in Gaëlic, signifies a promontory, and it is applied to a headland, either seaward—as it projects into a lake or into a plain, and from whatever place the unknown founder of this clan may have acquired the appellation, or however it may have become softened into Rose, the only probability is, that dwelling in such a locality, he would naturally be styled "de Ros." Ros is, indeed, a rose; but it is by no means likely that any kelt or clan would accept an appellation so little significant and so effeminate.

The Rosses, or Roses, were in other parts of Scotland as early as the time of King David I.; but the documentary history of the Kilravock family commences in the reign of Alexander II., at which time they held the lands of Geddes, in the county of Inverness, Hugh Rose appearing as a witness to the foundation of the Priory of Beaulieu, 1219. His son and successor, Hugh, marrying Mary, daughter of Sir Andrew de Bosco, of Redcastle, who inherited the barony of Kilravock through her mother, he obtained that addition to his possessions, the deed of conveyance being confirmed by charter from John Baliol, in 1293. He was succeeded by his son William who married Morella, daughter of Alexander de Doun, by whom he had two sons; Andrew, the second, ancester of the Rosses of Auchlossan, in Mar, and Hugh, his successor, who, in a deed of agreement respecting the Prior of Urquhart and the Vicar of Dalcross, is styled "nobilis vir Hugo Rose, dominus de Kilravock." His son Hugh married Janet, daughter of Sir Robert Chisholm, constable of the castle of Urquhart, by whom he received a large accession of lands in Strath Nairn, &c. He left a son, Hugh, who was succeeded by his son John, who was served heir to his father in 1431, and procured a charter de novo of all his lands, a feudal provision for the better security of property against adverse claims, so often preferred in those troublous times, and frequently as pretexts to cover the outrages consequent on feuds. The wife of this chief was Isabella, daughter of Cheyne, laird of Esslemont, in Aberdeenshire. Hugh, son of this marriage, built the old tower of Kilravock, in 1460, and it is related as somewhat marvellous that he finished it within the year.

The "Barons of Kilravock," or Kilraik, as it is pronounced intermarried with the first families in the north, and filled various situations of high trust and honour.

The castle is an old picturesque building, situated on the bank of the river Nairn. It is still inhabited, and contains some old armour, portraits, and family relics.

There is scarcely any family whose charter chest is more amply stored with documents, not only of private importance, but of great antiquarian interest, and we are happy to learn that a history of this distinguished clan may soon be expected from the pen of Cosmo Innes, Esq., a gentleman eminently qualified for the task.

Bonds of manrent, or contracts of friendship, were frequently made between different clans, and others, by which the parties bound themselves to "tak oppin upricht pairt in all and sundrie thair causis and querells," as is expressed in one between Kilravock, Lord Forbes, the Mac Intosh, and others, 1467, in which they "maid to uther the greit bodilye aith," touching "the haly Evangell," and declaring, that whoever should break any of the conditions should be held mansworn, renouncing the faith of Christ, and never to be received as a witness, "ne ly in kirk, nor Cristin berrial." In a deed of submission, executed in settlement of a dispute between one of the chiefs and two of his neighbours, about 1560, he facetiously signs himself "Hutcheon Rose, of Kilravock, an honest man, ill guided between you baith."

In 1704, this clan was accounted able to muster five hundred men, but Marshal Wade estimated their strength, in 1725, at three hundred only, and then he believed them to be well affected to his Majesty.

The ARMORIAL BEARINGS for Rose are, or, a boar's head couped, gules, between three water bougets, sable. Crest, a harp, azure; motto, "Constant and true."

The SUAICHEANTAS, or Badge, is Ros-mhairi fiadhaich, Wild Rosemary—*Andromeda media.*

The figure is represented at work with the cas-crom, or footplough, an ancient agricultural implement, now seldom to be seen. The artist has well shown both the position of the man while at work and the form of this primitive instrument. Forcing the head into the earth, to a depth of 8 to 12 inches, it is pushed along, and about 10 or 12 inches in breadth of the soil is raised by the shaft, which forms a powerful lever, and is very dexterously, and with great exactness, thrown to the left. One man can turn over as much in a day, with the cas-crom, as four men could accomplish with the spade; and its chief utility is in the workman being able to avoid the stones, which in most highland ground would disable a plough. Ten or twelve men are sometimes employed in this operation, which is one of the most picturesque exhibitions. " They arrange themselves in a line at the bottom of the hill, with their backs to the acclivity, and with surprising rapidity turn over the rough soil, forming an extended cut or trench, like a plough furrow. This is repeated as they gradually ascend the hill backwards, and the land so laboured is very productive."*

The dress is modern—such as worn by a respectable farmer. The pattern of the tartan is well made out in the kilt, or feile-beag, and it is a very pleasing specimen of the darker sort.

* Scottish Gaël, II., 91.

ROSE

The day before the battle of Culloden, Prince Charles dined at Kilravock Castle, with the laird and his lady, on which occassion his manners and deportment were described by his host as most engaging. Having walked out with Mr. Rose, before sitting down, he observed several persons engaged in planting trees, on which he remarked, "How happy, Sir, you must feel, to be thus peaceably employed in adorning your mansion, whilst all the country round is in such commotion." Kilravock was a firm supporter of the Hanoverian family; but his adherence was not solicited, nor his principles alluded to by his Highness. Next day, the Duke of Cumberland called at the castle gate, and when Kilravock went to receive him, he bluffly observed, "So you had my cousin Charles here yesterday." Kilravock replied, that he could not prevent the visit. "Oh!" says the Duke, as he turned away, without alighting, "you did perfectly right."

CLAN ROSICH, NA GILLE ANDRAS.

Ros is a Celtic word, descriptive of a brow, or point of land, and it is found in the different countries which have been possessed by that race. The name, therefore, as a personal designation, is local, and an individual holding the land, or there residing, was distinguished by the preposition *de:* hence there must have been individuals of this name in Ireland, Wales, and even in England.

The old Rosses of Scotland, however, were perfectly distinct from the others, and from their possessions lying in the extensive district so called, the presumption must be that it was their original seat. They are, at the same time, known in the Highlands by the appellation Clan Gille Andras, or the offspring of the follower of St. Andrew, one of the ancient earls having devoted himself to that Saint.

Their chief had great power, and obtained the title of earl in a very early age. In 1235, the Galwegians having risen in rebellion, Fearchar Mac an t-Sagairt, or son of the priest, then Earl of Ross, went against them, and having assaulted their army, defeated them with great slaughter. Alastair, who was earl in the middle of the thirteenth century, was grand justiciar of the kingdom, and his son William fell at Bannockburn, 1314, leaving a son, Aodh, or Hugh, who also fell in 1333, at the less fortunate battle of Halidown Hill. William, his successor, left no male heir, and his eldest daughter, Eupham, having married Sir Walter Leslie, of Leslie, Aberdeenshire, he, in her right, laid claim to the Earldom of Ross. His granddaughter, an only child, entered a convent, and resigned both title and territories in favour of her grand-uncle, the Earl of Buchan; but Walter having had a daughter, Margaret, who married Donald, Lord of the Isles, he immediately assumed the title, took possession of the lands in right of his wife, and made strenuous preparation to vindicate his claim. Mustering their hereditary followers—"the warmen of the Isles," and raising, by peremptory summons, the clansmen on the mainland, the whole rendezvoused at Inverness, and the first campaign was a raid through Morayland, to which no resistance could be offered. Continuing to advance, with an army as large as, perhaps, ever left the Highlands, amounting to upwards of 10,000, the sacking of Aberdeen was believed to be Donald's ulterior object, but when he had marched to within about sixteen miles of that city, he was met on the Muir of Harlaw, by the Earl of Mar, with about equal numbers, from the southern counties, when a most sanguinary and protracted conflict ensued. The victory was doubtful; Donald, by leaving the field, suffered the consequences of a defeat, but Mar was unable to pursue: his loss is said to have been 700, and that of the Highlanders 900, among whom were many chiefs and daoine-uasal of note, while of the Scottish nobility and gentry a surprising number were slain. Leslie, of Balquhain, a baron who lived in the vicinity of the field of battle, fell, with seven of his sons!

The claim of Donald must have been held good by the numerous chiefs who followed his standard, and King James I., on his return from captivity in England, created his son Earl of Ross. On the forfeiture of John of the Isles in 1476, the earldom reverted to the crown, and James, second son of King James III., was invested with the title of Duke of Ross, but he soon after resigned his whole lands, with the reservation of the Tomain nam Mòd, or Moot Hills, in each district, from which he took title, an ancient form by which his dignity and honours were secured. Subsequently the dukedom went through several parties; among others, the unfortunate Darnley. But to return to the descendants of the original family. William, last earl, had a brother, Hugh, of Rarichies, who flourished about 1360, and received a charter of the lands of Balnagouan, 1374, on whom, by clan law, the chiefship devolved. The influence of his nieces' husbands prevented the open assertion of his claim, and Paul Mac Tire, a man famous in tradition for his indomitable valour, and a near relation of the deceased earl, took command of the clan. The Balnagouan branch at last resumed their acknowledged authority, but their power was much broken, and the clan was nearly annihilated in a feud with the Mac Kays, who had given them frequent molestation. At last the Rosses, infuriated with repeated outrages, marched against their enemies, who were under the leading of Aongas Mac Aodh, of Strathnaver, and who, finding themselves so fiercely attacked, took shelter in the church of Tarbat, where several were slain, and Aongas and many others burnt in the edifice! To revenge this "cruel slaughter," Ian riach Mac Aodh, assisted by a body of Sutherlands, began to ravage the lands of the Rosses with unappeasable fury. The Laird of Balnagouan

ROSS

collected all his forces, and met the invaders, with whom the battle shortly commenced, and after a long and desperate struggle the Rosses were utterly overthrown; Alastair the chief, with seventeen gentlemen, and a great number of others, being slain. This battle is known as Blar Ault an charish, from the place where it occurred, and the clan seem never to have recovered its effects. In the beginning of the eighteenth century, David of Balnagouan finding himself the last of his race, sold the estate to General Charles Ross, brother of Lord Ross, of Hawkhead, parties in nowise related, but the circumstance is rather singular, that property so many centuries in possession should pass into the hands of others bearing the same name, and of such respectable antiquity and status. Ross of Pitcalnie is now the representative of the old earls.

In the twelfth century a knight of the name of Ross came from Yorkshire to Scotland, and settled there on the lands of Hawkhead, of which family we find John de Ross obtaining a *salvus conductus* through England to pay his devotions at the shrine of St. Thomas, of Canterbury, in 1362. These lairds were of considerable note among the barons, and were ennobled by the title of Lord Ross, in the time of James IV. In William, fourteenth earl, who died in the year 1754, the title became extinct. He was in the royal army under the command of Lord Loudoun, and when they attempted to surprise Prince Charles at Moyhall, he was thrown down and nearly trampled to death by the cavalry who were put to a rapid and disorderly retreat by the stratagem of a blacksmith, unaided by a single soldier. Sir James Lockhart, of Carstairs, who, by the courtesy of Scotland, which, in marrying an heiress, gives the husband her name, is ancestor of Lockhart Ross, of Balnagowan, Bart. He commanded the thirty-eighth regiment, and was wounded at Culloden.

In 1427 the earls of Ross brought into the field 2000 men; in 1715 the number was only 300; but in 1745 it was 500.

The Rosses of Scottish descent carry gules, three lions rampant, two and one arg. Crest, a hand holding a garland of laurel proper. Supporters, two savages wreathed about head and loins with oak, holding clubs, proper. Motto, "Spem successus alit." Borne by Balnagowan.

The SUAICHEANTAS is Craobh Aiteann, juniper.

The PIOBARIEACHD is Spaidseareachd Iarla Ros, or the Earl of Rosses march, composed in 1427.

The figure is in the doublet occasionally worn in the Highlands, the plaid in the half-belted form is the most graceful and useful now worn: the brogs are common in Argyle. He may be supposed a forester who has shot several ptarmigans.

NA SIA'ICH—THE SHAWS.

ANTIQUARIES and genealogists assent to the tradition, that the Shaws are descended from the great Mac Duff, Thane of Fife.

The renowned Malcolm Ceannmòr, who had long and sanguinary, but successful, wars with the turbulent tribes of the north, rewarded the services of his followers, by numerous grants of land, and in this way the family of Shaw was established in Moray.

It has been a favourite assertion, that the Mac Intosh branch of the Cattanaich, or Clann Chattain, is derived from these redoubtable Thanes, and in absence of other authority, their own tradition may be received as satisfactory, viz. that "the Seach, or Shaw," as Sir George Mackenzie designates the son of Mac Duff, was progenitor of this clan, whose possessions lay in the higher part of the beautiful strath of the river Spey.

The Rev. Lachlan Shaw, the learned and laborious historian of the province of Moray, sees no reason to doubt that all those of this name, both in the south and north, are the same people, but we must differ from him in this opinion. Saidh, pronounced Shà, is a Gaëlic appellation, quite distinct from the Saxon word Shaw, which is applied to a thicket, or copsewood, whence it became a personal designation common in England and elsewhere. The respective coat-armour, is besides, quite different thus showing that they themselves have no idea of any affinity of origin.

Rothiemurcus was the seat of the chiefs for many centuries. In the year 1226, King Alexander II. granted a charter of the lands to the Bishoprick of Moray, and the Shaws held them in undisturbed possession under the prelates of that See, until about

SHAW

1350, when the Cumins of Strathdallas obtained a lease, or wadset, on them, but the Shaws refused to give up possession, and an appeal to the sword was promptly adopted. The result of the first conflict does not appear to have been decisive, and James, then chief fell in the battle. He had married a daughter of Ferguson, a baron of Athol, by whom he left a son, who, on coming to age, attacked his adversaries, whom he defeated, killing their commander at a place since called Laggan na Chuiminaich : he thereupon purchased the freehold of Rothiemurcus and Baile an Easpuig which put a stop to farther controversy. "The unvaried tradition beareth," says the above reverend author, "that Shaw Cor'iacalich, or Buckteeth, was captain of the thirty Clan Chattan who fought in the memorable battle on the North Inch of Perth," the circumstances respecting which singular event are related under the Clann Dhai', or Davidsons, No. X. He died about 1405, and a rude stone in the kirkyard still remains to mark his resting place. He married a daughter of Mac Pherson of Clunie, by whom he had seven sons, the second of whom, called Fearchar, who died about 1440, was the progenitor of the Farquharsons, or Clann Fhiunla, who afterwards became so numerous and united in the braes of Mar. James, who succeeded, joined the army of Donald of the Isles, and was engaged in the battle of Harlaw, where he was killed, 1411, leaving, by his wife, a daughter of the Laird of Inverettie, a son and successor, Alasdair, surnamed Ciar, from his grey complexion. This chief, by a daughter of Stewart of Ceanchardin, left four sons, from whom are descended the families of Dail, Tordarrach, and Dailnafeart. By his wife, who was a niece of the Mac Intosh, he left a successor, John, who was father of Allan, whose son John, left Allan in possession of the honour and estates. This chief was forfeited for the slaughter of his stepfather, Dallas of Cantray, and the lands were purchased by the Laird of Grant about 1595.

The Shaws, although broken up as an independent clan, remained in considerable numbers throughout their ancient territories, and attached themselves either to the more powerful Mac Phersons or Mac Intoshes.

The chief resided in a strongly-constructed castle, built on an island, in a small lake called Loch nan Eillean.

The ARMORIAL BEARINGS of Shaw of Rothiemurcus are quarterly; first and fourth, or, a lion rampant, gules, armed and langued, azure; second and third, argent, a fir-tree growing from a mount in base, proper, and on a canton in dexter chief, of the field, a dexter hand, couped fesswise, holding a dagger, all proper. Crest, a demi-lion, gules, holding in the dexter paw a sword, proper. Motto, "Fide et fortitudine." The Shaws of the south of Scotland carry three covered cups, &c.

The SUAICHEANTAS, or badge, is that of the Clan Chattan —Lus nam Braoileag—red whortle berry, *Vaccinium vitis idea.*

The extraordinary mutiny of the Black Watch, now the forty second Royal Highlanders, has afforded the artist an interesting subject for the illustration of this clan, one of whom acted a prominent part in that unfortunate affair. The regiment, which had been recently embodied, was marched to London, in 1743, with the view of being inspected by His Majesty, but he having previously sailed to Hanover, Marshall Wade was appointed to review them. Those proud-spirited Gaël, had several grievances to complain of, and their discontent was so increased by an apprehension that they were to be sent abroad, contrary to the terms of enlistment, that the greater part set off in the silence of night for Scotland, and, avoiding the high road, went straight across the country, and had reached Oundle, in Northamptonshire, where they intrenched themselves in a wood. Meantime their route being discovered, a regiment of dragoons was sent after them ; but so far from showing any disposition to surrender, they declared their determination rather to be cut to pieces than submit. Some of the less daring having, on the persuasion of a clergyman in the vicinity, been induced to desert, and the others finding themselves surrounded, they were compelled, after some days, to surrender, when they were disarmed, and marched to London. Here the mutineers were tried, and three individuals were selected for execution. These were Andrew and Samuel Mac Pherson and Fearchar Shaw, and the examination of the latter, through an interpreter, showed great simplicity of character, with the most undaunted spirit. This unfortunate affair excited much interest at the time, and served to increase the disaffection of the Jacobites. It has, indeed, been alleged that the rising with Prince Charles, which took place two years afterwards, was hastened by this tragic occurrence, for, as the two Mac Phersons were sons of respectable gentlemen in Badenach, and Shaw being a native of the adjoining district, if not a tenant of their chief, and one likewise of the Clan Chattan, Clunie thought he had been pointedly ill-used in having his men selected as the victims. When the Prince landed, he therefore threw up his commission, and immediately raised his clan for King James.

Shaw is painted from a scarce old portrait of the above-mentioned unfortunate individual. The tartan had at that time a red stripe, which is now omitted, and the pattern resembles that of Sutherland, but, in making up the kilt, the blue interval is shown, which gives a sombre hue to the Breacan. The sash worn over the shoulder is peculiar to highland corps; the sporan, or purse, is of the genuine old form, as is likewise the bonnet, a much more convenient head-dress than the pile of ostrich feathers now worn. The pistol slung as here shown formed part of the highland arms at this period, and those who chose might carry a dirk.

SINCLAIR

CLANN SHINCLAIR—THE SINCLAIRS.

It has been maintained that the Sinclairs are not, strictly speaking, a Gaëlic clan, the surname being originally from France. William, son of the Comte de Saint Clair, a relative of the Conqueror, who came over with him in 1066, settled in Scotland soon afterwards, and was progenitor of all of the name in that country. The ancient Earls of Caithness were, however, an original race, the first recorded of whom is Dungald, who flourished in 875, and Sir William Sinclair, of Roslin, which was the first possession of those of the name in Scotland, having married a daughter of the Earl of Strathern and Caithness, by this early connexion with a Highland district, and holding so high a feudal position, they have fully acquired all that confers on them the rights of chiefship.

The chief went with his clan to Flodden, in which battle he fell, with a great number of his followers, anno 1513, and so strong an impression did this event make upon them that, to this day, no Sinclair will, without the greatest reluctance, dress in green, or cross the Ord Hill on Monday, for in such an array, and by that road, they marched on this disastrous expedition, when so many were slain, that scarcely a family of note had left a representative of their name.[*1]

George, sixth Earl, had no children, and finding himself very deeply in debt, he executed a disposition to Sir John Campbell, of Glenurchai', his chief creditor, of all his property, titles, and heritable jurisdictions, anno 1672. Glenurchai' thereupon took the title, and on the death of the Earl of Caithness, 1676, obtained a grant of all the possessions; but George Sinclair, of Geis, heir male, was not disposed to submit to this alienation of the honours of his family, but took possession of various houses and lands, and Earl John was consequently obliged to apply for military assistance; and, raising his own clan, he marched northwards and encountered the Sinclairs, when he obtained a decided victory, on which occasion his piper composed the piobaireachd called "Bodach an Briogas," in derision of Sinclair, who wore trows, which has ever since been the cruinn-eachadh, or gathering, of his clan.[*2] Having thus regained the property he placed garrisons in the castles to secure it, but Geis frustrated in his attempts by force of arms prosecuted his suit in Parliament, and it was found that his claims were just, on which Sir John Campbell relinquished the object he had so keenly pursued, and was created Earl of Breadalbane, &c.

The military achievements of the Sinclairs, from the power of their chiefs, were considerable. Their feuds with the Clan Gunn have been noticed in the sketch of that tribe; their misunderstandings with the Earls of Sutherland were more serious. George Gordon, of Marle, having been attacked and slain, the Earl sent 200 men into Caithness, in 1588, who ravaged the parishes of Lathron and Dunbeath, and were followed by Sutherland himself, who overrun the country, and besieged the Earl in Castle Sinclair, who made a long but successful defence, and to revenge this inroad, which is commemorated as Là na creach mòr, "the day of the great foray," he assembled all his clan and followers, and marched into Sutherland, severely retaliating on the inhabitants: finally, a battle took place in which they were victorious, and returned with abundant spoil. "In exchange hereof Alexander, Earl of Sutherland, sent 300 men into Catteyness, the same year of God, 1589, who spoiled and wasted the same, killed above thirty men, and returned with a great booty." The Sinclairs, nothing daunted, made an inroad with their whole force, and returned, "driving a prey of goods before the host," but the inhabitants having collected to the number of about 500, attacked the invaders at Clyne, who maintained a desperate fight until nightfall. When they reached Caithness they found Houston Mac Aodh spreading farther desolation through the unhappy country, who retreated so speedily as to elude the pursuit of the Sinclairs. These mutual "harrieships" are said to have been congenial to Highland feelings! We can only say, in the words of an old seanachai', that, if so, "there was good mischief those days!" The Sinclairs were in arms in 1745, and ready to join Prince Charles with 500 men; but the disaster at Culloden induced them to disband as the most prudent step.

President Forbes says that, in 1745, Mòr 'ear Gal' ao', as the Earl of Caithness is called in Gaëlic, could raise 1,000 men; but in the late war with France double that number were enrolled.

The Armorial Bearings of the Earl are—Quarterly: first az. a ship at anchor, oars in saltire, within a double tressure flory counterflory, or, for the title of Orkney; second and third, or, a lion rampant gules; fourth az. a ship under sail, or, for that of Caithness, the whole surmounted by a cross ingrailed dividing the quarters, sab., for Sinclair. Crest, a cock proper. Supporters, two griffins proper, beaked and membered or. Motto, "Commit thy work to God."

The Suaicheantas, or Badge, is a branch of conis, whins, or gorse, ulex Europœus.

Among the numerous cadets of this noble family must be noticed the Sinclairs of Ulbster, related to the illustrious house of Sutherland. In 1603, George, Earl of Caithness, made a disposition to his much beloved cousin, Patrick Sinclair, of the lands of Ulbster, and his brother John succeeded, from whom the present Sir George Sinclair, Bart., is ninth in descent. His venerable father, the late Right Hon. Sir John, a distinguished senator and statesman, has been pronounced one of the greatest benefactors to society, and he did more, by individual exertion, to improve the county of Caithness, than all

[*1] Sinclair's Stat. Account, viii. 156.   [*2] See No. 1, under "the Campbell's of Breadalbane."

192

the former proprietors together. With the true spirit of a Highland chief, in 1794, he raised a fencible regiment, and he was the first who extended the services of these troops beyond Scotland. He shortly afterwards raised another, and each was 1,000 strong, a proof of his enjoying a degree of respect and influence which very few men of much higher rank and more extensive possessions could boast of! The uniform of these fine battalions was a military Highland bonnet, with trows and scarf plaid of a handsome dark tartan. Sir John was induced to adopt this mode of dress, from having been misled by a silly paragraph which appeared in the "Scots Magazine," referring the origin of the kilt to a very recent period, an opinion which he subsequently repudiated. His superintendence of the publication of the originals of the poems of Ossian, is a labour for which "The Clans" are under a peculiar obligation, as it removed the doubts of many on that much contested subject.

The figure chosen to illustrate the Sinclairs is a Highland girl, and that she is unmarried we see indicated by her hair being bound with the stem, or snood. She is also bare-footed, the want of covering being no mark of low circumstances, but agreeably to a practice still very common. Her gown is of a blue home-made manufacture; a mixture of linen and wool, which forms a very economical and pretty material. A plaid scarf, of about three yards in length, is worn over the head, falling down gracefully before. This was usually fastened by a brooch of silver, brass, or copper, on the breast, and ladies were wont to indicate their political principles by the manner in which it was worn.*

* Burt's Letters from the Highlands, 1725.

SIOL SGEINE, NO CLANN DHONCHADH MHAR—
THE SKENES.

SKENE, of Skene, is an Aberdeenshire family, who resided in a parish of the same name, about twelve miles distant from the capital of the country, where the Gaëlic is no longer the native language, but the circumstance of its having ceased to be the mother tongue of a chief or part of his clan, is no bar to their claim of Highland descent. The Gaëlic, at no very distant period, was the prevailing speech of all who lived beyond the Grampian mountains, and the Parliamentary line of demarcation, which was drawn on occasion of passing the Act, prohibiting the use of the Highland dress, passed from the north side of Lochlomond, by the north side of the Forth, near Stirling, and comprehended the hill part of the county of Kincardine, the whole of Aberdeenshire, &c.; all that division of Scotland being accounted the native residence of the Highlanders.

But the Skenes have another claim to a Highland origin,—a current tradition being that they are descendants of the Clan Doncha', or Robertsons, of Athol; and W. F. Skene, Esq., F.S.A., &c. &c. has furnished us with several corroborative proofs of this descent. A second son of the chief of the Robertsons having crossed the mountain ridge, which separates Athol from Mar, passed down Strathdee, and ultimately settled in the district in which the family so long resided. The leader of this branch of the clan was designated Doncha', or Duncan mòr na Sgine and he is believed, with much probability, to have been contemporary with the first Lowland Earl of Athol, whose succession to this property was very likely to induce the discontented portion of the highland clan to leave their original seat. The "Baronage," it is to be observed, deduces the Robertsons from a younger son of Donald of the Isles, but on what authority does not well appear.

Skene seems to have long existed as a territorial appellation; hence the prefix de, applicable to place, le being always personal.

John le Skene, who signs Ragman's Roll, 1296, was probably the son of Duncan, whose son Patrick, signed the same document, and his grandson Robert got a charter of the lands of Skene from Robert the Bruce. The origin of this ancient family is thus more satisfactorily proved than by the admission of legends that savour of old women's tales,—the story, so often repeated, of some person rescuing one of the Scottish monarchs from a ferocious wolf, by slaying it with his sgian, or dirk, is the popular traditional origin of the name, and the hero is said to have lived in the time of Malcolm II. or about 1014. He would, therefore, be the first recorded in the family history. Although John the Skene and his son Patrick signed the bond of submission to King Edward I. of England, in 1296, on the accession of Bruce to the Scottish crown, he granted a charter, "Roberto Skene dilecto et fideli nostro, pro homagio et servitio suo, omnes et singulos terras de Skene, et lacum ejusdem, per omnes rectas antiquas metas et divisas suas," &c., dated 1318. Adam de Skene went with his followers to oppose Donald of the Isles, in his alarming advance from the north, and was slain at the battle of Harlaw, 1411. He had raised money for this service by mortgage on his estates, which proved a source of great trouble to his successors. Alexander joined the army of James IV. and fell with that chivalrous monarch in the disastrous battle of Flodden Field, 1513; and Alexander, his grandson, was likewise slain at the battle of Pinkey, 1547. The laird of Skene joined Huntly in his attempt to get Queen Mary out of the Earl of Moray's keeping, and lost his youngest son and several kinsmen in the consequent battle of Corrichie, 1562. Others of the family distinguished themselves in military service, both in this country and abroad.

The ancient family of Skene of Skene at last terminated in George, who was the twenty-first chief, and died without issue in 1824, when the possessions, which had been much increased by intermarriage and purchase, reverted to the present Earl of Fife, whose father had married Mary, sister of the above George.

Several families of respectability are descended of this house, of whom may be mentioned those of Dyce, Hallyards, Cariston, &c.

The castle of Skene is believed to have been the first stone and lime building in that district of the country called Mar; it consisted of a square keep of three vaulted stories, and entrance was obtained by a ladder placed against the second floor.

The ARMORIAL BEARINGS are gules, three sgians, or daggers, palewise, in fess, argent, hilted and pommelled, or, on the points of which, as many wolves' heads of the third. Crest, a dexter arm from the shoulder, issuing out of a cloud, and holding forth a triumphal crown or garland of laurel leaves, proper. Supporters, on the dexter a Highlander in his proper garb, holding in his right hand a sgian, and on the sinister a Highlander in a more simple habit, his target on the left arm, and his dorlach, by his side, all proper. Motto— "Virtutis regia merces." The Clann Dhoncha', or Robertsons of Athol, carry wolves' heads erased on the same field.

The Dorlach was the wallett, or haversack, of the highland soldiers, and is noticed in Baillie's Letters, under the year 1639. "Those of the English who visited our camp did gaze with admiration upon those supple fellows, the highlanders, with their plaids, targes, and Dorlachs."

A dirk of antique manufacture, supposed to be Duncan Mòr's, was carefully preserved in the charter chest, the safe keeping of which was probably a sort of tenure similar to those of some other families which we have had occasion to notice.

The figure given for this clan may be taken as the portrait of one of the lairds of Skene, dressed in the fashion which prevailed in the time of James VI. The doublet was then formed in this manner, embroidered and slashed out in Spanish style, as we see in the armorial supporters of Clunie Mac Pherson, and it was retained by the highlanders, long after it had gone out of use among other people. The belted plaid, which was formed of one entire piece, is of the clan tartan, from the pattern of an old kilt preserved in the castle of Skene. The Sword is from a curious weapon in possession of Henry Angelo, Esq., and we believe it to exhibit one of the first approaches to the cliabh, or basket hilt. The sporan is a very ingenious specimen of the old leathern purse, which was furnished with different pouches, curiously contrived to be closed by thongs of different colours, which were thus rendered ornamental. The Bonaid gorm is from the head on one of James the Fifth's coins, which being so covered, is called a bonnet piece. The brooch is similar to the celebrated brooch of Lorn, and the no less elegant one so long preserved in the family of Campbell, of Glenlyon.

NA STIUBHARTICH—THE STEWARTS.

FEW of the royal races of Europe can boast so long a line of unbroken ancestry as the Stewarts. From Fergus Mac Eirc, who reigned over the Scots in Argyle at the commencement of the fifth century, to James VIII., called the Pretender, there have been a hundred and ten kings of Scotland. Genealogists trace them through Bancho, Thane of Lochaber, slain by Mac Beth in 1043, to Allan, who was created Lord High Steward of Scotland, about 1100, which is the origin of this distinguished name, and the propriety of adhering to an orthography consonant with its rise is obvious. In the Gaëlic alphabet there is no letter w, and the French language being equally deficient, Queen Mary spelt her name Stuart, and thus introduced that form, which was adopted, on her return to Scotland, by her brother, the Earl of Moray, and several others.

There are many noble and distinguished families of the name in different parts of Scotland; those in the districts of Athole and of Appin were the most noted among the clans.

The early history of the race must be dismissed in few words, but the epoch of the last rising in favour of the exiled family appears an appropriate commencement; especially as the portrait of "the young chevalier," the gallant and "bonnie Prince Charlie," royal leader of his own and all other clans who followed him, is given as an interesting illustration of this work.

Now that this august family is extinct, and no fear exists of the Pope and the Pretender, "the unfortunate house of Stewart" is the general expression when it is alluded to, and it is singularly just. James I. was most inhumanly murdered in Perth, 1436; James II.

SKENE

was killed by the bursting of a cannon at the siege of Roxburgh, 1460; James III. was slain in a rebellion of his own nobles headed by his son, at the field of Bannockburn, 1488; James IV. fell at the disastrous battle of Flodden-field, in 1513; and James V. died of a broken heart, in consequence of the shameful conduct of his nobles, and defeat of his army at Solway, 1542! Darnley was blown up in his lodgings, and the fate of the lovely Mary is well known. Her grandson the martyr, Charles I. was beheaded, and although her son did not indeed meet with the doom of so many of his race, he was harassed with repeated plots and conspiracies, real or pretended. The escape of Charles II. was almost as wonderful as that of his successor, whom we shall more particularly allude to.

Prince Charles Edward, elder son of King James VIII. of Scotland and III. of England, appears to have indulged from his infancy, the sanguine hope that his family would be restored to their ancient crown and kingdom. That cherished anticipation strengthened with his years, and his highest ambition was to become the favoured instrument of so glorious an achievement.

The families who retained their attachment to the race of their ancient monarchs, had frequent correspondence, for several years, with the exiled court, and several influential chiefs of clans were commissioned, in name of the Jacobites, to negociate measures for a rising in the Highlands; indeed, "the hale dint and pressure" of this undertaking, it is evident, were to be laid upon the devoted adherents of the Stewarts in that country. The majority of them enthusiastically engaged in the romantic and ruinous attempt, and considering the relentless persecutions to which many of the clans had been subjected by the Stewarts, more particularly the Mac Gregors and Mac Donalds, they evinced a spirit of forgiveness and unextinguishable loyalty, scarcely if possible, to be paralelled in history. The persevering efforts which the Highlanders had made for the restoration of the Stewarts is truly astonishing; no reverses were sufficient to deter them from repeatedly taking arms. Under the Marquis of Montrose they had recovered Scotland for King Charles, and Viscount Dundee, by his victory at Killiecrankie, gave hopes of equal success, which were extinguished by his death. The Earl of Mar, in 1715, had an army, of which from his own want of military skill and energy he could make no serviceable use, and speedily allowed to dissolve. The Earl of Seaforth, in 1719, was overthrown in Glensheil; yet with all these severe discomfitures, the clans arose again to embark in a scheme infinitely more wild and romantic than the others.

The requisite assistance to carry this bold attempt into effect, was promised by Louis XV.; but whether the French court was really sincere or otherwise, that assistance was not afforded, at least to any efficient purpose. "The impatient Adventurer," raising what money he could, by borrowing money and pledging his jewels, engaged a small vessel of sixteen guns, put on board about 700 stand of arms, and with seven attendants only, set sail for Scotland with his father's commission of Prince Regent, to overthrow a powerful government, and regain the sovereignty of three kingdoms! He was joined in the channel by a sixty gun frigate, supplied by private individuals, containing a farther supply of arms, provided by his friends; but she was intercepted by a British cruiser and forced to return, while Charles, sailing on, landed in the west Highlands, the 24th of July,

1745, and proceeded to the residence of Donald Mac Donald, of Boradale. The success of an expedition commenced with such inadequate preparation, appeared to his friends so utterly hopeless that those who had been most anxious for his appearance, absolutely refused to move; but the fascination of his persuasions and his appeals to the honour of those who had encouraged his landing, subdued all their objections and dissipated those fears which were indeed too well grounded. The generous Cameron of Locheil, with his clansmen, and several Mac Donalds, repaired to the sequestered valley of Glenfinan, where he then was; and the 19th of August the celebrated Brattach bhàn, or white banner, was unfurled amid the fervid acclamations of the incipient army.

Meantime, hostilities had commenced by Mac Donald of Tierndrish, a gentleman of the Keppach branch of this clan, without waiting the formality of any declaration of war. With eleven men he attacked two companies of the First Regiment, or Scots Royals, when marching to reinforce the garrison of Inverlochie, whom he compelled, with some loss, to retreat, when a body of Glengarry's men coming up, they were taken prisoners to the number of seventy, and conducted to Prince Charles, by the Camerons, the very morning when his standard was to be displayed. Having issued a declaration, and assumed the highland garb, he marched forward, receiving additions to his scanty band, and the Government troops under General Cope sent to oppose him declining battle, he reached Perth September the 3rd, where he was joined by many gentlemen of influence. The Robertsons, Stewarts, Mac Gregors, and some other clans having come up, the little army, driving the dragoons before them, and fording the Forth, reached Edinburgh, which was taken on the 16th, by surprise. He did not succeed in getting possession of the castle; but, reinforced by the Grants of Glenmoriston, the Mac Lachlans, and others, the Prince marched against General Cope, who lay at Prestonpans, whom he surprised by a night attack, and totally routed in about six minutes! Cope had a strong body of well-mounted dragoons and six pieces of artillery, both of which were most effective arms against the ill-appointed highlanders, who had neither. The Stewarts and Camerons, rushing to the muzzles of the cannon, "with a swiftness not to be described," took them immediately by storm, and the whole were forced, from an irresistible onslaught with the broad-sword, to make a precipitate retreat.

Joined by reinforcements of the Mac Kinnons, Mac Phersons, Lords Elcho and Pitsligo with some horse, the Marquis of Tullibardin with 1800 men, and the French ambassador, who brought a small supply of money and arms; the whole body marched for England, which was entered on the 8th of November, and investing the fortified city and castle of Carlisle, they were taken with the loss of only one man killed and another wounded on the part of the Highlanders! Proceeding southwards on the 30th, the army reached Derby on December the 4th, having by skilful manœuvres got between the Duke of Cumberland's army and London. Here the Chevalier stopped short. The town is situated 126 miles from London, and it is to this day matter of surprise that an army so daring, did not push on with their usual celerity, which so often baffled their foes; but a council of war determined to march for Scotland, to the exceeding mortification of all the inferior clansmen, who loudly murmured when they found themselves on the retreat. They left Derby on the morning of the 6th, and arrived in Scotland on the 18th of December; having eluded two armies and gained the action at Clifton, where the Duke's advanced dragoons were routed by the Stewart and Mac Pherson battalions, who charged through hedge and ditch with the cleaming clai'mòr. This admirable retreat, in an enemy's country, was made in the depth of winter, and not only did they turn out early in the mornings, but marched at times by moonlight, and these men being clad in kilts or belted plaids, many without hose and some without shoes, must have been exposed to innumerable privations which their pursuers were very carefully protected from! By their own official report they did not lose fifty men during the whole time, and they had traversed upwards of 380 miles through a hostile country in forty days, including about sixteen days of halt, during which they conducted themselves, even by the Gazette account, with great moderation.

The Prince was grievously disappointed when it was determined to retreat; but although, had he reached London, many would have hailed his arrival with joy, he had little encouragement in his advance, the only reinforcement he received being raised by Francis Townley, Esquire, of Manchester, the uniform of whose regiment consisted simply of the white cockade, and a tartan scarf lined with white. Notwithstanding, it is the opinion of Lord Mahon, an able and dispassionate writer, that had the army marched onward, the Stewarts would have certainly regained the British throne.

On re-entering Scotland, 20th of December, the Highlanders marched to Glasgow, a city extremely adverse to them, on which they with the less hesitation levied a contribution to refit themselves. From thence they proceeded to Stirling, where they were joined by the Frasers, Mac Intoshes, Farquharsons, and a large body of other troops who were in arms for Prince Charles, under Lord Lewis Gordon, Lord John Drummond, Viscount Strathallan, and others.

At Falkirk, beside the auspicious field of Bannockburn, the retreating Highlanders gave battle to the Government troops, and the Stewart army was again victorious, defeating General Hawley's well-trained veterans, with as much celerity as in the previous battle of Prestonpans. While the main body was in England, Lord Lewis Gordon defeated and dispersed the Mac Leods and Munros at Inverury, on their march to dislodge him from Aberdeen. Charles had about 9000 men engaged at Falkirk; but the Highlanders began to retire to their homes with the spoils they had won; and as even the chiefs could not prevent them, it was resolved to retire to the north; and soon after the whole forces commenced their march to Inverness, where the different divisions were to be concentrated. Here they arrived, January 1746, when many of the chiefs went home to recruit. The castle of Inverness, which had been put in a state of good defence by Government not long before, was taken and blown up, and various successes were obtained in different parts of the country by the Highlanders. Lord George Murray, with some of his own men, and the Mac Phersons, made an expedition to Athole, where not only was the castle of Blair well garrisoned, but in every gentleman's house was a strong detachment of soldiers. In one night thirty of these posts were surprised, and with the exception of three

or four killed, every one almost was taken prisoner, without the loss of a single Highlander. Roy Stewart also made a night march, and captured a party of horse and infantry at Keith; but in Ross and Sutherland matters went very untowardly, and the whole body having been put in motion to surprise the Duke of Cumberland, who lay at Nairn, nearly twelve miles distant, the attempt proved abortive. Next day, 16th April, the Duke advanced to the field of Culloden, where Charles's troops were lying, and soon after the two armies were confronted, that battle commenced, which for ever terminated the hopes of the unfortunate Stewarts.

Many of the clans were absent in their own country, when this disastrous battle took place, and those who were engaged suffered not only from the fatigue of the night march, but from having been on the shortest rations for some days before. There were, however, the following clans drawn up, as we give them, right to left in front, opposed to an equal extent of line:—The Athol Brigade, Cameron, Appin, Fraser, Mac Intosh, Mac Lachlan, Mac Lean, Roy Stewart, Farquharson, Clan Ranald, Keppach, and Glengarry.

The Highlanders, for the first time during the campaign, were worsted,—the cannon made fearful havoc among their ranks, and after the five first-mentioned regiments had charged sword in hand with such fury as to annihilate several companies of the enemy, they commenced a retreat, irregular and sanguinary, but the left wing went off in a body, after an ineffectual charge by the Keppach Mac Donalds, and were not pursued. This division was met by the Mac Phersons, who had come down fresh from Badenach, and, exasperated by defeat, were eager to renew the battle; but to the exhortations of their chief, Clunie, to return and again lead on his troops, Charles paid no deference; he seemed to have lost his wonted fortitude, and gave up his cause as irretrievably ruined.

The direful scourging which the unhappy Highlanders received from the Duke's army, after their discomfiture, is an indelible stain on his memory. The country was ravaged in the most shocking manner; and the Prince, so lately inspired with a confidence strengthened by his astonishing successes, found himself a deplorable wanderer in the wilds. His narrow escapes, woful privations, and wanderings with Flora Mac Donald, have been often the subject of pen and pencil; great as were the calamities brought on them through his expedition, and well known as were his retreats, £30,000 was no temptation for the poorest Celt to betray his trust.

He at last got on board a French frigate, with some others, 20th September, and landed on the 29th at Morlaix.

Appin, the chief, had not gone out; and Stewart of Ardshiel led the clan, which evinced its usual bravery. He escaped from Culloden, but a great number of his officers and men were killed and wounded in their impetuous charge on the cannon and the Scots Fusiliers, before whom they were planted. When the standard-bearer was slain, one of the corps called Mac an t-ledh from Morven, tore the banner from the staff, and wrapping it round his body, carried it off.

The force of this branch of the clan was three hundred, but the Stewarts of Athol, Strathearn, and Monteith, according to General Stewart, of Garth, writing in 1821, amounted to nearly four thousand. There were many of the name in the Braes of Mar and Strathspey also; Colonel Roy Stewart, of Kincardine, in the latter district, an accomplished scholar and poet, who had served long abroad, was one of the most active and efficient of Prince Charles's officers, and commanded a battalion of four hundred men, with which he performed several daring and successful exploits.

The ARMORIAL BEARINGS for the name Stewart, is or, a fesse checky, argent, and gules.

The SUAICHEANTAS, or badge, is Cluaran, Thistle, *Carduus*; the national emblem. On ascending the throne of England, the oak is said to have been assumed, and from its not being ever-green, it was rendered typical of the family downfall.

The PIOBAIREACHDAN, complimentary and valedictory, in honour of the royal descendants of their ancient kings, were played proudly by the pipers of the Clann Stiubhartich, although none of them appear to have been the production of clansmen. A Failte, or salutation to King Charles, was composed in 1715, by the piper of the Chief of the Menzies', who was author of a similar welcome to Prince Charles, called " Thanig mo righ air tir am Muidart," being a burst of exultation on hearing that his King had landed at Muidart. The White Banner was saluted with a becoming pio-baireachd, and doleful are the strains of the "Cumha'achan," or lamentations on the departure of both Charles and his father—the former being composed by Captain Mac Leod of Rasa. There is also a piece composed in compliment to the Princess Sobieski, the mother of Prince Charles.

The standard under which the Highlanders marched, they called, as has been observed, Brattach bhan, or the white banner. According to Home, in his " History of the Rebellion," this flag was of a large size, and composed of red, blue, and white silk; but Henderson describes it as of a red colour, with the figure of a white standard in the middle, and the motto, " Tandem bona causa triumphans." It was borne in the centre of the column, by the clans, each having the honour of carrying it on alternate days.

A monument now marks the spot, in the wild secluded glen where it was first displayed to the delighted gaze of the enthusiastic Celt. It is a slender tower, the basement forming a lodge intended for use in the shooting season, and it presents inscriptions in Gaëlic, Latin, and English; the latter of which is in these words:—

ON THE SPOT WHERE

PRINCE CHARLES EDWARD STEWART

First raised his Standard,

On the 19th day of August, 1745,

When he made the daring and romantic attempt

To recover a Throne lost by the imprudence of his ancestors;

This column was erected

BY

ALEXANDER MAC DONALD, ESQUIRE, OF GLENALADALE,

To commemorate the generous zeal,

The undaunted bravery, and the inviolable fidelity

Of his forefathers, and the rest of those

Who fought and bled

In that arduous and unfortunate enterprise.

This pillar is now,

ALAS !

Also become the monument

Of its amiable and accomplished founder,

Who, before it was finished,

Died in Edinburgh, on the 4th day of January, 1815,

At the early age of 28 years.

STEWART

The upper portion of the figure appropriately illustrating this clan, is from a half-length portrait of the chivalrous Prince Charles Edward Stewart, whose adventurous attempt to achieve the conquest of the British kingdom has occupied so great a portion of the preceding pages. It is an original miniature in possession of Sir Charles Forbes Bart., of Newe and Edinglassie, which was taken immediately before or during the period of his brilliant campaign, and he is here represented in the costume he wore at his levees and balls, and in which he at times appeared among his troops.

On his first appearance at Edinburgh, he was not dressed in the Feilebeag, but is described as wearing a short Highland coat of tartan, but no plaid, a blue velvet bonnet, having a gold band around it, in which was a white cockade and cross of St. Andrew, carrying an elegant silver-hilted sword, and gold-mounted pistols. Subsequently he bore a target, mounted in classical silver devices. The star of the thistle was suspended around his neck, but he wore that of the garter on his breast. In a letter from the neighbourhood of Manchester, it is said " he was dressed in a light plaid, belted about with a blue sash, with a blue bonnet, and a white rose in it."

He would undoubtedly wear the Stewart tartan; but in those days the subject of clan patterns was not attended to, except among the people themselves; but the Breacan dearg na Stiubhartich, or red-coloured plaid of the Stewarts, is alluded to in songs. It would naturally be assumed by other clans in compliment to their leader, hence an old man who had been " out " in that affair, described the effect of a large body of men crossing a hill clothed with red tartan, contrasting with the dark-coloured heath, and seen at a distance " as if the hill were on fire." He is described, however, in " The Glasgow Courant," as otherwise arrayed, " in a green plaid of the Highland fashions, with a silver-hilted sword, a black velvet cap, and a white cockade."

There is no doubt he must have been under the necessity of wearing different suits as he could obtain them, and it is known that he was accustomed to part with his plaids, or portions of them to those, especially ladies, who were anxious to possess relics of the Prince, with whom they had become so fascinated. We have seen some of these tokens of remembrance: a small piece is carefully preserved by the Earl of Fife, at Duff-house.

It may be observed, that nothing gave the Highlanders so much delight as the Prince's adoption of their costume and manners. Dressed as themselves, he marched on foot at the head of his troops, or occasionally with the different clans—forded the streams, as at the Mersey on the 1st of December, when the water reached his middle— lay in the open field along with his hardy adherents; fatigues which seemed so little in accordance with his apparent delicacy of habit. He must, however, have enjoyed the most robust constitution to enable him to undergo so much personal hardship, with the mental harassment of commanding an armament from its composition, so difficult of proper regulation.

In contemplating the extraordinary proceedings, of which a rapid account has been given, we are struck with surprise at the state of society in which they could take place. Prince Charles landed with a sum less than 4,000 louis d'ors, and when he reached Perth one only remained in his possession. It is not to be supposed that the few chiefs who had then joined him could have brought much with

them; in fact the computed rental of the whole of the lairds that ever followed his fortunes did not amount to more than £12,000! The law of Clanship, or patriarchal rule, was then in operation; but one of the effects of this last " affair " was an act of the legislature which for ever broke up this primitive system, and thereby all hopes of any similar effort of the Gaël to bring " the auld Stewarts back again," were finally crushed. The chiefs had no longer the patriarchal influence over their clansmen; and the clansmen had no longer the wonted dependence on them as their natural protectors. Whether the social state of the Highlanders has been improved by the alteration, the many thousands who have left their native shores for distant climes, where they might obtain the maintenance which the Highlands no longer afforded them, and the deplorable state of destitution in which the remaining inhabitants are now, and have so frequently been, placed, will amply testify. Battalions of brave and hardy soldiers, nay, armies, have been drawn from glens and hills, where now the solitude is disturbed only by the bleating of sheep, and occasional strains from the pipe of the lonely shepherd.

The destruction of a " bold peasantry—their country's pride," has been feelingly deplored in the oft-repeated words of the poet.

Having brought forward, throughout the work, as far as the plan of the undertaking would admit, in condensed sketches of each clan, some of the most notable transactions in their respective histories, by which their individual position is elucidated; in this last portion, the proceedings of a confederated army of considerable strength, is more particularly detailed. The Gaël were from circumstances a military people, and it was a source of no small trouble for the Highland chiefs to preserve a balance of power among themselves. Ambition amongst them, as elsewhere, frequently led to open hostilities; and no combination of the smaller tribes was able to prevent the Campbells in the west, and the Mac Kenzies in the north, from gaining an ascendancy over many ancient clans, who were in nowise connected with those who brought them under subjection. It will be seen that the different septs were involved in frequent feuds or misunderstandings, which led to wars, on a small scale comparatively, but carried on with characteristic energy, military tact, bravery, and honour. In this sketch of the Stewarts a hearty co-operation is seen to take place, and all clan disputes give way to a spontaneous impulse of loyalty, generous and high-minded, although mistaken; and an army composed of discordant bodies, in many cases highly jealous of their individual honours, with high enthusiasm in the cause and hearty goodwill towards each other, attempt to achieve a conquest which no men less ardent would have dreamt of attempting. Such were the Highland troops of the olden time;—equally invaluable have they been in the armies of Britain, under the dynasty which has been called to her throne, and during whose sway the prosperity of these kingdoms has so amazingly advanced. Our gracious Queen has not an arm in her service more devoted or more emulous in support of the national honour, than her Gaëlic soldiers and subjects; nor has any portion of the community been more enterprising and successful as colonists and merchants in all parts of the world. It is no small matter of pride to the Highlanders, whose fathers so strenuously opposed the Hanoverian succession, that Her Majesty should take pleasure in their mountain homes, and patronise the manufactures which were once branded as felonious. The disarming act is in desuetude, and the Gaël may traverse their highland glens, or walk along the public streets, bearing their arms, without exciting the slightest dread that they will ever be used in treason or in any breach of peace. Many of the descendants of those whose lives were sacrificed and lands forfeited, have risen to a higher eminence in the walks of peace, than their ancestors could have ever attained in the highlands by the pursuits of war.

In closing these hasty sketches of the Scottish Clans, the manner in which a Highland army was regulated, or the military practice, according to the order of clanship, it may be suitable to describe. The clan was, of course, commanded by the chief, but that duty would devolve, in his absence, or from circumstances, on his son, brother, or nearest cadet, and the same rule of consanguinity was observed as to lieutenant-colonel, major, captains, lieutenants, &c. The chief stood, when the regiment was drawn up, in the centre beside the banner, supported by two relations, or foster-brothers, one on each side, and in battle the finest men and best armed were placed near to him as colonels. The same scale of relationship was adhered to as far as was possible throughout the line. They marched in a column three abreast, and when halted and formed in line, they simply faced about and were then three deep. The daoiné-uasal, or gentlemen, were in front, who were better armed than the others, having generally firelocks, and always swords, targets, pistols, and dirks. Many of the others had but swords, and some only pistols.

The pay of Prince Charles's troops was according to the following scale. A captain had 2s. 6d. a day; a lieutenant, 2s.; an ensign, 1s. 6d.; and a private, 6d.; but to those who formed the front rank 1s. was allowed as requisite for their station in life.

The known principles of the Stewart family produced the violent opposition of Protestants to the attempts of King James and Prince Charles; the Presbyterians, especially those of the west of Scotland, were in the greatest alarm, lest, if successful, they would bring in the restoration of Popery, to suppress which the country had so long struggled and paid so dear; and it was industriously spread that " Charlie's " men were all inveterate papists. They were not

all so—the Marquis of Tullibardine, Murray of Broughton, his Secretary of War, Locheil, the first man who joined him, and without whose acquiescence no other clan would have arisen, Macpherson of Clunie, were zealous Protestants, and so of many others, both noblemen and chiefs.

Jackson, in his view of the European armies, observes that the highlanders are the only troops who could look with a steady eye on a naked weapon, and, in allusion to their last rising, he says, "they are neither a ferocious nor a cruel people, for no troops probably ever traversed a country, which might be esteemed hostile, with traces of less outrage. They are now better known—their character is conspicuous for honesty and fidelity. They possess the most exalted notions of honour, the warmest friendship, and the highest portion of mental pride of any people, perhaps, in Europe. Their ideas are few, but their sentiments are strong."

We shall present a list of those noblemen who were in arms during this ill-matured invasion, in the centenary of which we have brought those illustrations of " The Clans " to a close.

The Duke of Perth.	Lord Balmerino.
Marquis of Tullibardine.	Lord Pitsligo.
Viscount Strathallan.	Lord Ogilvie.
Earl of Kelly.	Lord George Murray.
Earl of Kilmarnock.	Lord Lewis Gordon.
Earl of Cromartie.	Lord Lewis Drummond.
Lord Elcho.	Lord John Drummond.
Lord Nairn.	Lord Mac Leod, son of the
Lord Lovat	Earl of Cromarty.

The Hon. William Murray, afterwards Earl of Dunmore.

There were besides a number of baronets and others who favoured the cause, although they did not go " out," as the old Earl of Wemys, who sent him £500.

CLANN AN CHATTAOBH; NO, AN CINNEADH SHUTHERLANICH—THE SUTHERLANDS.

THE northern part of Scotland, comprehending the present counties of Sutherland and Caithness, received its name from the great clan Chattan.

Cattaobh is now applied to the latter division only, for at a very early period in Scottish history, the district south of the Ord mountain, became distinguished by the Norwegian appellation Sudrland.

It is supposed, that the Catti of Germany were the progenitors of the highland Cattanich or Cattans, and the popular belief is that they arrived from the continent about the beginning of the second

century; but, according to genealogies, the founder of the illustrious house of Sutherland was Freskin a Fleming, who is said to have come into Scotland in the reign of King William the lion; 1165—1214.

When first noticed in the national annals, the possessions of this family were in Moray, and those of that name are traced, in No. XI., to the same origin. The lands in Sutherland appear, from the above authorities, to have been acquired upon the forfeiture of the Earl of Caithness, in 1197, and by a deed, executed about 1211, and still preserved, Freskin conveys certain lands in that county to the archdeacon of Moray. That the original name was retained long afterwards, appears from several instances, as a salvus conductus to pass into England, in Rymer's Fœdera, granted in 1367, to William de Murref, son of the Earl of Sutherland, &c.

Allan the Thane, who lived in the time of Mac Beth, 1040—56, is placed by Sir Robert Gordon, in his elaborate history of the family as the first in its long and illustrious pedigree, and the title of Earl, whether conferred by Malcolm Ceann mòr, who reigned 1057—92, or Alexander II. in 1228, is undoubtedly the oldest in the kingdom.

Abundant as are the materials for a history of this clan, it can only, consistent with our plan, be treated with great brevity. William, who succeeded to his hereditary honours and estate in 1275, married the eldest daughter of Robert the Bruce, whom he actively assisted with his clan, making several incursions on the English borders, in one of which, he took the castle of Roxburgh, burnt Durham, and spoiled the country. He signed that spirited assertion of national independence, which the Scottish nobility transmitted, in 1320, to the Pope, wherein it is maintained, that by their will the Bruce was placed on the throne, from which they would not hesitate to remove him, if he proved undeserving. This Earl died at a great age, having enjoyed his title seventy-seven years.

The Earls of Sutherland fought with characteristic bravery in the battles which were so frequently taking place between the Scots and English, and many of them fell in the fields of their fame. They were also embroiled in repeated internal feuds, which they were generally able to quell by their valour, or repress by their pacific influence. The clans Mac Kay and Sinclair were troublesome neighbours, and the Gunns, although not so numerous or important as the others, were the very Mac Gregors of the north.

Through several centuries the history of this clan displays a series of the most rancorous feuds, mutual slaughter and alternate spoliation. The Sutherland nobles in becoming intermixed with the quarrels of others, brought several small tribes into notice by their patronage, who otherwise might have lived in obscurity, and contributed to advance the interest of others who were of more consideration.

The Thanes of Sutherland strenuously opposed the Danes and Norwegians, in their invasions of the north, defeating them at Drumlea, about the year 1031, and at Enbo, about 1259, where rude obelisks were raised to commemorate the events.

In 1517, an invasion of Sutherland, by the Mac Kays, took place, which led to a pitched battle at Torran du', in Strathfleit, in which the latter, after "a cruel fight, weill foughten on either side," sustained a sorrowful defeat, losing 216 slain on the field, and many others in the pursuit, the Sutherland men escaping with the loss of thirty-eight only. Donald and William Mac Kay led another expedition to retrieve their misfortune, which was met by their opponents, under the command of John Murray of Aberscors, at Loch Salachie, when, "after a sharp skirmish, both chieftains of the Strathnaver men were slain, with divers of their men, and the rest put to flight; neither was the victory pleasing to John Murray, for he lost there his brother John Roy Murray."

In 1522, John, chief of the Mac Kays, was completely overthrown at Lairg, and, submitting to his too powerful conquerors, gave a bond of manrent, or obligation of friendship, to Adam, then Earl of Sutherland. Donald, who succeeded John, taking advantage of the minority of the following earl, made an inroad on his possessions, 1542, burning and spoiling the country, but being intercepted, he was defeated at Ault an beà', and the booty recovered. Mac Kay acted with great valour, and, in his flight, turned on his pursuers, and killed William Sutherland, who first came up with him. The last battle between these clans took place about 1556, at Beann mòr, where the Mac Kays were again defeated, with a loss of upwards of 120 men.

The Sinclairs were determined enemies of the house of Sutherland, and they had influence to prevail with others to join in their aggressions. In the end of the 16th century, George, Earl of Caithness, their chief, when Alexander, Earl of Sutherland, was in wardship with Earl Huntley, took possession of the lands, and proceeded to remove all those of the name of Murray; but, in 1570, under the command of Uisdean, a determined leader, they threw themselves into Dornoch, their ancient property, where they bravely defended themselves in the castle after the town had been burnt, and obtained terms of capitulation. The life of excitement which these personages led will be seen by some farther account of "the troubles betwixt Sutherland and Catteyness."

In 1587, George Gordon of Marle, having offended the Earl of Caithness, he attacked him in his castle, where he stood out for some time; but in attempting to swim across the river Helmsdale, he was shot by the bowmen. In retaliation, the Earl of Sutherland, in the spring of next year, sent 200 men into Caithness, who ravaged the parishes of Latheron and Dunbeath, and, on their return, the earl himself entered the county with a great force, slew many of the inhabitants, burned Wick, and devastated the country.

Both parties seemed desirous of having a pitched battle, but, meeting on opposite sides of the Helmsdale, there could be no regular engagement; "yet they skirmished dayley, and divers were hurt on either syde with gunns and arrowes. The Southerland archers so galled the Catteyness armie that they forced them to remove their camp." In 1589, the Earl of Caithness sent a great force into Sutherland on a similar predatory excursion, which returned with very little loss, but it was quickly followed by 300 men, under John Gordon of Bakies, who carried home a great booty, after considerable slaughter. In 1590, Caithness assembled his whole strength, and again invaded Sutherland, where, in a short time, he collected a great number of cattle and other property, which were driven before the captors as they were on the return homewards. Meantime, the inhabitants of Sutherland had assembled to the number of about 500, and followed the enemy until they came up with them at Clyne, when, although inferior in strength, they commenced the attack, and "there ensued a sharp conflict, fought with great obstinacy on either syde, till the night parted them. Of the Sutherland men, were slain John Murray and sixteen common soldiers; of the Catteyness men, were killed Nicholas Sutherland, the laird of Fors, his brother, and Angus Mac Tormot, with thirteen others- divers were hurt on either syde. The next morning timely, the Earl of Catteyness returned with all diligence to defend his own country," but he was too late for effecting his object; whilst engaged in this memorable foray, Uisdean Mackay entered Caithness, which he "wasted, spoiled, and burnt, even to the gates of Thurso," carrying off a rich creach.

SUTHERLAND

"Thus," says Sir Robert Gordon, "they infested one another with continual spoils and slaughters, until they were reconciled by the mediation of the Earl of Huntley, who caused them to meet at Strathbogie, and a final peace was concluded betwixt these parties, in the moth of March, 1591."

Earl John, who died in 1514, left no issue, and he was succeeded by his sister Elizabeth, who had married Adam Gordon, of Aboyne, second son of Earl Huntley. In 1766, this most ancient title devolved on Elizabeth, twenty-third in succession, who was then an orphan, when there arose a keen competition for the Earldom and estates between Sir Robert Gordon of Gordonstoun, Baronet, and George Sutherland, Esq., of Fors. After genealogical researches and legal scrutinies of unexampled length, the question was settled in her favour by the House of Lords, 1771, and this interesting representative of a race so illustrious, lived long to enjoy her proud distinctions. In 1785, she married the Right Honourable Viscount Trentham, afterwards Marquis of Stafford and Duke of Sutherland; but, jealous of the extinction of her own more ancient title, she chose to be distinguished as "the Duchess-Countess." She died in 1838, leaving her honours and vast estates to the present amiable and patriotic Duke.

Clanship does not permit the transmission of honours by the female line, hence the late Countess, although Ban a Mhorear Chattaobh, the lady of the great man i. e. Earl of Sutherland, could not be chief. William Sutherland of Killipheder, who died in 1832, at a great age, and enjoyed a small annuity from her Grace, was accounted eldest male descendant of the old Earls. John Campbell Sutherland, of Fors, in the county of Caithness, is now considered the real chief.

The principal seat is Dunrobin, a strong baronial edifice, beautifully situated on the margin af the sea, built by Earl Robert, about 1097, which his Grace is to re-edify in a princely style.

The ARMORIAL BEARINGS are gules, three stars within a bordure or, charged with a double tressure, flory, counterflory, of fleur-de-lis, of the field, Crest, a cat, sejant proper. Supporters, two savages, wreathed around their heads and waists with laurel, each holding a baton over the shoulder, proper. Motto, "sans peur."

The SUAICHEANTAS, or Badge is Bealaidh chatti, the Cattans, vulgarly, Butchers Broom, *Ruscus occiliatus.*

The military force of the Sutherlands was estimated at 2000, who supported with great zeal the Hanoverian succession. In 1779, the Duchess raised a fencible corps 1000 strong, which was completed in twelve days, and in 1793, another body of clansmen were raised, which is now the Sutherland highlanders, or 93rd regiment of the line.

The figure is that of a highlander, in modern costume of the clan tartan "breasting the bræ" against one of those violent snow-storms which frequently burst out in the highlands, and compel the anxious shepherd to look after his fleecy charge, lest they get buried in the deep wreaths which are formed in the mountain hollows.

NA URCHDADAIN—THE URQUHARTS.

THE etymologies, which have been propounded for the explanation of the name of this clan, are sufficiently numerous and ingenious; but some of them rather far-fetched.

It has been generally supposed to signify "red earth," for no other reason apparently than that, in the opening sentence of Sir Thomas Urquhart's pedigree of the family, it is observed that Adam, from whom this facetious genealogist traces his descent, was framed of red earth. It is often impossible to discover the etymon of words, the component parts of which may be now obsolete, or become so corrupted, that they are not to be traced in the language to which they belong; in such cases, there is ample scope for the indulgence of conjecture. This is one of those personal appellations, which is evidently derived from locality. Urquhart, or Urchard, is

an extensive district in the county of Inverness, and there is a parish in Morayshire of the same name.

The talented but eccentric chief above alluded to, gives a genealogy of the Urquharts from the father of mankind, with amusing circumstantiality. A tribe, or family, bearing a territorial appellation has, without doubt, a claim to a higher antiquity than it is possible in most cases to determine, but, of course, he could not have believed great part of what he wrote. The pedigree, from a certain period, is, however, perfectly authentic.

There are records of the Urquharts, who were chiefs of the name, from the year 1306, when we find William Urquhart, of Cromartie, sheriff of the county, which office was afterwards made heritable in the family. In early ages, when individuals are of so

URQUHART

much importance as to receive royal charters and hold high national appointments, they must possess personal influence, or belong to a race which has attained distinction by public services.

This William married a daughter of the powerful Earl of Ross, and his son and successor Adam obtained charters of various lands; the estates being afterwards greatly increased by intermarriages with the Mac Kenzies and others.

Sir Thomas Urquhart, of Cromarty, who married Helen, daughter of Alexander, Lord Abernethie, of Saltoun, is remarkable for having been the father of no fewer than eleven daughters and twenty-five sons, of whom seven fell with honour in the battle of Pinkie, fought 1547.

He, however, who was the most remarkable personage in the line of chiefs, is the above-mentioned Sir Thomas, who lived in the time of King Charles I. and II. and whose life was singularly eventful.

When a young man on his travels, he was repeatedly called on to support the national honour, and he thrice evinced his patriotism and bravery by entering the list with "men of three several nations, to vindicate his native country from the calumnies wherewith they had aspersed it; wherein it pleased God so to conduct his fortune, that he suceeded in disarming his adversaries, and having generously spared their lives, they acknowledged their error."

He was knighted by King Charles I. on whose death he, with the Mac Kenzies, Munros, and other clans, took to arms, and raised the standard of Charles II. for which he was proclaimed traitor. He had a command in the royal army, which was defeated at Worcester, when he became prisoner, and, during his captivity, his affairs in Scotland went entirely to wreck; for as he had generously given up the rental of his estates to trustees for behoof of his creditors, they pillaged the lands and appropriated the rents; believing him dead, they actually abstracted the title deeds and other documents, while Leslie of Findrassie went so far as to make a predatory inroad on one of his chief vassals!

At this time he arrived from England, and although stern in the field, he was so meek and forgiving as to prevent his clansmen from resenting these numerous and galling injuries by deed of arms, a shorter method than the uncertain process of law. His property was at last sequestrated, when a choice collection of books which he had formed was dispersed, to his great sorrow. He wrote several works of an extraordinary character, and "under circumstances which pulled down the vigour of his fancy, and violentlie held it under." This fancy, which does not appear to have been very deeply depressed, was most fertile and amusing. While in prison he wrote "The Jewel," wherein he avers that he could introduce a universal language— new and surprising methods of calculation, systems of mathematics, and other matters of novelty and usefulness—which he offered to divulge, if his castle and lands were restored.

The death of Sir Thomas, like his life, was singular: he expired of joyous laughter, upon hearing that Charles II. had been restored.

The male line of the Urquharts of Cromartie terminated in James, who was a colonel of much distinction, and died without issue, 1741, when the chiefship of this clan devolved on the son of "the Tutor," who married Elizabeth, heiress of the ancient house of Seton, of Meldrum, in Aberdeenshire, 1636.

The ARMORIAL BEARINGS are or, three boars' heads erased gules, langued, azure. Crest, a demi otter, sable, crowned with an antique crown, or, and holding between his paws a crescent, gules. Supporters, two greyhounds, argent, collared and leished, gules. Motto, " Per mare et terras." The ancient motto is likewise borne beneath the shield—" Mean, speak, and do well."

The SUAICHEANTAS is Lus leth 'n t-samhradh, native Wall-flower, *Cheiranthus.*

The figure represents a female in the ancient and picturesque garment called Airisaid, which has been shown as otherwise worn, in illustration of Clann Mhathain, or the Matheson, in No. X. Although Martin, who wrote his description of the Western Islands in the latter end of the seventeenth century, says that this dress had not been in use for many years, we have met with old people in Inverness and Aberdeenshires who were able to recollect its being worn by some very aged females; hence the shoe buckles are introduced with propriety. Alasdair Mac Dhonuil, who wrote in 1740, alludes to it in one of his poems, as having been worn in his day.

The Airisaid was usually of lachdan, or of a saffron hue, but it was also striped with various colours, according to taste.